THE IOWA CLASS BATTLESHIPS

THE
IOWA CLASS
BATTLESHIPS
IOWA, NEW JERSEY, MISSOURI & WISCONSIN
MALCOLM MUIR

 Sterling Publishing Co., Inc. New York

Library of Congress Cataloging-in-Publication Data

Muir, Malcolm, 1943-
  The Iowa class battleships : Iowa, New Jersey, Missouri &
Wisconsin / Malcolm Muir.
      p.   cm.
  Originally published: Poole, Dorset : Blandford Press, 1987.
  Includes bibliographical references and index.
  ISBN 0-8069-8338-8
  1. Battleships—United States—History—20th century.   I. Title.
V815.3.M85   1991
359.3′252′0973—dc20   90-24927
                                                                CIP

10 9 8 7 6 5 4 3 2 1

Paperback edition published in 1991 by
Sterling Publishing Company, Inc.
387 Park Avenue South, New York, N.Y. 10016
Originally published in the U.K. by Blandford Press, Ltd.
© 1987 by Professor Malcolm Muir
Distributed in Canada by Sterling Publishing
℅ Canadian Manda Group, P.O. Box 920, Station U
Toronto, Ontario, Canada M8Z 5P9
Distributed in Great Britain and Europe by Cassell PLC
Villiers House, 41/47 Strand, London WC2N 5JE, England
Distributed in Australia by Capricorn Ltd.
P.O. Box 665, Lane Cove, NSW 2066
Manufactured in the United States of America
All rights reserved

Sterling ISBN 0-8069-8338-8

Frontispiece
The *New Jersey* shows
off her graceful lines
and balanced profile in
this port quarter
photograph taken
during her first Korean
tour in 1951. [NARS].

CONTENTS

PREFACE

'He who has his obituary published prematurely shall live long and happily ever after.' Anon.

I first saw battleships as a boy of 15 from a boat going up New York harbor in 1958. I was already absorbed in the big ships, an interest kindled by my father, a naval officer in World War Two, who had told me of the *Bismarck's* victory over the *Hood*. His short, but dramatic account of the sudden demise of the great British battlecruiser had sparked my imagination. While some of my fellows learned baseball batting averages, I pored over *Jane's Fighting Ships* at the nearby library as if my very future depended on my knowing the secondary battery details of HMS *Nelson* or the maximum speed of IJN *Nagato*.

Thus, it was with the greatest concentration that I gazed across the harbor at the vessels tied up in reserve at Bayonne. The unmistakeably graceful lines of two battleships marked them to be, without question, 'Iowas' (later I found out they were the *New Jersey* and *Wisconsin*). The gray day matched the gray paint of the silent ships, and both matched my mood. The sight made such a melancholy impression on me that I turned away and watched the Manhattan bustle on the starboard side of the boat.

My interest in battleships remained sharp, though, and I was anxious, when the *New Jersey* recommissioned for the Vietnam War, to get a glimpse of her. It was not to be: I was just starting my academic career, and my wife and I had small children and little money. When the *New Jersey* went back into mothballs at the end of the decade, I was sure that my last chance to see a living battleship had evaporated.

As I pursued my doctoral degree at Ohio State University in the mid-1970s, I made my avocation my dissertation topic. The documents pertaining to the American fast battleships had just been declassified at the Naval Historical Center in Washington, D.C., and I found in the voluminous files there more than ample material for my project. From this, I published several articles which prompted Blandford Press to ask for this more focused study on the 'Iowas' alone.

By that point, the great battleships were coming back into the fleet, and I was fortunate enough to be invited to the third commissioning of the *Iowa* on 28 April 1984. Even better, in fact much better, on 6 August 1985 the Navy flew me out to the same ship at sea off Norfolk for a 24-hour tour that went from bowsprit to shaft alley and through the barbette and gun house of turret No. 2.

During that morning, the ship fired her 16-inch guns at varying angles of elevation and degrees of train in order to take blast pressure readings. The spectacle proved as extraordinary as I had anticipated. The great flash, the gale of heat and the enormous noise were together briefly stupefying, then exhilarating. The shell could be seen as a black blur for a fleeting instant about 50 ft out of the muzzle; it could be heard for 20 seconds or so, sounding, to me, rather like the whir of truck wheels on a distant highway. When a gun was fired at maximum elevation, the shell would disappear without a trace over the horizon on that beautifully clear day. However, shot at a lesser angle and with a reduced charge, the shell would fall into the sea about eight miles out, and a geyser of water then climbed up and up for several seconds before cascading back.

In the course of the morning, the *Iowa* fired one full nine-gun salvo. I was watching from the bridge wings and, as I had expected, was enveloped in a tumult of smoke, heat and flash. The blast pressure was so great that it tore the open case from my camera and threw it down two decks. It was one of life's sweetest moments.

To do these ships justice in this book, then, I have gone through all the primary sources open to the general researcher. For the 1980s reincarnation of the battleships, I have, of necessity, relied on what has appeared in the open press, but there can be few secrets left about the battleships. While aboard the *Iowa*, I had the run of the vessel and was allowed to take pictures of anything I pleased except for some of the cryptographic equipment. Nonetheless, certain sensitive areas still do exist, such as the resistance of the ships to hollow charge warheads and concrete details of the *New Jersey*'s shooting at Syrian anti-aircraft sites near Beirut.

This work, then, is not a design analysis— that has been done definitively by Robert O. Dulin, Jr and William H. Garzke, Jr in *Battleships: United States Battleships in World War II* published by the Naval Institute Press in 1976. Nor is this a study of the evolution of design. That, too, has been covered, and in a most thorough manner, by Norman Friedman, in his *U.S. Battleships: An Illustrated Design History* released by the same press in 1985. There can be no point in redoing what has been done well.

Instead, the reader is here offered an operational history of the *Iowa*, *New Jersey*, *Missouri* and *Wisconsin*. Surprisingly little has been published about the activities of these ships in World War Two. The Korean War is virtually *terra incognita*. I have, to the best of my knowledge, examined every action and damage report ever submitted by the four vessels. These reports vary greatly as to value. Some are quite detailed and informative; others, perhaps reflecting a ship's time on station, are perfunctory. For instance, the *New Jersey*, on her 1951 tour in Korean waters, communicated so sketchily and so tardily about her activities in June that the chief of staff of the Seventh Fleet was moved to formal protest.

To flesh out these generally undemonstrative reports, I have corresponded with a number of the navymen who served aboard these ships. Their assistance has been valuable indeed, but it is only fair to single out FCCM Stephen Skelley of the *Iowa* who has made it possible for me to find my way through the maze of a 16"/50 turret, both literally and figuratively.

In fact, I owe a great deal to many people. At the Naval Historical Center, Dean Allard, Robert Cressman, Agnes Hoover, Michael Walker, Wesley Price and Martha Crowley all proved most helpful. Without the assistance given by John C. Reilly, it is doubtful that this study would have even got off the ground. Across the street in the Marine Corps Historical Center, Danny J. Crawford, J. Michael Miller and V. Keith Fleming helped to add a different dimension to the work. In Annapolis, Mary Catalfamo and Pamela Sherbert of the Nimitz Library and Patty Maddocks of the Naval Institute gave me significant aid. Paul Stillwell's insights, given both in print and in person, put right several of my misconceptions. The Oral History Collection, developed at the Naval Institute under his direction, offers a wealth of color and of operational analysis by retired navy personnel.

Of the officers, retired and serving, who answered my many questions, I would like to thank especially Vice Admiral Edwin B. Hooper, Rear Admirals John L. McCrea and Frank Pinney, Captain Gerald E. Gneckow and Commander Stanley W. Pawlowski. Several colleagues: Allan Millett, Harding Ganz, Carl Boyd, Archer Jones and Norman Friedman assisted in a variety of ways. Congresswoman Beverly Byron made my trip to the *Iowa* possible.

At my home institution of Austin Peay State University, Clarksville, Tennessee, James Nixon and Richard Gildrie, both 'ex-naval persons' have been most helpful; so have Preston Hubbard and Karen Pulley. In trying circumstances, Carolyn Haney did her usual speedy, accurate and intelligent job of typing and editing the manuscript.

My family and close friends have given essential logistical and emotional support. I owe a great debt of gratitude to Dwight, Lyman and Anne Wooster and to John and Helen Thornton, as they well know. Ann, Tom and Susan all put me up and put up with me. My father, who unknowingly started me in this direction, backed me in so many ways, as did my mother who died just as I was finishing my research. My two sons were indulgent of my odd hours and my often irascible moods. As for my wife, Carol, I never could have done the work without her support, and it is to her that I dedicate this book.

Malcolm Muir Jr
11 April 1986
Clarksville, TN

1 BATTLESHIPS FOR 'ECCENTRIC OPERATIONS'

The battleship, more than any other military instrument, made the United States a world power. Upon this one type of warship, the growing American Navy based most of its strength and lavished most of its attention from the 1890s until World War Two. By settling early on a formula of big guns and thick armor at the expense of speed, the Navy had consistently built burly, but slow ships. In 1938, the designers broke the mold. In one jump, they began planning the fastest battleships the world would ever see: the celebrated 'Iowa' class.

Before the Spanish-American War, American officers, such as Alfred Thayer Mahan, theorised that strongly protected battleships with big guns could 'bull' their way into enemy waters and force combat on their foe. The battle of Santiago in 1898 seemed to reinforce the validity of this vision. The ships of the Great White Fleet constructed immediately thereafter followed the pattern. When HMS *Dreadnought* rendered all of these vessels obsolete, the US Navy followed the British lead, but the new American battleships were generally a knot or two slower with marginally better protection and armament. Never content to be mere imitators, US naval architects experimented with turbo-electric drive for battleships. In the *Nevada*, the designers introduced the concept of all-or-nothing armor protection—quickly adopted by other navies. For hitting power, American planners embraced early on larger guns. They went to the 14-inch in 1910 and then to the 16-inch in the 'Navy Second to None' program of 1916. This gargantuan plan called for the construction of 16 immense vessels, each one larger than any extant warship. Ten were designed as battleships, the remainder as battlecruisers: ships that traded protection for speed.

All were to carry the 16-inch gun, a size new to modern navies. In August 1913, when the biggest weapon at sea was a 14-inch rifle firing a shell weighing about 1,500 lb, American ordnance experts began design on a 16″/45 gun. An increase in bore diameter by two inches meant almost a quantum jump in shell weight to 2,240 lb. Intended for the first four battleships of the 1916 program, eight of the weapons were ultimately carried by each of the three vessels of the 'Maryland' class that were completed.

As if the 16″/45 were not advanced enough, the second batch of six battleships and all of the battlecruisers were slated to receive the 16″/50. With a lengthened bore, this gun shot the same 2,240-lb shell farther and with more penetrating power.

Work on these immense ships (they would have displaced around 43,000 tons) was suspended during the last years of World War One, but with the Armistice, building began in earnest. The Navy ordered 150 16″/50 guns. By the time the entire building program ran on the shoals of the Washington Naval Conference, 71 of the weapons were ready and another 44 in varying stages of completion. This expensive stock then went into storage.

Not only did the Washington Treaty condemn most of the 1916 capital ships to the cutting torch, it also mandated a 10-year battleship building holiday (later extended to 15) and set limits—35,000 tons standard displacement and 16-inch gun caliber—for any future construction.

In 1936, the Japanese Government gave notice that it would not agree to a continuation of the treaty restrictions. Working in the greatest secrecy, the Imperial Navy had drawn up plans for massive battleships of 64,000 tons mounting 9-18.1″/45 guns firing a 3,200 lb shell. Two ships, the *Yamato* and *Musashi*, were laid down in 1937 and 1938 respectively. Both were launched in 1940 and joined the Japanese Fleet soon after Pearl Harbor. A third, the *Shinano*, was begun in 1940 but was transformed after Midway into an aircraft carrier. Japanese planners intended that these immense ships offset American quantity with Imperial quality. Calculating that new United States battleships would have to be small enough to fit through the Panama Canal, the Japanese intended to defeat these lesser vessels at extreme ranges with the biggest guns ever carried to sea.

American planners knew nothing whatsoever of the actual dimensions of the 'Yamato' class until very late in the war. True, rumors floated around of super-ships armed with 18-inchers, although some navy officers tended to discredit the tales as 'Nipponese rodent propaganda'.[1] But the Imperial Government's withdrawal from the treaty system was real enough.

So was renewed construction in Europe. Although Germany and especially Italy posed distant threats, their capital ships on the ways had to be taken into account. American planners considered, albeit rarely, the possibility that Italian battleships of the 'Littorio' class, building since 1934, might enter the Atlantic some day. German ships played a much larger role in American deliberations. Hitler's yards had started working on the *Scharnhorst* and *Gneisenau* in 1935. Reversing the usual order of naval design, these two battlecruisers featured good protection but a weak main battery of nine 11-inch guns. Fast and with a reasonably good range, the vessels seemed admirably suited for raiding (as indeed they later showed themselves to be).

Significantly more threatening, the Nazi government in 1936 laid down two larger ships. Reportedly designed to conform to the 35,000-ton limit still in effect, these battleships, the *Bismarck* and the *Tirpitz*, actually cheated on the treaty maximum by more than 9,000 tons. For their duplicity, the Germans got ships with a reasonably powerful armament (8-15"/47), a speed of 30 knots and stout armour. Both ships would take a harrowing amount of punishment before they went down.

As the tattered treaty system came to shreds, the British and French commenced their own programs in late 1936. The Royal Navy, desperately anxious for an agreement to hold down ship size and gun caliber, started work on the sort of vessels it hoped everybody else would build. The five ships of the 'King George V' class, of an actual 35,000 tons at standard load, mounted the weak battery of 10-14"/45 on a well-protected hull with a top speed of about 29 knots. The ships were regarded by many both inside and outside the Royal Navy as mediocre at best. In the end, though, they gave valuable service to the Allied cause, and the follow-on ship, the *Vanguard*, corrected many of their faults, although the war ended before she was commissioned.

As to the French battleships, the *Richelieu* and *Jean Bart* maintained the best traditions of their navy by being innovative and even peculiar. Their designers stuck reasonably close to 35,000 tons and still got good firepower (eight 15"/45), high speed (30 knots) and thick armor. To accomplish this juggling act, the French designers adopted the radical solution of placing the big guns in two quadruple turrets to concentrate both offensive and defensive weights. The French compromise was partially tested at Casablanca when the incomplete and immobile *Jean Bart* in Vichy service stood up fairly well to 16"/45 gunfire from USS *Massachusetts*.

American planners were not caught unaware by this foreign construction. Like their counterparts abroad, they sketched new designs during the 15-year treaty hiatus. Although the architects drew plans for some monster ships (one 1934 sketch projected a vessel of 66,000 tons carrying eight 20-inch guns!), the policy-making body of the navy, the General Board, intended to stay within the treaty limits, whatever they might be. American diplomats, hoping to avoid the expenses of an uncontrolled arms race, agreed with their British and French counterparts in 1936 to maintain the 35,000-ton limit and to restrict gun caliber to 14 inches. The American negotiators added two escape clauses. If the Japanese did not accede to the 14-inch limit, the USA would revert to 16 inches; and, if evidence emerged that a country was exceeding the 35,000-ton restriction, any of the three signatories could move to a 45,000-ton maximum.

When the Imperial Government refused, at the last moment, to go along with the 14-inch gun, the American designers immediately chose the heavier piece for the two ships voted by Congress. The *North Carolina* and *Washington* were forward-looking ships in many ways. Their armament of nine 16-inch guns set the caliber and layout for every American battleship built after them. This very heavy battery was made substantially more powerful by the quiet introduction of a super-heavy armor-piercing (AP) shell of 2,700 lb. The secondary battery was well ahead of all foreign designs except the British in being composed, not of separate anti-destroyer and anti-aircraft weapons, but rather of a dual-purpose gun of advanced design. This handy piece would be on active duty with the US Navy 50 years later.

The 'North Carolina' class was unusual in other ways. For the first time in history, the Navy built a fast battleship. Concerned about the speed of the Japanese capital ships, especially the 'Kongo' class battlecruisers, the American designers gave the 'North Carolinas' 27 knots, a six knot increase over existing US battleships. Large as this increase was, the new ships were somewhat slower than all their foreign contemporaries.

Speed had its price. Weight for propulsion, armament and good endurance had to be found somewhere—and, breaking a long American tradition, it came from protection. For many years, the navy standard required that a ship be strong enough to withstand the fire of its own guns at battle ranges. Designs that followed this criterion were labelled 'balanced', and early sketches of the *North Carolina* armed with the 14-incher had followed the rule. But when the General Board opted for the 16-inch weapon, there was no margin within the 35,000-ton limit to upgrade the armor as well. Unbalanced as the 'North Carolinas' might be, they performed well during the war.

Designers concentrated in the next class—the 'South Dakotas'—on righting the situation, but their success was only partial. The nine 16-inch arrangement of the 'North Carolinas' seemed sound enough and the heavy shell looked like a real winner, so the gunnery set-up was carried over to the new ships, lock, stock and barrel. Some officers were willing to accept a slower ship, but with foreign vessels already showing their sterns to American battleships, the speed of the new class was also pegged at 27 knots.

The weight for the improved protection had to come from somewhere, and the planners found it in sheer physical dimensions. By shortening the 'North Carolinas' 50 ft, the designers could upgrade the armor to resist 16-inch shells—the old 2,240-lb shell, not the super-heavy projectile. Thus the new ships, if not neatly balanced, would show a better equilibrium at least. They also proved to be exceedingly cramped for their crews, but their military qualities were potent indeed and would be demonstrated on a number of occasions at Santa Cruz, Casablanca, Guadalcanal and the Philippine Sea. Congress eventually authorised four of them: the *South Dakota*, *Indiana*, *Massachusetts* and *Alabama*. All entered service in 1942.

By the fall of 1937, some top Americans were getting increasingly nervous about the competitive adequacy of the new American ships. The principal concern was that Japan might have outsize ships under construction. Naval Intelligence reported as 'probably accurate', rumors from Italian sources that three 46,000 ton Japanese ships were already under construction. Were this actually the case, the situation would be analogous to the introduction of the *Dreadnought* at the beginning of the century when a large number of expensive new American battleships were rendered obsolescent at one stroke by a vastly superior ship.[2]

Accordingly, the General Board instructed the Bureau of Construction and Repair to investigate what sort of ship could be built on a displacement of 45,000 tons. That office sketched a number of alternatives, from a lengthened *South Dakota* with an extra turret to a very lightly protected, 35-knot cruiser-killer armed with 12 16-inchers. Then, in February 1938, Chief of Naval Operations (CNO) William D. Leahy asked for studies of ships with 18-inch guns.[3]

While the Bureau of Construction and Repair set about its work, representatives of France, Britain and the United States met in London to reconsider the treaty limitations. The three powers, alarmed at the reports of the oversize Japanese ships, asked the Imperial Government for assurances that it would not go beyond the 35,000-ton limit. When an evasive reply came on 12 February, the United States invoked the escalator clause allowing for a ship of 45,000 tons. The stage was now set for the 'Iowa' class.[4]

The *New Jersey* fires a salvo early in her World War Two career. The guns have a maximum elevation of 45 degrees, and a maximum depression of 2 degrees. They can be elevated at a maximum rate of 12 degrees of arc per second and the turret can be trained at 4 degrees of arc per second. Once fired, the gun recoils 48 inches to the rear in .43 seconds and is returned the 4 feet to battery by the recoil mechanism in .9 seconds. The gun itself is in motion for 1.33 seconds total. The ship herself does not move, contrary to the popular conception that she heels over from the blast. [USN]

A study in contrasts, the *New Jersey* fires her main battery about 25 years later off Vietnam. One shell can be seen at the far right edge of the photograph. Although the immediate impression is that the battleship has changed little over the years, a closer examination will reveal a number of significant differences. Note that the light anti-aircraft guns have been removed; that the radar sets on the secondary battery directors and the fire control tower have been updated; that the rangefinder has been removed from the rear of No. 1 turret; and that the conning tower has been enclosed. The basic impression of grace and power remains the same. [USN]

At this juncture, President Franklin D. Roosevelt intervened decisively in the planning process. More than any other chief executive—with the possible exception of his distant cousin Theodore, FDR possessed both the background and the inclination (unlike Jimmy Carter) to act as his own Secretary of the Navy. He knew a great deal about ships and was not loath to press his views on quite technical matters. Exasperated by this time at the unwillingness of the Japanese to avert an arms race, Roosevelt at a Cabinet meeting in mid-March told the ostensible Secretary, the aged and ailing Claude Swanson, that he wanted battleships larger than anything afloat. The President bore in on the details. He wanted, he said, a ship that could cruise at 15 knots for six months. More important, he wanted his battleship to be capable of the unprecedented speed of 35 knots. Swanson, always a proponent of large ships, was so taken with the concept that he proposed altering the last two ships of the 'South Dakota' class to these standards. However, plans had gone too far forward on those vessels; they would be completed as originally designed.[5]

Henceforth, Roosevelt took a continued interest in seeing the fast ships built. When some Congressmen balked at funding them, the President called the top naval expert in the House, Representative Carl Vinson, to the Oval Office to explain personally the necessity for them. With Vinson's prodding the legislature provided the money that Roosevelt wanted. The class would be named for its lead ship—USS *Iowa*.[6] Congress would pay for

them, but it was up to the Navy to work out their details. Much would depend on their uses. Over the next year, the General Board enthusiastically listed a number of missions that could be fulfilled only by battleships of very high speed and great offensive power. They could, of course, buttress the battle line, but they looked especially valuable for certain 'eccentric operations', as one officer from the War Plans Division put it.[7]

These missions included dealing with enemy battlecruisers (the 'Kongos') detached from the Japanese battle line. The 'Iowas' would also be perfectly suited for chasing down enemy heavy units operating, as the German ships were later to do, against trade routes. On the other side of the coin, the General Board envisioned the 'Iowas' acting as raiders themselves, or more presciently, combining with other ship types to form a 'striking force' in advanced areas. The General Board recommended making up such a force—in later parlance, a 'task group' of several 'Iowas', escorted by carriers and destroyers. Note that the carriers were quite clearly to play the subsidiary role in this formation.[8]

Some popular naval authors wrote in the 1960s and 1970s that the 'Iowas' had been designed specifically to protect the fast carriers.[9] Such reasoning is *post hoc ergo propter hoc*. As the war in the Pacific developed, the carrier became the dominant type, and the fast battleships made their most important contribution to the victory over Japan by guarding the flat-tops. But that mission was an unintended one, as indeed were most of the duties that the fast battleships carried out. No one on the General Board in 1938–39 suggested, at least not for the record, that the 'Iowas' would fuel destroyers, rescue downed fliers with their floatplanes, serve as fighter direction ships or shell enemy shores. In fact, the 'Iowas' accomplished almost none of the tasks for which they had been designed; instead, they did invaluable work at totally unintended missions.

Largely responsible for this classic design was Capt. Allan J. Chantry, the head of the Design and Construction Division of the Bureau of Construction and Repair. Chantry had graduated first in his 1906 Annapolis class. He had received a master's degree in naval architecture from MIT and had won rapid promotion. During World War Two, as the manager of the Industrial Department of the Philadelphia Navy Yard, he supervised a work force of 42,000 in the construction of almost 1,300 vessels including several carriers and the battleships *Washington, New Jersey* and *Wisconsin*.

In designing the 'Iowas', Chantry worked within certain basic guidelines. The ships had to fit through the Panama Canal locks which were 110 ft wide. The vessels could draw no more than 36 ft of water at extreme full load; otherwise they would be unable to enter certain major harbors and docks. Pacific operations dictated a long range. The ships were to carry protection adequate to resist the 2,200 lb 16-inch shell.

They were also to be armed with 9-16″/50 guns. As Chantry began his major structural planning, he operated on the crucial assumption that the turrets, being designed by the Bureau of Ordnance, would measure 37 ft 3 inches in diameter. That office had submitted those dimensions to Chantry's bureau at a General Board meeting on 6 April 1938. The Bureau of Ordnance then pushed ahead with an improved, but *larger* design without informing its opposite number. An *imbroglio* of grand proportions lay ahead. At least the gun size had been agreed upon, and a fine choice it was: the 16″/50 Mk 2. Made for the defunct ships of the 1916 program, these heavy and powerful weapons had been stored since 1922. On hand and paid for, the rifles were about 17 per cent more powerful than the 16″/45 going into the 27-knot battleships.[10]

The General Board had briefly considered three other guns. The 18″/48 with a projected shell weight of 3,850 lb was rejected partially because only six could be mounted on a ship of the mandated size. The 16″/56 offered little advantage over the 16″/50 other than range, and suffered from excessive barrel wear. The 16″/45, while the lightest of the guns under study, did not have as much range as the Navy wanted. (See Appendix B)[11]

Completing its work on the new turret design in early November, the Bureau of Ordnance shipped the completed drawings over to Construction and Repair. Incredulous officers there realised in examining the plans that Ordnance's barbettes were too big to fit into their hull. Five months of work appeared to have gone down the drain. The General Board meeting to find some way out of the mess was 'stormy'. The 16″/45 turret would fit, but then the Navy would have bought nothing for their 10,000 tons over the earlier ships but six

knots. Another alternative lay in returning to the type of turret designed for the 1916 ships, but a number of significant improvements would go by the board. Fittingly, Ordnance, which had caused the predicament, provided the solution: a lighter 16″/50 gun dubbed the Mk 7. Narrower at the breech than the Mk 2, the new gun made possible a 37-ft 3-inch barbette with the only sacrifice being the crowding of the two turret training pinions.[12]

The 16″/50 was the most destructive gun ever mounted on an American ship. It fired at a 45° elevation the 2,700-lb AP shell or the lighter 1,900-lb high capacity bombardment projectile (HC) to a maximum range of 24 miles. Compared to the 16″/45, the longer weapon had a higher muzzle velocity and greater penetrating power, except against horizontal surfaces, such as armored decks, which were punished more severely by the steeper final trajectory of the 16″/45.

Ordnance experts regarded the 16″/50 as a 'natural', that is, a balanced, reliable and extremely destructive weapon. Thus when the Navy came to design its next battleships, the 'Montana' class, it kept the 16″/50 and simply added one more turret. These very large ships of 60,000 tons were intended to resist the heavy 16-inch shell, and yet planners found it extremely difficult, even with 15,000 additional tons, to make the ship proof against the 16″/50. At a General Board meeting in the summer of 1939, two officers were discussing the relative merits of the 16-inch versus the 18-inch gun:

Admiral Greenslade: Inasmuch as we are finding it almost impossible to protect our ships [the 'Montanas'] against the 16″/50, what enemy could put 18-inch guns on a ship and protect it [against 18-in shells]?

Admiral Furlong: They could not protect it against our 16″/50.[13]

If the 16″/50 was a balanced gun, it unbalanced the ship. It was impossible to protect against it adequately on 45,000 tons, so Chantry and his bureau had to be content with providing enough armor to keep out the 2,200 lb 16-inch projectile. The designer accomplished this job by marginally upgrading the protection scheme of the *South Dakota* by thickening the turret faces, for example. Later claims exaggerated substantially the *Iowa*'s armor. For instance, the 1984–85 edition of *Jane's Fighting Ships* claims that the *Iowa* was

The *Missouri* on the ways at New York Navy Yard, 3 October 1941. She had been laid down on 6 January, and her bottom plating is virtually finished. Most of the workers in the center of the ship are standing on the middle layer of her triple bottom. The ship's keelson projects like a tongue toward the water, and on each side of the keelson can be seen the supports for the battleship's two inboard shafts. After the *Missouri*'s grounding on Thimble Shoals in January 1950, erroneous reports circulated for decades that her keelson was warped by the accident. [NARS]

designed to resist 18-inch shellfire. Still, the ship's protection was impressive indeed. The lower armor belt sloped inward to increase resistance by presenting an angled surface to incoming shells, measured 556 ft in length, was 12.2 in thick, and weighed 1,556 tons per side. Worked into the second and third protective decks were 4,255 tons of armor. In the end, each *Iowa* consumed slightly over 10,000 tons of armor. Underwater protection against torpedoes, mines and diving shells was also beefed up by more effective division of the machinery spaces. The General Board even gave some thought to armoring the bottom of the hull, but ruled it out because the weight would have increased the draft too much.[14]

Defense against the growing aircraft menace also received substantial thought. The excellent secondary armament of the earlier ships was repeated: 20 5"/38 in 10 mountings. Firing a 55-lb shell out to 18,000 yards, the gun was heavy enough to hurt light vessels and land targets as well as handy enough to make an excellent anti-aircraft piece.

The situation regarding the light automatic weapons was much less satisfactory. Original plans called for three quadruple 1.1" and 12 .50 caliber machine guns. The latter weapon was far too light to be effective; the former was too unreliable. Neither would actually ever be mounted on an 'Iowa' class ship.[15]

Offensive and defensive capabilities had to be balanced, not only against each other, but also against certain other basic requirements. To operate in the broad reaches of the Pacific demanded great endurance. Her maximum loading of 9,320 tons of fuel oil would take her almost 15,000 miles at 15 knots (11,700 at 20). Endurance also meant adequate provisions, weighing over 1,485 tons, for her complement of 117 officers and 1,804 bluejackets. In all, an 'Iowa'-class battleship had a designed displacement of 53,900 tons, but laden for a war cruise, she might leave port at almost 60,000 tons.

Another absolute prerequisite was that she fit through the Panama Canal which dictated a beam of less than 110 ft. Thus, she would be a

long ship, partly to get the volume she needed, but also to get the speed. As built, the four ships varied in length by a few inches, but at 887 ft, the difference was academic. Unlike their bluff predecessors, the lines of the 'Iowas' were unusually fine which helped them make their designed speed of 33 knots. To drive a mass of more than 50,000 tons of steel to this velocity, they required the most powerful engineering plant ever installed in a battleship.

The vessels cost about $125 million to build. The first pair was authorised on 17 May 1938 and named *Iowa* (BB 61) and *New Jersey* (BB 62). The Navy Department and White House had been deluged with letters and petitions from New Jersey urging that a battleship be named for the state. One New Jersey Congressman complained that over the Navy's history, most of the original 13 states had been honored with several ships bearing their names. There had been five vessels called USS *Massachusetts* for instance, but only one *New Jersey*. President Roosevelt, who took an interest in naval minutiae, was ultimately so bedeviled by this unimportant but touchy issue that he established a system. New battleships, he said, should be named for states 'which for the longest times have not been represented by ships named after them'.[16] This neat formula rescued Roosevelt from one of the most pestering Congressmen, Harry S. Truman of Missouri. That Senator had been pushing for a battleship *Missouri* since the 'North Carolinas' had been authorised. Under FDR's new rule, the next two battleships, voted by Congress on 6 July 1939, would be dubbed *Missouri* (BB 63) and *Wisconsin* (BB 64).[17]

Before any of the four 'Iowas' were laid down, the Navy was asking Congress for more. The most recent strategic studies and war games had shown them to be extraordinarily valuable. The War Plans Division pointed out that they were needed in the Atlantic to counter German or Italian raiders. In the Pacific, their speed might even enable them to force a reluctant Japanese fleet into the long anticipated showdown with the slower American battle line.[18]

The outbreak of World War Two obviously added a dimension of urgency to all defense planning. German raiders in the fall of 1939 showed themselves to be both aggressive and competent. More worrisome were intelligence reports that the Japanese had under construc-

The *Illinois* at Philadelphia 7 July 1945 with work going forward very quickly. She had been laid down a little over six months earlier and was by this point over 15 percent complete. Her starboard boiler in boiler room No. 1 peeks over the top of the transverse bulkhead.
Note the line from the overhead crane attached to the starboard boiler in her aft boiler room (No 4). Closer to the camera, her foresection is being built up, and the triple bottom is visible in varying states of completion. The *Illinois* was the last of the class to be started, and she would be cancelled five weeks after this picture was taken. [USN]

With the armor for the lower part of No 2 barbette erected, the *Wisconsin* on 8 July 1942 had been on the stocks for 18 months. She is only about 20 percent complete, but she would be ready for sea in 21 months. It is just possible to make out the uptakes of her eight boilers. Protecting them is the citadel with its 12.1-inch belt inclined at 19°. Note that the armor on No 2 barbette angles in at the bottom sides. The result is a saving in weight with no loss in protection since the belt will be extended forward past No 1 turret. [USN]

tion eight new battleships of about 40,000 tons with 12 16-inch guns and 'speed presumably high'. Admiral Stark successfully pleaded with President Roosevelt in November for two more 'Iowas', but Congress did not act on the administration's request until France fell.[19]

That debacle—and the fear that England would go down next—galvanised the legislature to rush through on 19 July 1940 the 'Two-Ocean Navy' bill. It authorised the construction of the five slow giants of the 'Montana'

Part of the light anti-aircraft and the secondary 5″/38 batteries are evident in this shot of the *Missouri* early in her career (probably 1945). Between the two groups of men in the foreground is a 20 mm Oerlikon. This 70 caliber weapon had a rate of fire of 450 rounds per minute. A 40 mm quad mount can be seen directly ahead of the 20 mm and another atop turret No 3. Each barrel could fire a 2 lb shell 160 times a minute. The 5″/38, depending on the training of its crew, could put perhaps 20 54 lb shells in the air per minute. Its proximity fuse—a miniature radar set fitted in the nose of the shell—proved especially deadly against aircraft, even though a test by the *New Jersey* in November 1944 showed that 13 percent of the rounds were duds, 54 percent were prematures and only 33 percent functioned as designed. Note the 17.3-inch thick face plate on turret No 3. [USN]

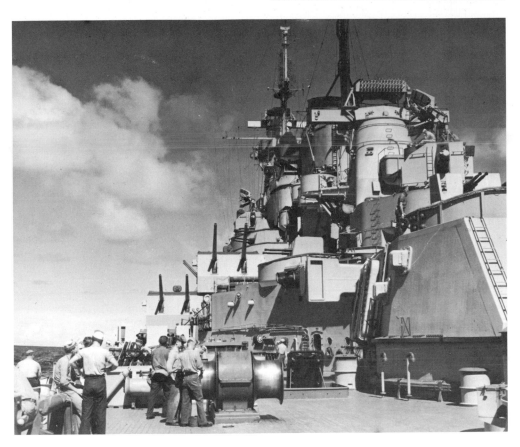

class plus two more 'Iowas': the *Illinois* (BB 65) and the *Kentucky* (BB 66). Some top officers actually preferred the two smaller ships with their five knot speed advantage. One General Board member remarked in 1940, 'If any country built any 75,000 ton battleship we would handle it with two 45,000 ton battleships.'[20]

Not one of these battleships of the 'Two-Ocean Navy' was ever completed. The 'Montanas', suspended on 20 May 1942 after the Coral Sea action, were cancelled 21 July 1943. As for the *Illinois* and *Kentucky*, about 15 per cent of the materials had been gathered for them, when in April 1943, the Bureau of Ships proposed diverting their machinery to 'Midway' class carriers. Admiral Ernest J. King, the CNO, shot back, 'I cannot acquiesce in a complete cessation of BB construction; these ships with their combination of gun power, 32-knot speed and ability to withstand damage are highly valuable and more than justify expenditure of the time and materials required for their construction.'[21] In fact, King wanted their construction accelerated, not postponed.

The two embryo ships came under attack again later in the year from the Office of War Mobilisation. King took the issue to Roosevelt who gave 'specific instructions' that the ships be kept in the program.[22] By the summer of 1944, King found the *Iowa* and *New Jersey*, which had recently joined the fleet, to be so valuable that he instructed the Bureau of Ships to prepare plans for an 'improved ... 'Iowa' adaption for progress in design and to guard against attrition in this category'. The plans were to be ready once the *Illinois* and *Kentucky* were finished.[23]

On 6 December 1944, Norfolk Navy Yard laid the keel of the *Kentucky*; on 15 January 1945, Philadelphia Navy Yard began the *Illinois*. Work went ahead very quickly: King hoped to get them both to sea before the end of 1946, but the surrender of Japan caused the cancellation of the *Illinois*. Norfolk, somewhat further along with the *Kentucky*, proceeded until August 1946. After a two-year suspension, desultory construction began again, this time with the thoughts of completing her to a radically different design (see chapter 8). She was floated out of her dock on 20 January 1950, more to free that facility than anything else.

Thus, only the four 'Iowas' authorised before the war were ever finished. The name ship was laid down by New York Navy Yard within one week of the fall of France; the *New Jersey* followed at Philadelphia, Chantry's yard. She was started 16 September 1940 at the height of the London Blitz. The same yards began the other two in January 1941, the *Missouri* at New York, the *Wisconsin* at Philadelphia. That early start for the *Iowa* and *New Jersey* meant that they joined the fleet more than a year before their sisters. Immediately following Pearl Harbor, those ships that were closer to completion received a higher priority rating. For instance, the 17 December 1941 list placed the *Iowa* and *New Jersey* in precedence group No. 3, behind only the four 'South Dakotas' and five carriers. The *Missouri* and *Wisconsin* were in group No. 8, behind all submarines, light cruisers and destroyers. After Midway, the *Iowa* and *New Jersey* were moved down the list, but they always maintained their place ahead of the latter pair.[24]

The *New Jersey* with her original radar outfit. Dressed in Ms 21 camouflage, she is carrying her full complement of three aircraft at the stern. [USN]

Building a battleship was, of course, a complex process. The various bureaux submitted contract plans to the New York Navy Yard which made the working drawings, both for its own force and for Philadelphia. Approximately 20,000 working plans were needed for one 'Iowa'. Included in this number were 700 ordnance plans, 6,000 hull plans, 2,400 electrical plans, and 2,700 machinery plans. During the building process, these plans were frequently updated or changed altogether as a result of combat experience or technological advances in equipment.

As one example, the light anti-aircraft bat-

The *Wisconsin* six months later on 12 January 1943. Note the wedge-shaped forward transverse bulkhead (with the worker on its top edge) just forward of the barbette for No 1 turret. This large plate of armor was designed to protect the ship from shells fired by an enemy vessel operating off the bow. In the *Wisconsin* and *Missouri*, this armor piece was 14.5 inches thick; in the *Iowa* and *New Jersey*, only 11.3 inches. At the time this photograph was taken, the *Wisconsin* was over 35 percent complete with almost 10,000 tons of material erected. She will be commissioned in 15 months. [USN]

U.S. WISCONSIN
BB-64
STERN VIEW LOOKING FWD. PORT SIDE.
NY YARD, PHILA. JAN 12 1943

tery was at first completely altered in composition and then continuously increased. As noted, the original specifications called for 1.1-inchers and .50 caliber machine guns, but neither were satisfactory weapons. In April 1941, the General Board ordered a total change-over to the Swedish 40 mm Bofors and the Swiss 20 mm Oerlikon. By replacing the original outfit with 16-40 mm in quad mounts and 8 single 20 mm, the new battery added 85 tons—a negligible displacement increase on a 45,000-ton vessel, the Board reasoned.[25]

A negligible figure it might be, but not for long. On 11 July 1942, two more quad Bofors were approved to make the 'ultimate' battery of 24 40 mm. Shortly after the Santa Cruz fray in which the *South Dakota* shot down 26 Japanese planes, the CNO's office wanted a minimum of 40 40 mm and 55 20 mm. Barely a month later, that office was approving as the 'ultimate close-in battery' 18 quadruple

mounts (17 for the *Iowa*). A route slip attached by the Bureau of Ships carried the anonymous but accurate remark, 'the use of the word "ultimate" can be classed as wishful thinking'. True enough. The *Iowa* mounted in the end, 76 40 mm and 52 20 mm; her three sisters, 80 40 mm and 49 20 mm.[26]

Similar drastic changes were made in sensors and in command facilities. With radar in its infancy in 1939 the ships, as designed, would have carried no sets at all. By 1944, a forest of antennas sprouted topside. A Combat Information Center (CIC), designed to keep command and control stations appraised of the tactical situation, was added when the first two ships were virtually complete. Admiral King personally approved a delay of two weeks in the *Iowa* so that she could be fitted with one.[27]

Changes such as those just described caused endless headaches for the building yards. The commandant of New York Navy Yard complained two days before Pearl Harbor that the Bureau of Ships had been remiss in keeping him informed about the switchover in anti-aircraft guns. He noted with some bitterness, 'Attempts to get the matter settled have been made at various times during the past half year ..., but the solution appears as remote now as in the spring of the year'.[28]

The planner's job was made tougher by the fact that he also had to deal with hundreds of subcontractors all over the United States. In the wartime transportation tangle, crucial items often were delayed or went astray completely. As a consequential example, the 100-ton rudder post for the *Wisconsin* was cast at Eddystone, Pennsylvania. The barge carrying it to Philadelphia in the dead of winter was trapped by ice for two days.[29]

Working with such huge pieces of metal became routine. For instance, the barbette for turret No. 1 weighed 417 tons, but came in only seven segments, which fitted around the turret complex and were held together by keys made at the yard.

To assemble the diversity of equipment necessary for an 'Iowa'-class battleship challenged the most skilled of managers. Such a ship requires over 1,100 telephones, over 5,000 lighting fixtures and 14,000 valves (some weighing almost half a ton) for her 42 miles of piping. The pumping system could handle 125,000 gallons a minute, and the distilling plant could make 100,000 gallons of fresh water from the sea daily.

The labor involved in building a battleship was prodigious, of course. The Philadelphia Navy Yard calculated that the *Wisconsin* took 2,891,334 man-days to construct. The work could be dangerous; two men were killed while building the ship. But from a later vantage point, the craftsmanship was of a high order—high enough, in fact, to be cited in the 1980s by advocates of battleship re-activation as a strong point in favor of the 'Iowas'.

Launching such a big ship was always a moment of high drama. It was also a most complex operation which involved determining such factors as the launching weight of the hull, its maximum velocity down the ways, its drop-off speed, and where the ship would pivot when the stern became waterborne. All of these variables had to be figured out before the ship was even started so that the slipway could be designed to take the weight of the battleship's structure. Prior to launching, the

vessel would be held by six 300-ton hydraulic triggers. If the hull failed to move once the triggers were dropped, six hydraulic rams would give it a shove.

The launch of a vessel as important as an 'Iowa'-class battleship was always attended by appropriate ceremonies, although the urgency of wartime kept them short. For instance, before the *Missouri* slid down the ways on 29 January 1944, Senator Truman gave a short address. Admiral Halsey then spoke to the workers via a radio broadcast. His words were prophetic indeed, 'We have a date to keep in Tokyo. Ships like the *Missouri* will provide the wallop to flatten Tojo and his crew'.[30] Truman's daughter broke the bottle of Missouri wine (one state temperance chapter had asked unsuccessfully that Missouri spring water be used). The ship was launched, and then the workers were back at their jobs. The whole process took 15 minutes. It was a proud day for Harry Truman. He had fought hard to have a ship named for his state, and when he became president, he saw to it that his battleship was the center of attention. No president in American history has been so closely associated with one particular naval vessel.

In fact, state societies often took pride in 'their' ships and provided amenities for 'their' crews. The *Iowa* received a fine silver service that had belonged to her famous Spanish-American War predecessor; it remains aboard BB 61 to this day. The people of New Jersey gave the first CO of BB 62 a 'slush fund' of $500 to spend for the crew's benefit. When three seamen from the *Wisconsin* wrote home bemoaning the lack of coffee percolators on

The *New Jersey* being readied for launching at Philadelphia one year after Pearl Harbor. The propellers and rudders have not yet been fitted in order to avoid damaging them during the launch. The massive rudder posts are castings weighing over 100 tons each. Note the two roller conveyances (resembling ladders laid flat) extending from under the ship. These facilitated the removal of the vast quantity of timber from the shores, cribs and keel blocks that were dismantled. To launch an *Iowa* took almost 3000 men working for over seven hours. [USN]

The *New Jersey* takes to the water, 7 December 1942. Note the exuberant worker standing on the ways, which were slathered with 26 tons of grease. Once the hull began moving, she took almost a minute before she was waterborne. She reached a maximum speed of about 25 feet per second (or 17 mph). [USN]

The *New Jersey* hits the Delaware River a little over 80 percent complete. Her 5-inch mounts are aboard but the big gun turrets will take months to install. She has her anchor chains rigged as drag lines and a bower anchor (which can just be made out on her starboard side) was set up for quick release in the event of an emergency. The happy dockyard worker standing on the greasy way is still cheering, and the steam from the battleship's superstructure shows that the ship's whistle is sounding in celebration as well. It was an emotional time; almost 2,000,000 man days had been invested in the ship by this point.

their ship, citizens from that state donated 30.

Once a battleship had been launched, one of the most ticklish of operations lay ahead: the installation of the turrets. As with the ship itself, the turrets were extremely complex mechanisms; each weighed over 1,800 tons and cost about $1.5 million. The basic structural components of the turret such as the electric deck sub-assembly were heat treated to 1,050° F, a process to ensure stress relief that took over three days. These components were then assembled in the yard's turret shop. Here, all the systems for training and elevation, gas ejection, ventilation and the like were fitted, as were the projectile and powder hoists, the wiring and the sprinkling system. In other words, the turret was completely built ashore, tested, and then torn down into sections weighing as much as 350 tons apiece and then reassembled inside the ship. Despite the ponderous weights involved, the last job required precision. Special gauges ensured that the turret's placement was accurate to within $\frac{1}{4}$ inch of level and $\frac{1}{64}$ inch of center. The entire turret installation process took about one month.[31]

Only then could big guns finally go into the ship. The 16"/50 rifles had started life as forgings made by Bethlehem or Midvale. A few were finished at the brand new Naval Ordnance Plant at Pocatello, Idaho, but most of the forgings went to the 'Big Gun Shop' established in 1886 at the Washington Navy Yard. Here, in the heaviest industrial facility ever established in the District of Columbia, the forgings were bored out and finished to tolerances of 1/10,000 of an inch. And here, the worn-out guns would return to be refurbished, the 68-ft long weapons being stood upright and sunk into a shrinking pit. In this oven, the barrel was expanded by heat and the liner, shrunk with cold water, was pulled out and replaced.[32]

As the battleship was finishing, key members of the crew arrived well before commissioning. Even that ceremony by which the vessel officially became a part of the Navy did not mean the end of the construction process. Much finishing work remained, and then the myriad of parts needed to be rigorously tested. The *Wisconsin*, for instance, hoisted her commissioning pennant on 16 April 1944. After trials, she departed on her shakedown cruise on 31 May. She returned to Philadelphia on 10 August to put right the problems that her exercises had revealed. This work took until 24 September. Thus, more than five months of hard toil by her crew and by the yard had been necessary after her commissioning to make her fully operational.[33]

Given the size of the 'Iowas' and the relatively low priority accorded them by planners once the United States had entered the war, the shipyards had worked with extraordinary rapidity. Using as a yardstick the time between laying down and commissioning as the source of comparison, New York Navy Yard built the *Iowa* in 32 months, the *Missouri* in 41. Philadelphia produced the *New Jersey* in the same time as the *Iowa*, and turned out the *Wisconsin* in less than 39 months.

Employing the same measure, foreign production was not as quick. British yards performed as follows: *King George V*, 45 months; *Prince of Wales*, 48; *Duke of York*, 51; *Anson*, 56; *Howe*, 60; *Vanguard*, 58. Brest Navy Yard built the *Richelieu* for the French Navy in 56 months. The *Jean Bart* took 12 years, but she was, of course, an exceptional case.

For the Axis, the Italian firms constructed the *Littorio* in 66 months, the *Vittorio Veneto* in 65 and the *Roma* in 45. The *Bismarck* commissioned 49 months after work had started on her, the *Tirpitz* took 52 months. Given the huge size of the *Yamato*, Kure Navy Yard certainly did a creditable job by building her in 49 months. Mitsubishi spent 53 months with the *Musashi*.

Thus, the 'Iowas' were rushed to completion more quickly than any other modern battleships—with the exception of their immediate predecessors, the smaller 'South Dakotas' (which also had the highest possible priority since they were close to completion in early 1942). Speed of construction was not the only feature that elevated the 'Iowas' over their foreign contemporaries. Their military qualities made them, in theory, more than a match for any World War Two battleship except the *Yamato*. In actuality, even that Imperial giant would probably have lost a gunnery duel to an 'Iowa'.

2 SWIFT SHIPS—BIG GUNS

The architects of the 'Iowas' succeeded in producing one of the classic warship designs of any time. Aesthetically, the ships were distinguished by graceful—from some angles, almost feminine—lines. Militarily, the ships were set apart, then and for decades to come, by their long-barrelled 16-inch rifles and their extraordinary speed. Taken together, these two features would ensure their very survival long after every other battleship had vanished from the world's oceans.

The 'Iowas' are certainly one of the prime candidates to prove the aphorism 'If it looks right, it is right.' It is impossible to see these ships without realising, almost instinctively, that they were *intended* to please the eye. Capt. Chantry had that rare sense of line, of balance, of what is right that is more often seen in the work of Italian exotic car designers. True,

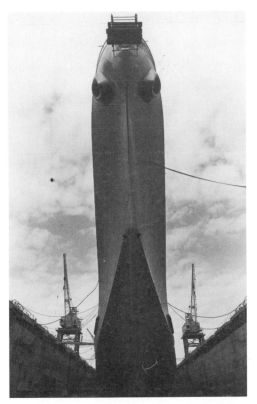

The bulbous bow form of the *Iowa* class is quite apparent in this photograph of the *New Jersey* taken at Long Beach in February 1982. Coupled with the ship's great length, this bow form is a major asset in developing high speed. [USN]

most of the *Iowa*'s peers were impressive in appearance. The British ships, the 'Bismarcks', and the 'South Dakotas' all had in common a certain muscular blockiness—rather the look of a heavyweight boxer. The *Richelieu* and *Jean Bart* were interesting rather than attractive. The 'Yamatos', despite their massiveness, appeared well-proportioned. The Italian ships, as might be expected, were handsome, and so were the 'North Carolinas', hardly surprising either since they too had come from Chantry's bureau. But the symmetry and sweep of the 'Iowas' singled them out as a classic example of the designer's artistry. In searching for parallels, one thinks of Humphrey's *Constitution* or Attwood's *Hood*. Later, additions to the 'Iowas', such as the antennas and electronic gear, detracted somewhat from their silhouettes, but their fluid lines remain essentially unspoiled.

Of course, naval architects sketch implements of war, not works of art. The fine hull lines of the 'Iowas' had a utilitarian purpose: the pursuit of speed. The sheer forward is to keep the vessels as dry as possible; the narrow hull form forward and the length of the design both made for high speed.

To provide the requisite power, the Navy prepared the greatest engineering plant ever installed in a battleship. Four propellers were driven by four double reduction geared, cross-compound turbine units, each rated at 53,000 shaft horsepower. The machinery spaces were subdivided into eight separate compartments so that even the unluckiest of torpedo hits (one damaging a bulkhead separating two compartments) would flood only one-fourth of the power plant. With just four boilers operating, the *Wisconsin* reported that she could develop 27.5 knots.[1] The turbines were driven, of course, by steam from the ship's eight boilers. They put out more power than their precursors in the 'South Dakota' class, and they proved very reliable in service. The battleships often operated continuously for up to two months during the latter days of World War Two, and the captain of the *Wisconsin* was

Left: The fine lines of the 'Iowas' helped give them their speed as well as their good looks. The fragile-looking bow never met the test of battle damage, although the earlier *North Carolina* (BB 55) was torpedoed just forward of turret No 1 and came through reasonably well. Nonetheless, in 1943, a number of design studies for modified 'Iowas' tried to improve their resistance to torpedo hits in that area with more armor and a broader hull form at a loss of a couple of knots in speed. This photograph taken in 1968 shows the *New Jersey* just before her stint in Vietnam. [USN]

Above: The housing for one of the *Iowa*'s main reduction gears, made by Westinghouse. Since propellers work best at 200 rpm or lower and the steam turbines at several thousand rpm, this gearing reduced the revolutions that would be transmitted to the shafts. With its fine tolerances, the reduction gearing is vulnerable to sabotage by disgruntled sailors who could easily disable the entire unit with a handful of metal chips. During the Vietnam conflict, a number of American ships spent months in port repairing such damage. Today, this housing on the *Iowa* is festooned with heavy locks. [NARS]

convinced his machinery could stand up to four months of steady use.[2]

Nonetheless, such a pace wore on the equipment, and occasionally the ships were troubled by some equipment failures. For instance, the *Wisconsin* in her first sortie with the Pacific Fleet in December 1944 suffered blown gaskets on by-pass lines of the bulkhead stop valves for boilers No. 3 and No. 4. Replacing the gaskets took two hours; in the meantime, the ship was forced to lock up No. 2 shaft when a steam leak forced the securing of two lube pumps.[3]

The *New Jersey* lost her No. 3 main engine off Wonsan, North Korea, 16 July 1951, when lubricating oil pressure to that engine dropped. The damage was serious enough to require a three-week stint with the repair ship *Ajax* which replaced oil seals, bearings and carbon packing for the turbines.[4]

The boilers also provided the power for the ship's eight turbo-generators. These, in turn, furnished 10,000 kw to the 900 electric motors aboard. Most of them gave no trouble, but the main drain pump motors made by Diehl failed repeatedly, as did air compressors made by the same concern.[5]

As the fastest battleships ever built, the top speed of the 'Iowas' has always been the

Right: One of the eight boilers on the *Iowa* shortly after her commissioning in May 1943. Made by Babcock and Wilcox of New York, these units were the usual two-drum, double-furnace, single-uptake type. They operated at a pressure of 600 psi with a superheated steam temperature of 850° F. Even at an easy cruising speed, this station was noisy, windy, and hot, and the clothes worn by the three reflect those conditions. Forced draft did provide gales of ventilation to certain spots. [NARS]

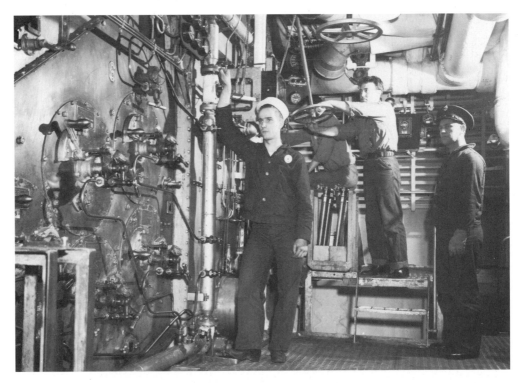

The main turbine gauge board on the *Iowa* shortly after her commissioning. The large wheel to the left is the ahead steam valve; the smaller one to the right is the astern valve. The instrument at bottom left shows that the captain is calling for two-thirds speed ahead. The large gauge in the box above the control wheels is a shaft revolution indicator, showing, at this moment, a shaft speed of 57 rpm. Directly above it is a steam temperature gauge which has a redline of 850 degrees and is currently reading a safe 650 degrees. [NARS]

The third deck passage above the machinery spaces on the *New Jersey*. This passageway, called Broadway, resonated with the vibration of the engines; one ex-officer remembered as a midshipman feeling as if he were standing on 'the fringes of hell'. The overhead monorail proved a great boon in moving heavy equipment, and it allowed the transfer of shells between the fore and aft turrets. The passage, extending down the center line of the ship, could be closed off by a number of watertight doors. [USN]

The rpm and ship speed indicators on the bridge of the *Iowa*, May 1985. Note that the speed of each shaft is shown separately and that the ship is easing along at 5 knots. Although the maximum reading on the shaft indicator is 200 rpm, that speed is sometimes exceeded. The ship speed indicator goes to 40 knots which is ample. Above the face on the latter instrument is a button to change the illumination of the dial from white to red light. [Author]

subject of some controversy, in large part because they never ran formal measured-mile trials. They were designed for 33 knots, but a number of supposedly authoritative commentators such as *Jane's* credited them with a service speed of 35 knots. This figure seems too high, at least for World War Two. They generally left port at a full load displacement of about 57,000 tons, and since all fuel oil burned was replaced with salt water ballast, the ships operated at that displacement. In December 1943, the *Iowa* at 56,928 tons attained 31.9 knots on 221,000 SHP. The machinery was designed for an emergency 20 per cent overload (or 254,000 SHP), which would have allowed the *Iowa* to touch 33.5 knots. These rough calculations are borne out by wartime experience. When the *Iowa* and *New Jersey* tried to run down the fleeing Japanese destroyer *Nowaki* off Truk in February 1944, the battleships with throttles wide open reached about 32.5 knots according to the *Iowa's* pitometer log. The American vessels had probably lost a knot to bottom fouling.[6]

However, the higher figure might well be accurate for the ships later in their careers. During the Korean War, they had lost the catapults and most 20 mm guns with their ammunition and crews. The *Iowa's* Captain during her Korean tour, William Smedberg, remembered getting his ship over 33 knots. The *New Jersey* ran machinery trials before her Vietnam deployment and reported making

35.2 knots at 207 RPM, although her command history maddeningly makes no mention of her displacement. Still, the figure seems believable in view of the fact that the ship had lost all of her 40 mm mounts and was operating with a much smaller crew than normal. The 1980s reactivation added weight again, especially with the armored box launchers for missiles, and the *Iowa* in 1985 slightly exceeded 32 knots at 205 RPM.[7]

The entire issue of top speed, while interesting, seems a bit trivial. In the real world, the ships always could make whatever speed was required of them—with the single exception of the chase at Truk where two or three more knots might have made a difference. But in carrier task force operations, the 'Iowas' had no trouble keeping up.

The requirements of actual operating conditions late in World War Two are reflected in the action reports submitted by the battleships. For instance, the *Missouri* supported air strikes against Okinawa and Kyushu from 28 May to 10 June 1945. During the period, she averaged 17.9 knots: the maximum that she needed was 27. Similarly, the *Wisconsin* in her first deployment in December 1944 spent 283 hours underway. Of that time, she operated on four boilers for 230 hours and put all eight on line for 53. Her average speed for the entire period was 18 knots; several times she made 27 but never for more than 30 minutes at a stretch. Two months later, the same ship reported a 4-

The twin-skeg hull form of an 'Iowa'. The skegs provided a clean flow of water to the inboard five-bladed propellers. Skegs could not be fitted to the outboard props because skegs there could not be aligned with the shafts. The massive size of the twin rudders helps give the 'Iowas' their superb maneuverability. [USN]

hour run averaging 26.7 knots. On another occasion, her CO required 30 knots for 20 minutes.[8]

Korean operations sometimes dictated high speeds. Smedburg later said:

Frankly, I handled the *Iowa* just like a destroyer, and we travelled fast. We travelled around 30 knots most of the time. We could do 32 and ofttimes did out in Korea. I had no fuel restrictions, and I was often ordered to go from one spot to another where I had to make 28 to 30 knots to do it. The only problem was we had stern tubes that fit in the bearings so loosely that when I got up to 30 knots, the chief petty officers had to abandon their quarters aft because they were shaken up like Mexican jumping beans. And I always tried to slow during the meal hour so that the petty officers could sit down and have their meals, if I had to make a high speed run.[9]

Another major asset of the 'Iowas' was their extraordinary maneuverability, an attribute vividly remembered by virtually all of their COs who were interviewed many years later.

These officers compared the handling of the 'Iowas' with that of a destroyer, but with the important distinction that the 'Iowas' would actually turn inside the much smaller ship.[10] Destroyers assigned for the first time to a formation with an 'Iowa' often disbelieved this fact at their peril. The destroyer, relying on its small size and nimble handling to get out of trouble with the bigger vessel, would sometimes come too close to the battleship. As the CO of the *Missouri* recalled the situation:

When a turn signal came up to make a 60- or a 90- or a 120-degree turn for the whole task force, I immediately had to go on the TBS [talk between ships] to tell them [the destroyer] ... 'don't turn until we've turned inside of you.' well, they wouldn't believe it and a couple of times we had to back full, reverse the rudder, and everything else to keep from cutting them in two. One time I took his flagstaff off his stern with the bow of the *Missouri* because he wouldn't believe us and he continued to leave his rudder over. I was screaming at him to take his rudder off and go straight, anywhere. . . .[11]

The *Iowa* demonstrates
the nimbleness of her
class as she snakes
through an 'S' turn.
At 25 knots, with a 35
degree rudder, her
tactical diameter was
773 yards, and she would
take two minutes, 40
seconds to turn 180°. In
such a sharp turn, the
ship would slow to 16
knots, even though
engine speed stayed the
same, because of the
increased drag on her
hull. The *Iowa* is shown
here on 28 October,
approaching Pearl
Harbor after her single
tour in Korea. [USN]

Some COs became almost cocky with their
ships. Capt. Jimmy Holloway actually ran the
Iowa into a floating drydock at five knots and
then backed her down full (see Chapter 3).
During the Korean war, Smedberg in the same
ship was returning from a bombardment mission to a carrier task group:

I was coming back to join the carrier group—I
always operated the *Iowa* as a destroyer—and I
picked up the carrier group dead ahead, just before
dawn. I was ordered to join at dawn. I came in at 30
knots. I came in through the two lead destroyers,
came in between the two carriers, whipped around,
and was in absolutely perfect position at the center of
the formation. I was assigned the guide station at the
center of the circular formation, and ran up my
'affirm posit,' which means that I am in position. It
was as beautifully done a job as you've ever seen,
thanks to my young officers who were working the
mooring board and so forth. I expected a well done,
but instead of that I got a blast:

'You have seriously endangered this whole form-

ation by entering at high speed. In the future, you
will always enter this formation from the rear.'[12]

Later, Smedberg made exactly the same
maneuver with a new admiral: '[I] came
smartly into position, and, bang, a big well
done came out from the flagship.'[13]

In handling, the 'Iowas' differed from lesser
ships in other important ways. Despite the
great output of an 'Iowa' engineering plant, the
horsepower-per-ton ratio for the battleship
was 3.7 to 1, for cruisers 6.5/1, and for destroyers, 19/1. Thus an 'Iowa' accelerated
slowly, but once at speed, the vessel possessed
tremendous momentum. When the *New Jersey*
ran machinery trials in 1968, her CO ordered
'full astern' as the ship was making 35 knots.
She took two full miles to stop. Thus, with this
great inertia in mind, battleship COs had to
make early—and correct—decisions.[14]

An 'Iowa' also presented a challenge to
smaller ships coming alongside. With her
broad underbody and great wake, deep hollows
form behind the battleship's stern and forward

Taking it green, the *Iowa* drives into heavy seas during World War Two. One of her commanding officers, watching from the bridge, wondered at such moments whether her bow structure would stay on. The heavy cruiser *Pittsburgh* lost hers in weather like this in June 1945, although the *Iowa*, *Missouri*, and *Wisconsin* came through without damage. Indeed, these battleships remain among the fastest rough water ships in the world today. [NARS]

The *Missouri* slams through heavy seas off Japan, probably in June 1945. Four months earlier, she had suffered some storm damage to the two 40-mm quad mounts (Nos 1 and 2) seen here covered with canvas. The shields to the guns had been so dished in that they pushed the pointer and trainer's handwheels out of line. Mounts Nos 16 and 17, just forward of No 3 main battery turret, were also especially vulnerable. Note that turret No 1 here has been trained far to starboard. In the February storm, heavy seas had sprung the left rangefinder and window shutter, slightly damaging the left optics. [NARS]

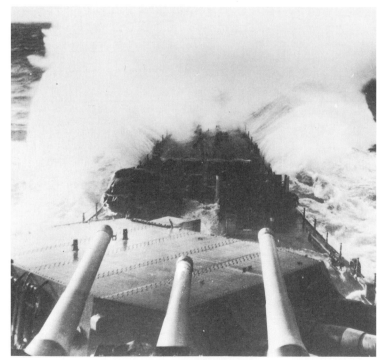

Below: Mess aboard the *Missouri*, September 1948. By this point, the serious overcrowding experienced by the ships during World War Two had been alleviated. As a truism, it was often noted that the ships were miniature cities with their own tailor, cobbler and barber shops, with storerooms of every conceivable description, and with complete hospital and dental facilities. Note the photographer's assistant with the supplementary flash at the top of the picture. [NARS]

Folding bunks on the *New Jersey*, 1943. With two men sleeping side by side, the utter lack of privacy is quite obvious. The battleships went to war in 1944 with close to 3000 men aboard, and the maze of passage-ways confused many new sailors. One *Wisconsin* bluejacket, after looking for a friend in another division for three days, finally wrote a postcard: 'Meet me on deck beside turret No 3 at noon.' [USN]

The *New Jersey*'s sick bay, fall of 1943. Note the complex of overhead ventilation ducts, fire mains and deck drains. [USN]

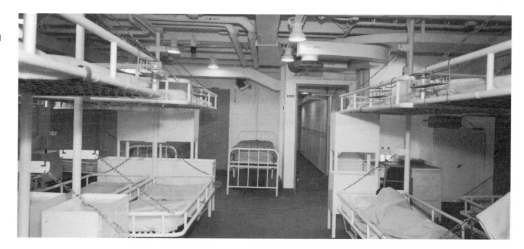

The captain's cabin on the *New Jersey*, fall 1943. [USN]

However spartan, the captain's cabin in the *New Jersey* in 1943 looks luxurious in comparison to the crew's quarters. Rank has its privileges and also its necessities. Note the telephone, clock, safe, fan, and reading lights. Captain Carl Holden apparently was a mystery buff: two of the 'Saint' series lie on the top shelf. Underneath them stand a *Bartlett's*, a *Webster's* and a collection of *National Geographic* maps. [USN]

The *New Jersey*'s chart house, fall 1943. [USN]

The bridge and conning tower of the *New Jersey*, 11 October 1943. The original open bridge had not proved satisfactory in the *Iowa*. Top officers were supposed to fight the ship from inside the conning tower, and their vision slits are visible inside the enclosed bridge. [USN]

of the screws. Smaller ships coming alongside, in consequence, were instructed to stay even with the battleship's bridge and not drop astern. Vessels that disregarded this procedure sometimes paid for their carelessness. On 4 November 1944, the destroyer *Colahan*, passing mail to the *New Jersey*, fell too far back and was drawn into the big ship's port quarter by screw current suction. Although no one was injured, the destroyer's anchor damaged stanchions, lifelines and chocks on the *New Jersey*. A similar accident occurred in the Korean War when the destroyer *Rowan* was pulled into the stern of the *Missouri*.[15]

In port, an 'Iowa's' handling changed completely. Quick and responsive on high seas, the battleship in shallow water acted like 'a dead log', in the words of one officer.[16] For a variety of hydrodynamic reasons, a battleship with only a fathom of water under her keel responds to the rudder very sluggishly, and usually the engines had to be employed to help steer the ship. But shallow water makes life more difficult for the battleship officer in another way: his ship's speed becomes less predictable. Acceleration is slower and slowing more rapid than usual. In ports like New York or Norfolk, an 'Iowa' often has less than five feet of water under her bottom, and consequently, the big ships ordinarily rely on tugs for even the simplest movements.

Transiting the Panama Canal was always a sensitive operation. In the locks, the battleships had just inches of water under the bottom and less than a foot of clearance on each side.

They would always scrape a bit as they were towed into the locks at two or three miles an hour. For instance, when the *Wisconsin* went through for the first time in early October 1944, her CO tried to save the paint by draping mattresses and fenders over the side. As she was leaving one lock, cross currents bashed her against the side and dished in 12 ft of plating.[17]

In rough weather, the ships were usually quite steady. One of the COs of the *New Jersey* remembered her bow quivering as the ship drove into very heavy waves, and he wondered if she might lose her fore section as the heavy cruiser *Pittsburgh* had done. In certain seas though, the battleships would roll. During a NATO operation in the North Atlantic in September 1953, the *Iowa* registered a 26° roll each way (at the same time, HMS *Vanguard* experienced a 15° roll). The 'Iowas' have always been wet ships. The *Missouri* reported in August 1950 after she passed close to the eye of a hurricane, 'with normal loading and even moderate seas, *Missouri* takes considerable water across the fantail'.[18] The vessels also especially shipped water where the hull narrowed forward of No. 1 turret. Nonetheless, they are the only ships in existence capable of staying with the big carriers in really heavy weather.

Life aboard the battleships was spartan during the first two years. When the light anti-aircraft battery ballooned during World War Two, the vessels became grossly overcrowded. Designed for a complement of 1,924 officers and men, the *Wisconsin* left Philadelphia for the war with 2,724 aboard. Troughs in the heads and the four-high berths did not allow even a modicum of privacy for the men.

Accommodations for the officers were not exactly generous. Despite their size, the battleships had surprisingly small staff facilities. In action, the top officers were supposed to be at their battle stations inside the heavily armored conning tower, but the view through the vision slits was poor, and the quarters were cramped. Consequently, the CO would often exercise his authority from the bridge. In the press of active duty, some battleship captains lived at their stations. John McCrea of the *Iowa* spent 68 consecutive days and nights on the bridge of his ship without once going to his cabin three decks below. Rear Admiral Olaf Hustvedt, the commander of BatDiv 9, lived inside his flag conning tower. He slept on a cot and visited his cabin only to shower.[19]

Supplies sometimes grew scarce on an operation, especially because the smaller ships
called upon the battleships for provisions. The
experience of the *Iowa* in October 1944 can be
regarded as fairly typical. She started the
month 20 tons short of fresh meat, a problem
aggravated by the fact that her allowance was
identical to that of the 'South Dakotas' which
had 500 fewer men aboard. The *Iowa* also
reported severe shortages of rags, cordage and
lumber. During the month, she transferred 45
tons of provisions to cruisers, destroyers and
tankers, including 400 gallons of ice cream to
the oilers. Her action report noted, 'At no time
were any requests for fresh provisions
refused'.[20]

Despite these problems, the Iowas generally
had the reputation of being happy ships. The
battleship mystique was real enough. The *New
Jersey*'s re-enlistment rate in 1969 during a
most unpopular war was 80.7 per cent. The
Iowa's cruise book for the Korean conflict
boasts:

There is no ship that sails the seven seas whose guns
are mightier than ours. No ship afloat has engines
more powerful. No battleship in the world has
greater ability to withstand the punishment and
survive than we. This is our ship.[21]

For many officers, the command of an 'Iowa'
represented the apex of their careers. Robert
Lee Dennison regarded the *Missouri* as 'the
premier command in the navy for a captain' in
1947; William Smedberg called the *Iowa* 'the
greatest command that a man could have at
sea'. Charles Melson took over the *New Jersey*
during the Korean War and reflected later,
'There was more personal satisfaction in commanding this big ship than any other assignment I had.' Another *New Jersey* CO, Tony
McCorkle, exclaimed upon learning of his
posting to that ship, 'After this job, everything
will be downhill.'[22] In 1946, Rear Admiral
Raymond D. Tarbuck requested the *Iowa*.
Told that he would have to turn in his flag rank
to get her, he did so without hesitation. He
later reminisced:

I had her out in mid-Pacific, and it was a lot of fun
twisting her tail ... In the open sea at full speed she
was just grand, like flying 58,000 tons of steel. For
this thrill—I had turned in my stars. It was my last
chance to feel the call of the high seas.[23]

The interior of the *New Jersey*'s conning tower in 1943. The thickness of the armor may be gauged by the two vision slits in the port side. Two periscopes are clearly visible; less obvious is a speed indicator (the black round instrument above the switchbox to the left) reading 12 knots. Many officers disliked the conning tower for its limited visibility. [USN]

The massive conning tower armor on the *Iowa* can be clearly discerned by a glance at the 17.3-inch thick door. Note the periscopes on the top, and the narrow vision slit on the starboard side. [Author]

The business end of a 16″/50. The photograph was taken aboard the *New Jersey*, 18 June 1951, on her first Korean tour of duty. The rifling grooves in the liner can be seen somewhat indistinctly. Note the SK-2 air search radar high atop the ship's fire control tower, and directly under the radar, the Mk 38 main battery director with its arms projecting and its blocky fire control radar on top. The director obtains the target bearing and range as well as the level and cross-level angles for the fire control system. It held a crew of seven and could be rotated either manually or electrically. The rangefinder element measures 26½ feet across; the director also contains a 12 power spotter's periscope (for target and fall-of-shot observations) and a time-of-flight buzzer which sounds just before the projectiles hit, thus helping the spotter in identifying the ship's salvo. [USN]

The *Iowa* firing a 16-inch salvo during Operation UNITAS in the Caribbean Sea, 5 August 1984. Note the projectile caught by the camera as a blur in flight. Some of the target and HC projectiles used during and shortly after World War Two were fitted at the base with an orange tracer, so that the shells could be followed by eye. One sailor described them as 'glowing like bolts from hell'. Today, it is possible to get a glimpse of a projectile as it leaves the muzzle if it is fired with a reduced charge. An *Iowa* fire control master chief said of a practice in the fall of 1985: 'In a surface shoot against an iceberg off Greenland, I saw a number of blue painted projectiles in the instant before impact or near miss. This was a full charge shoot at 13,000 yards.' [USN]

Intimately associated with this attraction was the 16″/50 gun, the most powerful rifle ever mounted in an American ship. Weighing 120 tons and 68 ft long, this weapon could fire, per minute, two AP shells weighing 2,700 pounds apiece to a distance of 22.8 miles. To house this new weapon, the Bureau of Ordnance designed a turret with a variety of improvements. Compared to the double turret of the World War One era, the new triple turret featured better protection, a lower silhouette, a welded structure and much improved compartmentation. In the magazines, the new concentric rotating projectile rings were generally safer and easier for the personnel in everyday use. The rings also made feasible ammunition handling in rough seas.

Increased safety was also bought by a system of interlocks between the gun house and the powder handling room. In the former, the cradle and spanning tray, which were operated automatically by electric-hydraulic drive, reduced the time required to load the guns and the fatigue of the crew. Reversible projectile hoists eliminated the need for auxiliary hoists.[24]

By later standards, the turrets were labor intensive. Each required a crew of 77 men: 30 in the gun house, 4 on the electric deck, 30 in the two projectile handling flats and 13 in the powder handling room. The turrets were also marvellously complex pieces of equipment, and their design and operation was covered in minute detail by the turret manual (OP 769), a volume of almost 500 pages that, by itself, showed the care which the United States Navy lavished on the 'Iowa'-class battleships.

33

The projectiles—the Navy eschewed the term 'shells'—were also more than met the eye. The AP 'bullet' had to withstand the great stresses of firing and rotational forces (a 16″/50 projectile turned at 4,000 RPM as it left the muzzle). It had to cut through armor specifically designed to keep it out without breaking up or glancing off and then—and only then—explode. To accomplish these difficult tasks, the 16-inch AP shell was made of a chromenickel steel given a heat treatment to harden the nose while the remainder of the shell body remained softer and less brittle. Onto this body was soldered and peened a hardened cap designed to stress the armor plate and to prevent a ricochet. To give the shell adequate aerodynamic performance, a ballistic windshield was fitted onto the cap. A load of dye was usually placed under the windshield to color the shell splashes so that a ship could identify its own. In any case, the projectile body contained the explosive charge, and of the 2,700-lb AP shell weight, this charge amounted to only 41 lbs. It was a substance called Explosive D, or ammonium picrate, a crystalline powder which was slightly inferior to TNT in explosive strength, but it had the great virtue of withstanding severe shock—a prerequisite if it were to penetrate thick armor

before exploding. In fact, Explosive D was loaded into the projectile with a hydraulic press. Following the shell's impact with armor, or water or earth, the AP charge was set off by a base-detonating fuse (of lead azide) which functioned after a .033-second delay during which time the projectile had travelled 48 to 66 ft through the target ship, ocean or enemy bunker.

The 16-inch bombardment shell was less esoteric. Usually called a high capacity (or HC) projectile, it indeed contained more of the Explosive D, but only 153 lbs of the substance. Usually equipped with a point detonating fuse on the tip of the nose, the HC shell was timed to explode only 1/100 second after impact. It is this shell which makes up the bulk of an 'Iowa's' ammunition load today, as has been the case since World War Two. In Vietnam, the *New Jersey* carried a total of 1,202 rounds, 95 per cent of which were HC projectiles. In addition to their service ammunition, the battleships also carry inert practice rounds and drill projectiles. These cheaply made projectiles substitute admirably in turret exercises and target shoots when the Navy would prefer

Two 16-inch HC shells come aboard the *Iowa* at Sasebo, Japan, on 15 May 1952, in preparation for her return to the bombline, Korea. Caps protect their point detonating fuses. The *Missouri*, in the fall of 1950, was the first battleship to reammo at Sasebo, and all the specialised equipment—the shell sling cradles, eye bolts and projectile trucks—had to be brought from the United States. Working with 1900-pound shells like this pair was always inherently dangerous. Serious accidents have been few, but one man on the *Wisconsin* was injured when a 2700-pound AP shell fell five decks down an ammunition strikedown trunk in 1944. [USN]

16″/50 projectiles being loaded aboard the *New Jersey* off Norfolk in the spring of 1968. Under the ballistic cap of an AP or target projectile, there is a load of dye to facilitate spotting the fall of shot. The *Iowa*'s dye colour is orange; the *New Jersey*'s, blue; the *Missouri*'s, red; and the *Wisconsin*'s, green. [USN]

The silk powder bags weigh 110 lb each for the AP shell and 50 to 55 lb for the HC round. The gun captain and the cradle operator are spreading out the first batch of three charges on the spanning tray so that the second batch of three will fit between them. Note that the circular black powder ignition charge quilted onto the end of the bag faces away from the gun. This charge must always be loaded next to the primer vent, and the quilted end is therefore dyed red. No new powder has been manufactured for 16-inch charges since the Korean War. This picture was probably taken aboard the *New Jersey* in the fall of 1944. [USN]

to avoid the expenditure of HC shells, each of which cost $1,352 at the time of the Korean War. In fact, no assembly line for 16-inch ammunition exists at the time of writing, but the extant rounds are in excellent condition. Most of the shells fired by the *New Jersey* in Vietnam had been made during the late 1930s, and they gave an excellent performance.[25]

To drive a 2,700-lb shell at 1,700 miles per hour over 20 miles took 660 lbs of powder; the lighter HC shell was usually fired with half that amount. The Navy used several types of propellent, but all were derivatives of nitrocellulose. The powder was formed into tubular

grains which were almost an inch long and perforated by seven holes to ensure uniform burning. These grains were sewn up into unbleached silk bags designed to burn completely. If any smoldering residue remained in the barrel, it could ignite the powder bags for the next round before the breech was locked. The resulting explosion, called a blowback, could be catastrophic. While bombarding Makin on 20 November 1943, the old battleship *Mississippi* suffered a blowback in No. 2 turret which burned 42 men to death.[26]

For reduced charges, the propellant grains were dumped into the silk bags; for full charges, the grains were stacked. Since the dumped grains occupied more space, the reduced charges weighed about 55 lbs each, the full charges a hefty 110 lbs. The identity of the charge was stenciled on the bag with information on the lot number. As far as possible, charges from one lot were kept together since different blends had slightly different ballistic properties. Quilted to one end of each powder bag was a black powder ignition charge which had to be loaded facing the rear of the gun. The black powder in turn was ignited by a primer

After every salvo, the guns come down to their 5° loading angle, and then an innocuous-looking puff of white smoke issues from the muzzle. After all the sound and fury, the sight is almost comical in its contrast, but the reason behind the operation is deadly serious. The bore must be purged of any smoldering remnants of powder bags to avert a blowback (see text). The air blast also expels any of the dangerous gases (such as carbon monoxide, ammonia, hydrogen and methane) generated by the propellant combustion. In fact, the turrets are ventilated by eight independent systems which supply air to all levels but the powder handling room. The intakes for these systems are at the rear of the gun house or under the turret overhang. This photograph was made aboard the *Iowa* in August 1985. [Author]

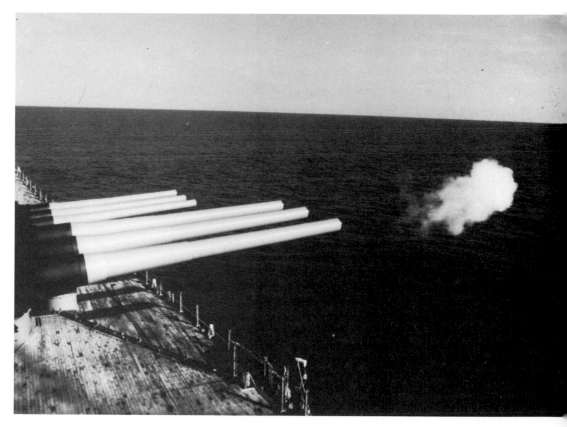

fired either by percussion or more usually by electricity.[27]

Despite a substantial drop in muzzle velocity, gunners preferred to use reduced charges if at all possible to save on barrel wear. For instance, 100 AP rounds fired with full charges would shave .281 inches of metal from the inside of the bore. After 316 such shots, the battleship would be shooting a 16.5-inch gun. This situation was not a happy one. Barrel erosion led to decreased muzzle velocity because as the projectile was rammed, it seated further down the bore. Fuse performance degenerated from the shock loading on the fuse components as the projectile hit the rifling. Accuracy fell off with muzzle velocity variation or with insufficient projectile spin rate caused when the shell's rotating band failed to grip the rifling tightly enough.[28]

Reduced charges greatly prolonged the life of a gun. For instance, the AP projectile with a reduced charge was less than 1/10th as hard on the gun as the service charge, and fired with the lighter charges only, a gun could be expected to last over 3,000 rounds. The trade-off was a drop in muzzle velocity from 2,500 f/s to 1,800 f/s. Fortunately, the recent introduction of Swedish additive and cooler-burning powders has cut the erosion rate to insignificant levels (see Chapter 9).

The charges for the HC projectile sometimes caused trouble early in the ships' careers. The powder bags were occasionally mis-shapen, and these tended to tumble from the hoist to the loading tray. The gun captain and the cradle operator had to catch these 55-lb bags to prevent them from falling into the gun pit. In the confusion, the risk arose that the rearmost charge would be loaded into the gun backward (with the black powder ignition end facing the muzzle). The *Missouri* suffered such a failure off Korea, in February 1951, so did the *Wisconsin* when she was shelling Okinawa, on 24 March 1945. In the latter case, as the gun was being reprimed, a trickle of smoke issued from the primer vent indicating that a hangfire was in progress. The ship's action report theorised that the rearmost bags tumbled in the powder chamber when the gun was elevated and emphasised, 'Reduced charge bags *will* fit sideways in the powder chamber.'[29]

Ensuring the accuracy of the 16″/50 at normal battle ranges demanded a complex fire control system. To oversimplify, gunnery con-

trol officers, in planning for a ship-to-ship engagement, had to consider the following variables: the speed and course of their battleship, the speed and course and range of the enemy vessel, the pitch and roll of their ship, the speed and direction of the wind, the type of shell and charge to be used, the state of their guns regarding bore erosion, and at normal battle ranges the curvature and rotation of the earth. Such a wide array of variables mandated some sort of computer system which, in turn, demanded a reliable method for spotting and correcting the fall of shot. The system developed for the 'Iowas' was almost labyrinthian. Three principal components made up the system: the directors, computers and stable elements. The main directors (two Mk 38s) determined target range, bearing and level angle. The stable elements (two Mk 41s) were gyroscopes which measured the level and cross-level to stabilise the fire control system. Both fed data to the two Mk 8 analog computers (generally called the rangekeepers) which then calculated the aiming point for the guns.[30]

There was a great deal of redundancy built into the system, so that the failure of any one component could be quickly bypassed. For example, all the turrets were (generally) controlled by one of the main battery directors working in concert with the main battery plotting rooms. In the 'automatic' mode, the guns were aimed by either plotting room directly (through receiver regulators). In the 'indicating' mode, the turret crew aimed the guns by matching pointers with signals from the plotters. As a back-up method of operation,

16-inch reduced charges being loaded aboard the *New Jersey* in August 1968 before her departure to Vietnam. Each canister holds three bagged charges which weigh about 160 pounds (less the container). It is essential to keep the charges in air-tight containers; otherwise the ether and alcohol mixture will evaporate, and the performance of the powder would be adversely affected. Worse, the loss of these volatile elements leaves a powder with high, rather than low, explosive characteristics; that is, a powder that will explode rather than burn. The result would be a ballistically dangerous substance that might explode the gun. [USN]

Rangefinder for turret No 3 of *Iowa*, May 1943. The rangefinder pointer (farthest from the camera) keeps the rangefinder lines of sight on the target in elevation (to follow the roll of the ship). The rangefinder operator (center) is in charge of the large, 46-foot base length instrument. He generally serves as back-up to the primary or secondary armament directors unless his turret is acting as the director or is under local control (see text). At right, the rangefinder trainer maintains the lines of sight on target in deflection or azimuth motion. Note the large deflection handwheel connected to the highly polished, round deflection indicator dial. The box structure above and to the right of the trainer is the range transmitter whose signals go to the turret officer's switchboard and from there to the main battery switchboards in the plotting rooms. After World War Two, these transmitters were deactivated. The turret rangefinder has a maximum range of 70,000 yards and is much more accurate than the rangefinder in the Mk 38 anti-aircraft directors. Consequently, this rangefinder was sometimes used to track low-flying aircraft as the *Wisconsin* did at 50,000 yards on 24 January 1945 with 'excellent results'. [NARS]

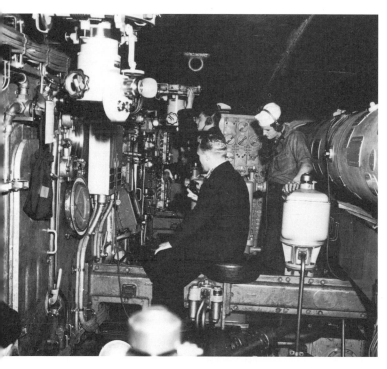

Turret officer's compartment—*Iowa*, May 1943. Fully manned, this location would hold six. The front of the large circular rangefinder cuts across the back of the compartment. Just beyond the bulkhead at left lie the gun pits, cradles, spanning trays and the guns themselves. The bulkhead serves as a flame barrier; one gun crew could be lost without losing the entire turret. The turret officer stands at his periscope with his fire controlman in the white hat behind him. Seated closest to the camera is the computer operator who takes over fire control calculations when the turret is on local control. Note the hatches leading to the guns, the untended turret captain's periscope and the square announcing system control box in front of the computer operator whose body hides most of his auxiliary computer from the camera. His padded seat is perched atop the rammer chain housing for the center gun. The white tank immediately to his rear houses the hydraulic fluid supply for the center rammer. A small portion of the right rammer chain housing can be made out at the level of the turret officer's thighs. The ring attached to the turret roof is used for chain falls to move heavy turret equipment for repair purposes. Visible between the turret officer and the fire controlman is the transfer switchboard with its rotary disc switches.

A turret officer's fire control station on the *Missouri* on her way out to Korea in 1950. By the officer's left hand is the transfer switchboard. The top six switches all relate to turret train. Behind the officer's head is his periscope. The indicator panel over his right shoulder tells the status of the three guns in the turret. A gas ejector air supply gauge is attached to the bulkhead at upper left; the auxiliary computer lower left. [NARS]

Seaman A. W. Fehndrich mans the phones at the dead reckoning tracer table in the main plot room of the *Missouri*. The map shows that she is engaged in a practice shoot at the Kahoolawe range before moving on to Korea in the late summer, 1950. Each battleship has two main plotting rooms, and the entire fire control system is designed with a great deal of redundancy (see text). [NARS]

This main battery switchboard can be seen behind the tracer table in the preceding photograph. The fire control switchboards are points of convergence from which the various elements of the fire control system can be activated and connected. Numerous alternate circuits can be set up in the event of casualties to a portion of the system. There are 130 'J' type rotary switches on each of the two main battery switchboards. [NARS]

however, one turret was able to act as the director for the other two, and with the same two basic types of operation: 'automatic' and 'indicating'. Finally, if all else failed, a turret crew could fire their three guns under local control, that is, completely independently, with all calculations being made in the turret. Thus, the turret officer had also to learn the duties of a director officer.[31]

Fire control officers were immeasurably assisted in the early 1940s by the development of radar. Shell splashes made easily discernible echoes on the scope, so that blind firing became possible in conditions of reduced visibility. In fact, the projectile itself could be followed during its flight as a small, weak moving echo. Certain limitations existed: echoes from direct hits or near misses were lost in the target echo; several shells landing close together could not be distinguished separately; deflection spotting was more difficult than spotting for range. Nonetheless, radar proved early in World War Two to be an invaluable asset, and the 'Iowas' were fitted, while still under construction, with two SG-1 surface search sets, two Mk 8 radars for their Mk 38 directors, four Mk 4s for their 5-inch directors and an SK air-search radar. The big Mk 8 sets were often very useful in picking out terrain features to fix a ship's position for a shore bombardment.[32]

Radar was of no help, however, in spotting the fall of projectiles ashore because their impacts were not visible on the scope. In fact,

bombardment of enemy positions on land offered its own set of challenges to which the 'Iowas' had increasingly to adapt as support of friendly forces became their primary mission. Before World War Two, not one US Navy gun system was designed with shore bombardment in mind. Quite by accident, then, the 16"/50 proved extremely well suited to the task, although a wide variety of problems, such as reverse slope spotting and communication with troops ashore, took practice to solve.

Some of the early radars showed themselves to be vulnerable to blast damage. For instance, in just one bombardment in July 1945, the *Iowa*'s big guns sheared struts on her SK and cracked its frame. After every salvo, her SG set went blind, but it was reset immediately. The antenna cover on another set was caved in.[33]

In fact, the enormous blast pressure from the big guns always demanded respect. Generating overpressures of more than 50 PSI close to the muzzle (and 7 PSI up to 50 ft away), the 16"/50 blast could do significant damage to the battleship. For instance, during five days of action off Korea in March 1951, the guns of the *Missouri* split vent ducts and welds, fractured the deck in two places, loosened teak planks, and did superficial injury to the hull structure and fittings in the vicinity of turret No. 3. Similarly, when the *New Jersey* engaged in a trials shoot on 17 April 1968, her guns blew life rafts out of their racks and tore apart an accommodation ladder stowed near the aft

The *Missouri* firecontrolman is standing at one of the Mk 41 stable verticals. An integral part of the fire control system, their gyroscopes measure and transmit, both electrically and mechanically, level and cross-level to stabilize the fire control system. The sailor is gripping the firing keys. Any one of the three, which are connected to different circuits, can touch off as many guns as are programmed to fire at the moment. Identical sets of keys are in both plotting rooms and in the director's. The guns can also be fired locally from the turrets. [NARS]

The Mk 8 range keeper is an analog computer that solves the complex fire control problems and transmits the information necessary to aim the guns. The Plotting Room Officer (the lieutenant at right) is giving the order to fire; he knows the guns are ready through a series of 'turret ready lights' and two alternate telephone circuits. This photograph was part of the series taken aboard the *Missouri*, as is the next. The forward plotting room is close behind the barbette to No 2 turret; the after plotting room is located just ahead of No 3 barbette. Both are sited behind the belt armor and under the armor decks. [NARS]

turret. Several on-lookers lost their hats overboard.[34]

Surprisingly, the 5"/38 was harder on the crew than the main battery. As one sailor described the experience of the concussion from the 16-inch guns: 'is tremendous, but it builds up. It's like being hit by a slow truck wrapped in sofa cushions. The 5-inchers, damn them, hit you like a plank.'[35] And they could hurt. Twelve men aboard the *New Jersey* off Okinawa suffered badly enough from 5-inch blast to need medical attention. During that same operation, seven *Wisconsin* sailors were put under medical supervision for several days for chest and nasal problems due to the 5-inchers; two more men suffered first and second degree flash burns from the stubby weapons. The preceding year, Rear Admiral Hustvedt, seated on the starboard side of *Iowa*'s bridge, was literally blown out of his chair by the unexpected discharge of the nearest 5-incher whose muzzle was perhaps 25 ft away. The admiral suffered permanent damage to his right eye.[36]

But the whole point was to damage the enemy, and the battleship guns would certainly do that. A 16-inch AP projectile would penetrate 30 ft of reinforced concrete. A single HC round landing in a South Vietnamese jungle would create a helicopter landing zone 200 yards in diameter and defoliate trees for 300 yards beyond that. HC projectiles often gouged out craters 50 ft across and 20 ft deep. Of course, the shells arrived at supersonic speeds and thus gave no warning whatsoever.

Unfortunates on the receiving end usually found battleship gunfire very demoralising.[37]

However, the 'Iowas' had been designed in large part to fight other battleships, something they never had a chance to do. Yet it is interesting to speculate for a moment as to the results of a possible showdown with their Axis counterparts. The operative word here must be 'possible'. Because the *Iowa* and *New Jersey* came into service in the fall of 1943, an engagement between the American ships and the French or Italian battleships was clearly out of the question by that time.

However, the *Iowa* was briefly stationed in the North Atlantic to guard against a sortie by the *Tirpitz*, the sister of the *Bismarck* sunk two years earlier. These enemy ships were very well protected against shells at close range—a central consideration for German designers in the mid-1930s before radar cleared away the mists of the North Sea and the Atlantic. The US Navy calculated after the war that the German magazine armor was proof against the light 2,240-lb AP shell to about 25,500 yards.

But the *Iowa* fired the heavy 2,700-lb AP which would have penetrated the German vitals at the longer ranges that the American officers preferred and that the better American radar made possible. Add to this overwhelming advantage the American superior speed of two or three knots (and thus the ability to choose the range), and the *Iowa* should have been able to make short work of the *Tirpitz* had the two ever met.[38]

The outcome of a duel between the *Iowa* and the *Yamato* would have been much more problematical and the two ships missed each other only by the narrowest margin at Leyte Gulf (see Chapter 3). The guns of both ships could penetrate the other's decks above 35,000 yards. During the daytime, the American ships with the advantage of air control—and thus of aerial observation—should have been able to hit the Japanese ships over the horizon. Hindsight certainly dictates that the *Iowa* should not get too close to the *Yamato*, and presumably, the speed advantage of the American ship would have come into play here. Had the contestants met at night, as was entirely possible during the later stages of the battle, the far superior American radar should have told heavily. It must be emphasised too that the *Yamato* would have fought not just the *Iowa*, but the *New Jersey* as well. In fact, had

Halsey played his cards right, a full scale fleet action would have occurred.[39]

Of course, this comfortable scenario might not have held. Admiral Willis A. Lee, the American gunnery expert, might have decided to close quickly with the Japanese to finish them off. At these lesser battle ranges, the thicker side protection of the *Yamato* could have proved decisive. Even at this late stage of the war, American intelligence still rated the *Yamato* as a relatively conventional vessel with 16-inch guns. Then, too, the element of chance has often been critical in war. The *South Dakota* should, by all calculations, have made short work of IJN *Kirishima* at Guadalcanal in November 1942. Instead, in a confused night action, the old Japanese battlecruiser gave far more punishment than she received until the fresh *Washington* bailed out her compatriot.

Still, it is hard to avoid the conclusion that the 'Iowas' were the most formidable battleships ever constructed. Although their armor was not as thick as the *Yamato*'s nor their guns of equal caliber, the Japanese AP shell was not that much heavier (3,219 vs 2,700 lbs). More to the point, the American guns could penetrate the Japanese decks at extreme range. Whoever got in the first good hits would probably have won. With her superb fire control system, they probably would have been by the *Iowa*.

3 TO WAR

With the first of the 'Iowa' class commissioning in mid-1943, the ships entered service at a time when the chances were ebbing for action against Axis battleships. As the tempo of the Allied offensive increased, aircraft were becoming increasingly the dominant naval arm. Yet the large expenditure of resources on the big-gun ships paid dividends. The *Iowa* and *New Jersey* found plenty to do.

The name ship entered service first. Capt. John L. McCrea presided over the commissioning of the *Iowa* at New York on 22 February 1943. Two days later, she began her shakedown cruise in the Chesapeake and continued her working-up throughout the spring and summer along the Atlantic coast. On 16 July, the ship suffered substantial damage when she scraped bottom while navigating Hussey Sound to enter Casco Bay, Maine—a very tricky passage.

The twisting, narrow channel required Capt. McCrea to maneuver the 888-ft long ship through a tight 'S' turn in waters made trickier by strong currents. However, the *Iowa* had shown her nimbleness in close quarters in New York harbor and had, in fact, already made the trip into Casco Bay five times without incident. As McCrea confidently took his ship in at 12 knots, he was startled to hear from his station on the bridge a ghastly scraping sound as the ship's bottom was gouged by a rocky outcropping. McCrea initially thought that 'something had gone wrong with some

machinery in the ship'.[1] Inspection showed the damage to the port side to be serious. Rivets were sheared; the plating was bulged at one point; a seam had parted; and several rips in the hull had ruptured 16 fuel tanks. The damage extended from frames 76 3/4 to 139 3/4 (a distance of 252 ft) with indentations in the bulge up to 30 inches deep. All transverse floors were bent over 62 frames (248 ft), and sections of 64 floors and frames had to be cut out and refurbished. Virtually all the steam heating coils and the adjacent piping were damaged, and 18 hull plates required replacement.

The *Iowa* spent over a month at Boston Navy Yard under repair, and Capt. McCrea's career lay on the line. His prior record as a smart shiphandler helped him. Admiral C. F. Bryant, Commander of Battleships, Atlantic Fleet, recommended McCrea's retention especially on that ground. Final exoneration came from President Roosevelt who took a personal interest in the case because McCrea had been his naval aide.

Ready again for action on 27 August, the *Iowa* headed for Argentia, Newfoundland to stand distant watch on the *Tirpitz* as the Allies prepared resumption of convoys to Russia in the fall. Less than two weeks later, the *Tirpitz* flexed her muscles by bombarding Spitzbergen. However, any chance for an *Iowa-Tirpitz* gunnery duel (see Chapter 2) evaporated when the German ship was mined on 22 September

The *Iowa* in early April 1943. She has been in commission for barely six weeks. The roof of turret No 2 is devoid of any anti-aircraft guns, as is her bow. Because there is, as yet, no enclosed bridge, her three conning tower levels are visible. Note that the censor had blotted out all her radars. [USN]

by British midget submarines. Ultra intercepts revealed to the Allies the extent of the damage, and the *Iowa* was freed for other duties.

On 25 October, the *Iowa* entered Norfolk Navy Yard for almost two weeks of maintenance. The Yard devoted special effort to putting in top shape the brickwork on the boilers, for the battleship had been selected to take President Roosevelt and a top-ranking delegation at high speed to North Africa for the Cairo and Teheran meetings with Chiang Kai-Shek, Stalin and Churchill. Specially installed for the President was a bathtub—the only one fitted aboard a fighting ship in the Navy.

On 11 November, the *Iowa*, after having discharged virtually all her oil, headed up the Potomac as far as practicable. She first took aboard the Joint Chiefs of Staff party headed by Admiral King, Gen. George C. Marshall and Gen. 'Hap' Arnold. The next day, the presidential yacht *Potomac* came alongside and FDR, Harry Hopkins, and Admiral William Leahy boarded the *Iowa* with no ceremony at Roosevelt's specific direction. Altogether, the top officials with their retinues totalled 80 more or less important people to be quartered aboard the *Iowa*.

Back at Hampton Roads, the dignitaries were ordered to stay below decks for the sake of security. FDR held up the sailing of the *Iowa* until five minutes after midnight on 13 November, so that the voyage would not start on a Friday. One of FDR's aides wondered if the gesture reflected genuine superstition on the part of the President, or whether he was playing the role of the old salt.[2]

Two escort carriers, the *Block Island* and *Santee*, positioned along the route provided continuous air coverage, although Capt. McCrea complained that he often learned a plane was on station only when it signalled by lamp, 'I go'.[3] More visible were the three destroyers in constant attendance. Because of the speedy crossing (24.6 knots average) and the short range of the escorts, three destroyer groups relieved each other in turn.

The crew of the *Iowa* found time for much anti-aircraft practice, and the escorting destroyers found the *Iowa* a perfect target for torpedo drill. On 14 November, the *William D. Porter* accidentally fired a torpedo at the *Iowa*. The timing could hardly have been worse: FDR and all the passengers were on deck watching anti-aircraft practice. Although the destroyer immediately notified the *Iowa*, the

The bathtub installed in the *Iowa* for FDR's convenience. This was the only such plumbing fixture in the United States Navy. Located just off the captain's cabin, it is still aboard the battleship. [USN]

wake of the torpedo, set to run at a depth of 16 ft and a speed of 46 knots, was initially invisible in the rough seas. Capt. McCrea went to available full power (29 knots at the time) and turned toward the *William D. Porter*. At that point, the after gun watches spotted the torpedo about 1,000 yards from the *Iowa*'s starboard quarter. The anti-aircraft batteries opened fire, and after what seemed a very long time to Admiral Leahy, the torpedo exploded close by with the force of a depth charge.

No material damage was done, but the incident made the Navy 'look badly' before the top-ranking officers in the Army. The *William D. Porter* reported that moisture had caused a short in the firing mechanism—an explanation that Capt. McCrea found unsatisfactory. Ultimately the President ordered that no one be punished for the accident. But as each successive group of destroyers joined up, McCrea ordered them not to use the *Iowa* as a target in torpedo drills.

As the battleship neared Gibraltar, she traded her third group of three destroyers for an escort of the cruiser *Brooklyn* and five British and American destroyers. The ships ran through the Straits at 27 knots in the dark, but Spanish searchlights silhouetted the task force for almost 30 minutes. The Allied force countered the unwelcome light with a destroyer-laid smoke screen.

The *Iowa* reached Mers-el-Kebir where the presidential party disembarked. Fueling was cut short after only 700,000 gallons of oil had been loaded (about one-half the amount desired) because Admiral J. H. D. Cunningham, RN, warned the *Iowa* to leave the Mediterranean as quickly as possible. The ship's arrival, he said, would be known to the enemy within hours, and he felt that the *Iowa* made just the type of 'profitable target' that the

Germans would attack with guided bombs. Only two months before, the Luftwaffe had sunk the *Roma* and damaged the *Italia* and *Warspite* with 'Fritz-X' missiles.[4]

The *Iowa* therefore hurriedly left Mers-el-Kebir shortly before sunset, passed Gibraltar again in the dark, and crossed the Atlantic to Bahia, Brazil where she spent a day topping off her bunkers. She then headed east once again to pick up the presidential delegation at Dakar, but that harbor had to be avoided since torpedo protection for the anchorage was judged inadequate. The *Iowa* therefore waited two days at Freetown, Sierra Leone to rendezvous on 9 December with FDR and party who arrived, after an all day flight from Tunis, aboard the French destroyer *Gazelle*.

The return trip was slowed by the inability of the escorting destroyers to maintain high speed in bad weather. Nonetheless, the westward run of 3,941 miles was made at an average speed of 23.6 knots. Before boarding the *Potomac* on 16 December, Roosevelt, as 'the chief shellback of them all' congratulated the crew on crossing-the-line. They certainly had been on the move. In the 33 days since the President had first come aboard on 13 November, the ship had been underway 713 out of 808 hours and had covered 16,161 miles. The machinery had functioned perfectly, and the crew had refined their combat skills.

They would soon need them, because on 2 January 1944, the *Iowa* left Hampton Roads for the Pacific as flagship of Battleship Division 7, under Rear Admiral O. M. Hustvedt. Making up the other half of the division was the *New Jersey*. The second ship of the class had commissioned on 23 May, three months after the *Iowa*. Under Capt. Carl F. Holden, the *New Jersey* had worked up in the Caribbean and Western Atlantic during the summer and fall. 'A happy ship', one of her officers called her.[5]

After transiting the Panama Canal on 7 January, the two new battleships reported to Raymond Spruance's Fifth Fleet on 22 January. Although some of the veteran aviators resented the snappy appearance and win-the-war attitude of the battleship sailors, Rear Admiral Frederick Sherman remarked to Capt. McCrea, 'Thank goodness you people are here. From here on, I shan't have to worry about providing our own anti-aircraft coverage.'[6]

The ships saw quick service in just that role. They sailed the next day to support carrier strikes against Kwajalein and Eniwetok. Although no enemy planes appeared, three weeks later the *Iowa* and *New Jersey* fired their weapons in anger for the first time in the sweep against the Japanese bastion of Truk on 16 February. Spruance planned the operation

The *New Jersey* as completed in the summer of 1943 with an open bridge. She lacks the four 40-mm quad batteries that will be mounted in pairs at the sides of turret No 2 and in front of turret No 1. Note the three sailors on her after funnel, and her full complement of three OS2U Kingfishers. These slow and clumsy float planes later showed their value in rescuing downed aviators; one of the *New Jersey*'s aircraft picked up three aviators under fire from Guam and taxied them 15 miles to safety in early June 1944. Still, some top officers proposed as early as November 1942 that the catapults be traded for more anti-aircraft guns. The General Board disapproved. [NARS]

The *New Jersey* in Casco Bay, Maine, on 29 November 1943, immediately prior to leaving for the South Pacific. Her bridge is now enclosed, and she bristles with anti-aircraft guns, including the recently added 40-mm mounts forward and the two 20-mm Oerlikons in the very eyes of the ship. Serving these weapons on her bow must have been an exhilarating or terrifying experience with the sea rushing by on all sides. The battleship is painted in Ms 21 which she would wear for most of the rest of the war. [USN]

The *New Jersey* anchored off Hampton Roads with the French *Richelieu* in the background. Refitted in the United States following battle damage inflicted by the British at Dakar, the French battleship served in the East Indies during the closing stages of the war and narrowly missed catching the Japanese heavy cruiser *Haguro* which was sunk by the battleship's destroyer screen. The *Richelieu* then went to Vietnamese waters after the Japanese surrender; the *New Jersey* would follow her 22 years later. [USN]

partly to cover the Eniwetok landings, but he also hoped to catch some major Japanese units in their lair. Alerted by reconnaissance planes over their base, most of the Japanese ships fled, but a few stragglers offered Spruance a chance for surface action. With his flag in the *New Jersey*, Spruance formed up Task Group 50.9 with the two 'Iowas' accompanied by the heavy cruisers *Minneapolis* and *New Orleans* and four destroyers. Sherman's carriers provided continuous fighter coverage. Weather conditions could hardly have been better: visibility 15 miles; sea condition two; force five wind. The crews were most enthusiastic.[7] As the task group moved to cut off the enemy ships, a Japanese plane suddenly darted through a cloud and dropped a bomb which exploded about 100 ft off the starboard side of the *Iowa*. Spray drenched the forward main battery turrets, and some of the personnel on the bridge, including Admiral Hustvedt, dove for cover, but no damage was done.[8]

Shortly thereafter, a spotting plane from the *New Jersey* reported three enemy ships 25 miles from the task group. Within minutes, lookouts could see carrier planes on their bombing runs, smoke and a large explosion. At 33,000 yards, Spot One in the *Iowa* sighted a light cruiser, the *Katori*, dead in the water. In its damaged condition, this training ship was misidentified by the *Iowa* officers as an 'Aoba'-class heavy cruiser with the after stack blown off. A small minesweeping trawler, the *Shonan Maru No. 15* and two destroyers, the *Maikaze* and the *Nowaki*, were soon visible as well. The battleships increased speed to 30 knots, and, at 1527, opened fire for the first and only time in their careers at enemy warships.

The *New Jersey* made short work of *Shonan Maru No. 15* with her port 5-inch battery. As the two battleships swept by the wreckage, 'the lone Japanese survivor defiantly shook an oily fist' at the pride of the US Fleet.[9] The *Iowa* concentrated on the *Katori*. Firing 46 16-inch HC and 124 5-inch shells, gunnery officers had the satisfaction of straddling the enemy cruiser with all eight salvos. Just after the fourth, the *Katori* shuddered and took a heavy list to port. She sank stern first, having been under fire for only eleven minutes.

The *New Jersey*, in the meantime, had shifted her attention to the *Maikaze*. Heavily damaged and barely 7,000 yards off, the destroyer was smoking so heavily that she could

45

hardly be seen. When she rolled over, her after gun was still firing. More dangerous were the Long Lance torpedoes. Three narrowly missed the *Iowa*: one passed down the port side from ahead; the second went by close under the stern; and the third broached only 150 yards ahead on the port bow and was taken under fire by the anti-aircraft batteries which had standing orders to shoot instantly at any torpedo. So far, the battleships had made a clean sweep, but the second destroyer, *Nowaki*, was fleeing fast. Both the *Iowa* and *New Jersey* pursued at flank speed. With the *Iowa*'s pitometer log reading 32.5 knots, Capt. McCrea called for more steam. His chief engineer replied that 'he had plenty of steam, but no place to put it as the throttles were wide open'.[10] The *New Jersey* and *Iowa* opened fire at a range of 35,000 yards. Both ships straddled the *Nowaki* on the first salvos, but the destroyer was disappearing in the sun glare, haze and distance. At 38,000 yards, the guns were under full radar control, and Spruance ordered cease fire at 39,000 yards. At 22 miles, these were the longest range shots ever fired by a US battleship against an enemy vessel. The *Nowaki* escaped with what must have been a deeply shaken crew; she would not be so lucky at Leyte Gulf.

Admiral Spruance then directed the battleships to break out their largest American flags, and the task group, thus adorned, swept completely around Truk. In the strictest sense, the gesture was militarily unnecessary, but the symbolism was unmistakable.

In their first combat test, the new battleships had performed well. The crews spent 27 hours at general quarters and had eaten four meals at their battle stations. The turret crews had taken a breath of fresh air on deck when the situation permitted.

The battle did point out a number of problems, however. The Combat Information Center (CIC) functioned well, but it had proved extremely crowded with standing room only for most of the personnel—a real hardship over the extended period. Officers found it very difficult even to move from one plotting board to another. Desk space for taking notes and working codes was so scarce that the captain's sea cabin (adjacent to the CIC) was used. Ventilation was quite poor, and too many loudspeakers in such a confined space added to everyone's discomfort.

Two problems had cropped up with the

main battery ordnance on the *Iowa*. The firing lock of the center gun of turret No. 2 failed on the first salvo fired at the *Katori*. A new lock was installed, but not until after the action ended. On the left gun of No. 3 turret, the crew found a small burr on the breech plug. Caused probably by too high plug-closing air pressure, the burr was honed down while the *Iowa* fired at the escaping *Nowaki*, so that gun did not participate in that phase of the battle.

The radars performed well, but not flawlessly. The splashes of the 16-inch shells were 'easily discerned' by Mk 8 radar at 39,000 yards. The 5-inch guns firing at the *Katori* were under full radar control because of main battery smoke. However, the forest of 16-inch and 8-inch (heavy cruiser) splashes made it impossible to determine the mean point of impact of the smaller projectiles. On the *Iowa*, both SG radars were put out of action for about ten minutes when vacuum tubes jumped from their sockets. The forward FH (Mk 8) kept working even though 39 bolts holding the polyrods were sheared off by blast pressure from the main battery.

Despite the problems, the SK radars and sky plots kept track of all the planes in the air, the *New Jersey* acting as fighter director until she suffered troubles with her VHF transmitter.

BatDiv 7 (Rear Admiral O. M. Hustvedt commanding): *New Jersey* nearest the camera and *Iowa* in the background on their first sortie with Spruance's Fifth Fleet. Note the peculiar dull black and haze gray paint scheme on the *Iowa*. She eventually returned to Ms 22. The photograph was snapped by a *Bunker Hill* aviator on 24 January 1944. [NARS]

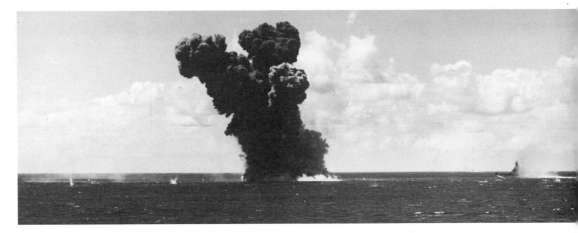

Action off Truk. The *New Jersey* blasts the hapless minesweeping trawler *Shonan Maru No 15*. The powder smoke from the battleship's 5-inch battery wreaths her port side. [USN]

The end of the *Shonan Maru No 15* as taken from the *Iowa*. [USN]

The CIC (Combat Information Center) in the *New Jersey* shortly after her completion. Usually called 'Combat,' the CIC processed tactical information and kept an up-to-date comprehensive picture of all friendly and enemy forces in the ship's vicinity. A last-minute addition to the 'Iowas', the CIC was located in a former powder magazine. By late 1944, complaints were legion of crowding, inadequate ventilation, and the need for certain types of equipment, especially projection type plotting boards and 10-channel VHF for fighter direction. The installation pictured here is the first aboard the *New Jersey* in 1943, and its jerry-built nature is perhaps evident. [USN]

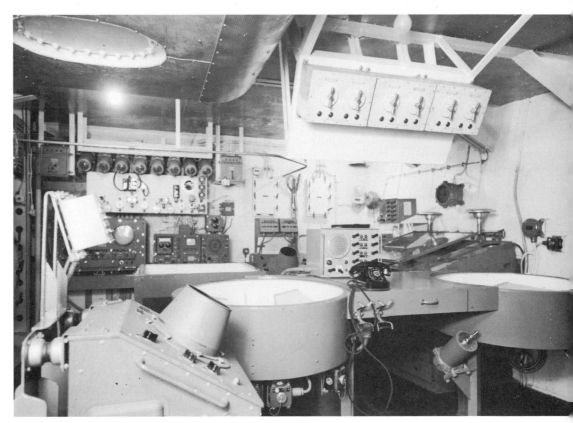

The *Iowa* took over the task, picked up a bogey on the SK radar at thirty-two miles, and vectored fighters from *Cowpens* which downed the Japanese floatplane.

The most serious mishap of the sweep came late in the day when the *Iowa* shot down an SBD [Dauntless dive bomber] which appeared suddenly at low altitude headed directly toward the ship. Attacked just this way early in the afternoon, some 40 mm gunners below the bridge opened fire despite repeated loudspeaker warnings of 'friendly plane'. The nervous gunners heard 'enemy plane'. As a result of the tragedy, the terms 'own plane' and 'bandit' were substituted.[11]

A month after the ride around Truk, the two ships tried their first shore bombardment. The victim was Mili Atoll in the Marshalls. The operation on 18 March was designed to give the crews the opportunity to perfect their bombardment techniques by shooting slowly and methodically. Each ship was to fire four three-gun salvos during alternate ten minute periods. The ships' Kingfishers assisted by Hellcats from the *Lexington* spotted for range; Top Spot provided the deflection readings. The two ships opened fire at a range of 15,000 yards and quickly destroyed a large camouflaged building and ammunition dumps. Planners had also noted the location of a suspected coast defense battery. Under fire from the battleships, these guns proved very real and surprisingly fiesty. The artillery pieces, only four in number and of 4.7-inch caliber, straddled the *New Jersey* several times and hit the *Iowa* twice.

The first shell exploded against the left-hand side of turret No. 2. Fragments entered the left pointer's sight port and demolished his telescope. Another jagged piece of metal broke the left window of the Mk 52 rangefinder. Twenty feet of the weather and gas seal on the left side of the turret was torn off, and the splinter shield of the starboard side No. 1 40 mm mount was peppered with fragments, none of which penetrated. The second shell exploded on impact four feet below the main deck at frame 134 and tore a hole 30 × 50 inches in the ship's side and cut an air escape line from the fuel oil overflow as well as a degaussing coil. Damage could have been worse. In 40 minutes, almost 20 shells landed within 500 yards of the *Iowa*. Shrapnel from some of these bursts was recovered in the after sky defense stations. The officer who wrote the ship's action report was

The *Iowa* after her quarrel on 18 March 1944 with a Japanese 4.7-inch coast defense gun on Mili. The 9.5-inch turret side plate has been barely scratched, but the weather stripping and gas seal suffered. [USN]

The second hit on the *Iowa* at Mili. Note the damaged degaussing cable and how the side plating has been peeled back. The *New Jersey* escaped any direct damage, but the ship underwent two operational failures in turrets Nos 1 and 2 (see text). [USN]

bemused to note that one of the fragments was 'a small, twisted piece of a US buffalo nickel, bearing the first three letters of the word "Liberty"'.[12]

Despite silencing three of the guns, the two battleships found the fire of the fourth so galling that they drew off to 20,000 yards. In the post-mortem summary, *New Jersey* officers concluded that the personnel, under effective fire for the first time had performed 'ably and well'. Equipment failures were minor for the most part, but irritating (see Appendix H).

In evaluating their shore bombardment technique, gunnery officers found their performance mixed. The *Iowa* had fired 180 rounds of 16-inch HC (high capacity or bombardment) ammunition; the *New Jersey* 187. The gunnery officer of the *Iowa* felt that the ship should have used AP (armor piercing) shells

The *New Jersey* shelling Tinian, on 13 June 1944, seen from the *Iowa*. The Mk 37 director shown here controlled the fire of the 5-inch mounts against aircraft. On 25 November 1944, a director like this one on the *New Jersey* ran away in train because the power head contacts stuck. By the time control had been regained, the Japanese aircraft had made its attack. [NARS]

Just completed, the *New Jersey* shows two of her Mk 37 secondary battery directors with the early FD radar sets on top. The main battery director has been swivelled around so that only its starboard end is visible. It is surmounted by the FH fire control radar, and that set is about 150 feet above the waterline. To enable the 'Iowas' to pass under the Brooklyn Bridge, their foremasts retracted. Stack gasses sometimes proved to be a serious problem; the *Wisconsin* complained of their effects when her formation steamed directly downwind in January 1945. Note the 40-mm quad mount in the immediate foreground and the 20-mm Oerlikon manned by black mess stewards. [USN]

against the coast defense batteries, 'We put several salvos right on the emplacements, and after each, as the smoke and dust rose, four gun flashes would appear as the Japs [sic] got off another salvo. Our HC projectiles ... had no effect on the heavy concrete emplacements'.[13] As for the 5-inch batteries, they had fired rapid down ladders to prevent smoke and dust from shorts obscuring later salvos. However, when the secondaries fired at the same target as the 16-inchers, it was impossible to spot the 5-inch shells.[14] Still, the ships had acquitted themselves well at Mili in what was essentially a practice shoot against live targets.

On 1 May, the *Iowa* and *New Jersey* got another opportunity, this time at Ponape. The principal target was the large airfield. Equipment performance improved: the *New Jersey* experienced no radar failures whatsoever and found the Mk 8 a great asset in firing an accurately controlled bombardment. The *Iowa* lost two fuses in the Mk 4 radar in Sky 1, but both were replaced immediately. With fire control largely performed by the vessels' float-planes, the battleships started fires in Ponape Town and in barracks and stores areas near the airfield. The army headquarters building was utterly demolished with debris strewn all over the river. The three airport runways were raked from one end to the other. Despite intelligence reports of Japanese 16-inchers on the island, the Japanese forces suffered through all this shelling without making any response.

At the same time that the *Iowa* and *New Jersey* were learning the techniques of shore bombardment that spring of 1944, they were also getting their first chance to put their anti-aircraft guns to good use. During the Palau operation of 29 March, the *New Jersey* fired at night on two enemy planes flying low and slow. The Mk 8 radars in the main battery directors assisted in tracking the targets for the 5-inch battery, which opened fire at 11,000 yards. The Mk 8 clearly observed the shell bursts, and the corrected salvos bracketed one plane which disappeared from the radar screen. The other plane turned hurriedly away. Of the 163 5-inch

49

shells expended, two-thirds were equipped with the new proximity fuse. The Navy was so determined to keep a dud round from falling into Japanese hands that whenever officers anticipated action near enemy shores (as at Ponape on 1 May), all proximity-fused shells were removed from the turrets to avoid the inadvertent firing of one in the heat of action.[15]

During the June invasion of Saipan and the subsequent battle of the Philippine Sea, the *Iowa* and *New Jersey* again fought in both the anti-aircraft and shore bombardment roles. In a night engagement on 12 June, the *New Jersey* dodged one aerial torpedo and then shot down her attacker at close range with 20 mm bursts. The next day, she and the *Iowa* with the other fast battleships shelled Saipan and Tinian. The *Iowa* blew up one ammunition dump 'in a most spectacular fashion', but because the battleships stood off at ranges above 10,000 yards, analysts ultimately judged the results as disappointing.[16]

The Imperial Fleet reacted to the Saipan landings with its first whole-hearted challenge in well over a year. In anticipation of massive assaults by the Japanese carriers, Admiral Spruance formed a separate task group of his fast battleships and put them directly in the path of those enemy attackers who managed to escape the American fighters. Action came fast and furious. The *New Jersey* in five minutes fired on six planes; the *Iowa*, missed by a torpedo from a Kate, splashed that plane and downed at least two more. Admiral Hustvedt aboard the *Iowa* could see several columns of smoke arising from aircraft wreckage at one time.[17] Later Japanese assault waves took detours to avoid the battle line and get at the carriers. Therefore, Spruance's experiment would not be repeated; in the future, the fast battleships would stick close to the flattops.

By concentrating the battleships, Spruance also hoped to give them a shot at destroying the Japanese Fleet, but Admiral Willis A. Lee, having seen the *South Dakota* badly damaged at Guadalcanal in a confused close-quarters fray in the dark, turned down the chance for a night encounter. Some of his subordinates were quite disappointed, especially when Lee's attempt to catch the fleeing Japanese by daylight was aborted because the battleships were forced to slow down to 14 knots to fuel escorting destroyers.

If too cautious employment of the battleships at the Philippine Sea had allowed the

The battleships often served as hosts for top officers. Here, Admirals Nimitz and Spruance meet aboard the *Iowa* off Majuro Atoll in the Marshalls, on 8 April 1944. [USN]

bulk of the Japanese surface fleet to escape, their too impetuous handling by Admiral William 'Bull' Halsey cheated them of their best chance for a gunnery duel at Leyte Gulf. Briefly, the Japanese hoped to lure Halsey away by using their carriers—essentially impotent because of the losses in June—as bait. If Halsey would charge the red flag, Japanese surface units, headed by the *Yamato* and *Musashi*, would pass through San Bernardino Strait and attack the cargo and transport ships.

Halsey fell for the ruse. Flying his flag in the *New Jersey*, he uncovered the strait by taking all of the ships toward the carrier decoy force at high speed. Officers on the *Iowa* were unanimous in believing that Halsey was making a major mistake, as did Lee. But early in the morning of 25 October, the fast battleships, with battle flags flying under a cloudless sky, had less than one hour to steam before opening fire on the hapless carrier force. However, for hours Halsey had been hearing calls for help from American vessels suffering under the *Yamato*'s 18.1-inch shellfire. The great Japanese battleship had slipped through the unguarded strait. Halsey doubled back. With 300 miles to go, he was forced to slow to fuel destroyers and finally detached the *Iowa* and *New Jersey* with three light cruisers and eight destroyers to hurry ahead at 28 knots. The task

A desperate fight off Luzon on 25 November 1944. The ships of TG 38.2 take evasive action: the *Cabot* is closest, the *Iowa* (still in her peculiar paint scheme) is at top center and the burning *Intrepid* can be made out just under the tail of the aircraft taking the photograph. The *Iowa* complained in her action report of several 40-mm misfires and of one 40-mm gun that did not return to battery, but all guns were firing by the end of the battle. [NARS]

group reached the strait three hours too late. Only the crippled *Nowaki*, the escapee from Truk, fell victim to the cruiser screen. The *Iowa* saw her sink. With the break of day on 26 October, both battleships catapulted their floatplanes, but all they found were oil slicks and floating debris. A few prisoners were brought aboard the *New Jersey* for interrogation by Halsey's staff.

Continued successes against Japanese aircraft provided a partial salve for this frustration. Shortly before the Leyte Gulf fiasco, the *Iowa* shot down a Judy diving fast at a range of three miles with 108 40 mm and 23 20 mm. Another, clearly hit by tracer shells in the engine and right wing, crashed only 300 yards away—close enough to see the bright red Japanese 'meatballs' painted on the wings.[18]

On that same day, 14 October, gunners from the *New Jersey* spotted a Judy crossing astern at 200 knots, tracked the bomber for two seconds, and shot it down in 12 more. However, officers complained that the ship, flying Halsey's flag and stationed in the center of the formation, often had her fire masked by other vessels. The danger was a real one. Later in the month, the *Iowa* took machine gun fire from the *Intrepid* that cost one sailor his eye and wounded another. The *Iowa* protested: 'It is not necessary to shoot up our own side in order to shoot down Japs.'[19]

But accidents were bound to occur with the increasing intensity of the Japanese aerial threat. During October alone the *Iowa* counted 43 planes shot down in her vicinity. And at the end of the month, on 29 October, the ships fired at their first Kamikazes. The *New Jersey* set afire a Judy headed straight for the *Intrepid*, but the blazing plane crashed into the port gun galleries of the carrier.

That same flattop was victimised again on 25 November when the Kamikazes made a concerted effort against the Third Fleet. Shortly after noon on a brilliant day with scattered cumulus clouds, the *New Jersey* picked up 15 'bandits' on radar. By 1230, the first were in sight. During the next 30 minutes, the suiciders adopted the new technique of approaching at low level and then climbing rapidly for a final suicide plunge.

The battleships fought well. The *Iowa* hit one Jill on the first shot at 6,500 yards with a proximity fused 5-inch shell. The aircraft disintegrated. The rangefinder operator of the Sky 4 director reported that at one instant, he was looking at an airplane and in the next, all he could see was a propeller and radial engine flying through the air. In ten minutes, the *Iowa* fired 78 5-inch shells and over 6,000 rounds of machine-gun ammunition at seven planes and

claimed three definite kills: two Jills and a Judy. The last went into a tight spin directly over the ship and crashed only 100 yards off the starboard bow. The machine gunners in the bow were ordered to abandon their stations for fear that the plane would crash directly on them. They 'were evidently of the same opinion as the sector officers since they lost no time in moving aft'.[20]

A Zeke, although winged by both the *Iowa* and *New Jersey*, crashed the *Intrepid*. Two more of the Japanese fighters, coming apart under anti-aircraft fire, glanced off the *Cabot* and *Hancock*. The *New Jersey* later reported that she had fired on seven planes. Two exploded; three more were definitely hit and crashed; the sixth was probably brought down by the *Iowa*, and only one escaped. The *New Jersey* compiled this excellent score despite her station still in the center of the formation.[21]

A reinforcement for the fleet: The *Wisconsin* is seen here on 11 November 1944 tied up alongside the salvaged hulk of the *Oklahoma* at Pearl Harbor. Although the two ships are reasonably similar in beam, their difference in length is quite evident. The Marine Corps detachment is lined up by the portside of No 1 turret. The ships are protected by torpedo nets. The *Wisconsin*'s crew engaged in scrounging up extra radio equipment in Hawaii, having learned that her standard allowance was by no means adequate. [USN]

The *New Jersey* digs her nose in, late 1944. Turret No 1 is now level with waves; her stern is high above the surface, and the waters there are roiled by her propellers. [NARS]

The *New Jersey* shakes free. The water cascading off her forecastle smashes into No 1 turret. Her stern is now almost awash and the float planes are in peril. The *Missouri* would lose two helicopters to a storm like this in the summer of 1950. The carrier in the background is probably the *Hancock*. [NARS]

The constant steaming and frequent action were taking their toll on men and machine alike. For instance, *Iowa* officers noted that the radar equipment, while still operating, was in 'serious' condition. The Diehl main drain pump motors, always a source of trouble, were incapacitated, some totally. Excessive wear in the strut bearings was leading to an increasingly worrisome vibration whenever the ship exceeded 25 knots. Thirty-two men were on the injury list, including two seriously hurt by a heavy sea at night and another who lost three fingers in an ammunition scuttle. One officer attributed the problems largely to fatigue and noted on 1 November that the last liberty for the crew—actually for one watch—had been in Panama on 7 January![22]

Happily, the Third Fleet spent early December at Ulithi allowing the battleships time for replenishment and upkeep. The crews sunbathed on the atoll, played baseball and drank their meager beer ration of three cans per man. They also welcomed the *Wisconsin*, commanded by Capt. Earl E. Stone. Launched barely a year before—on Pearl Harbor day 1943, the ship hoisted her commissioning

pennant on 16 April and ran her shakedown cruise out of Trinidad: a highly creditable record, for many of her men at commissioning had never before been aboard a ship.[23]

The *Wisconsin* joined Halsey's force just in time to experience the great typhoon of 17 December that sank three American destroyers. The *New Jersey* came through unscathed, but the newest battleship was less fortunate. Hit by giant waves even on turret No. 2, the battleship lost a plane swept completely off the port catapult. Another OS2U was so badly damaged as to be worthless. Antiaircraft mounts suffered, and both whaleboats were demolished on their skids. Most tragic, lookouts could see lights and hear whistles from unfortunate destroyermen in the huge seas.[24]

The typhoon also washed a plane off the *Iowa*. Worse, the storm aggravated the already serious shaft vibration noted among the ship's problems during the previous month. Suddenly on 23 December, at an easy 18 knots, the No. 3 shaft began vibrating badly, and officers felt a heavy pounding all the way on the bridge. The entire fleet slowed to 15 knots so that the

Iowa could lock the shaft. Inspection by the ship's engineers showed that the shaft had dropped three inches in its strut bearing and in consequence, a deep groove was worn into the metal. Temporary repairs could take place in an emergency drydock, but the battleship would be forced to return to the West Coast for a major overhaul.[25]

The nearest drydock capable of accommodating the *Iowa* was *ABSD–2* at Manus. Halsey sent not a 'can you' but a 'you will' message ordering the dock readied for the *Iowa*. The commanding officer in charge of *ABSD–2*, R. K. James, worked for 72 hours to move the damaged cruiser *Canberra* and two destroyers out, to reset the blocks for the *Iowa*, and then to re-pump the dock.

The battleship came 'roaring in' to Manus at dawn, Christmas morning. As James stepped onto her bridge, he met her new CO, Capt. Jimmy Holloway, an officer with a reputation for slick ship-handling. Although James, according to Navy regulations, should have taken control, Holloway headed the big ship toward the dock, about 11 miles up the bay. Moving at six or seven knots through the mooring area, the *Iowa* had ships rolling wildly. Holloway swept right past the tugboats which were supposed to tow the battleship into the drydock. One hundred yards from *ABSD–2*, James protested, 'Captain, you've got to back her down—you're going to wreck my dry dock block set-up.' Holloway paid no attention, entered the dock at four or five knots, and about half way in, ordered 'full speed astern'. The *Iowa* 'shook like a damned destroyer and stopped just where she should be'. Sharp ship-handling indeed, but James was:

... just absolutely shattered because I know what damage he's done. He's swept the dry dock blocks out from under his ship by reversing his engines full, inside the dock. I had warned him of this, and I said, 'I cannot dock you now. We've got to sit here until I find out what's happening below.'[26]

James sent divers to dog down blocks knocked out of place. One was overlooked, and it punched a hole in the side of the ship when the water was pumped out. After cleaning up, James noticed that he had a gray streak in his hair.

After a full year of operations, the *Iowa* and *New Jersey* had compiled a solid record of achievement. From ferrying the President across the Atlantic, to topping off thirsty destroyers, to serving as flagships, the new battleships had shown their usefulness to the fleet in a variety of support roles. In the test of combat, their sole surface fight at Truk had been exciting but not very productive. Their best chance for the ultimate gunnery duel—*Iowa* and *New Jersey* vs. *Yamato*—was so botched by the aviator Halsey as to make battleship officers then (and battleship advocates today) cringe. But against aircraft, and especially in the last ditch defense against suiciders, the new ships showed their value. They would have plenty more opportunity to confirm that appraisal off Iwo Jima and Okinawa.

The *Iowa* in *ABSD-2*, 28 December 1944. Her shaft has dropped noticeably off center. [NARS]

As the *Iowa* sailed for home and the *Missouri* joined the fleet, American forces prepared to deal the final blows to a faltering, but still defiant Japan. As part of the wide-ranging carrier task forces, the four 'Iowa'-class battleships would face the massive Japanese Kamikaze assaults off Okinawa. There, the big-gun ships would also bring their main batteries into action again for the first time in many months. Then, in the summer of 1945, the battleships would bombard Japan itself, and, as the Imperial Government gave up the fight, world attention focussed on the *Missouri*—center ring for the last act of World War Two.

This new ship, the last of the 'Iowa'-class to be finished, had been rushed to completion even more quickly than the *Wisconsin*. Christened by Margaret Truman, the Missouri senator's daughter on 29 January 1944, the battleship was commissioned on 11 June. She worked up in Chesapeake Bay under Capt. W. M. Callaghan, left Norfolk on 11 November, and arrived at Ulithi on 13 January—less than one year after she had been launched. Her chaplain later remembered that she was not a 'happy' ship, in contrast to the *New Jersey* on which he had served. The *Missouri*'s crew had an unusually large number of draftees, many of whom had left families, for whom military service represented real sacrifice.[1]

When *Missouri* reached Ulithi, Admiral Marc Mitscher temporarily made her his flagship. Halsey was off on a foray into the South China Sea with three carriers plus *New Jersey* and *Wisconsin*, in hopes of catching the battleship-carriers *Ise* and *Hyuga* which had so narrowly escaped destruction at Leyte Gulf. The American task force came very close to Indochina (the *New Jersey* would see those waters again over two decades later), but the Japanese vessels were anchored safely at Singapore. Upon return, the *New Jersey* lost her status of fleet flagship when Halsey hauled down his pennant and Spruance took control of the renumbered Fifth Fleet.

The three battleships left port almost immediately to cover the carriers in raids against Japan prior to the Iwo Jima assault. Shielded by punishingly bad weather, the task force closed the home islands and dealt airfields and other installations there severe damage from the air. Spruance then moved to provide direct support for the Iwo Jima landings, and on 19 February, the *Missouri* and *Wisconsin* got their first taste of combat. When they picked up on radar a number of cautious intruders on a clear half-moon night, the ships made smoke to reduce visibility. The *New Jersey* then drove away one plane with a few 5-inch shells; the *Missouri* did better. She reported later: 'It was a great boon to the morale of this ship to open fire for the first time against an enemy target and to splash the bandit with the first few bursts at a range of over 9,500 yards, at night.'[2] *Enterprise* night fighters identified the victim as probably a Helen. The *Missouri* did echo the persistent concerns about friendly fire and recommended that the task groups keep at least 18,200 yards apart, that is, outside the range of the 5″/38. However, the radars were performing well. The *Missouri* reported that her IFF provided positive identification of American planes out to 100 miles. Her SK-2 air search radar was able to track B-29s at 160 miles.

In fact, the battleships were working into a routine that they would maintain for the rest of the war. Operations were virtually constant.

Wearing the showy Ms 32/22D camouflage scheme, the *Missouri* works up in the Atlantic in the summer of 1944. She painted this over with the more conventional Ms 22 before going to the Pacific where she teamed with the *Wisconsin* to form BatDiv 9 under Rear Admiral E. W. Hanson. She was the last American battleship completed. This photograph, although heavily censored, does show the square bridge that the *Missouri* carried on completion. [USN]

The *Missouri* is here viewed from the bow during an anti-aircraft practice. Note the flak bursts overhead and the 40-mm mount at maximum elevation ahead of No 1 turret on the port side. These mounts were especially susceptible to storm and blast damage. Clearly visible is the SK search radar above her main battery Mk 38 director and the Mk 12 anti-aircraft fire control radars mounted on the Mk 37 AA directors.

For instance, the *Missouri* in February spent three weeks underway and travelled 8,080 miles at an average of 18 knots. From 17 March to 10 May, the *Wisconsin* was at sea for the entire 58-day period during which she covered 25,706 miles. Similarly, that ship steamed 18,188 miles during the last 45 days of the war (to 15 August).

All that travel took a lot of energy. During the last period operating at speeds from eight to 26 knots, the *Wisconsin* consumed 82,542 barrels of fuel (for an average of 190.6 gallons per mile). She rendezvoused with 10 oilers which passed her 127,164 barrels of oil. The apparent net gain was cancelled by the fuel the battleships passed to destroyers: 49,948 barrels to 71 of the smaller ships.[3]

In fact, the battleships became increasingly valuable at the Sisyphean task. By topping off the always thirsty escorts in the combat zones that the tankers dared not enter, the battleships were jokingly called 'armored oilers' by the sailors. To fuel one destroyer generally took 30 minutes; often a battleship pumped oil to two escorts simultaneously—one on each side. As frequently as it was performed, the fueling routine always retained an edge to it. The entire task group had to slow to 15 knots or less, depending on the weather, in the combat zone. The danger of collision was magnified. Fueling hoses and manila messengers parted frequently. When the hoses separated, they sent oil spray over everything. The 'fueling trademark' for the deck crewman was the rope burn. More serious accidents badly injured sailors. One 20 ft high wave over the bow of the *Wisconsin* in February washed all 12 men on the forecastle away from their stations. One sailor was pinned so tightly behind a 20 mm ammunition box that the container had to be removed before he could be freed. Four others suffered broken bones.

No wonder that that battleship recommended as 'a matter of urgent military necessity' greater pumping capacity. With five pumps,

the ship was able to push across 300 gallons per minute. The *Wisconsin* wanted to triple that rate. Given the press of operations, however, the alteration was not made. Still, by the end of the war, the *Wisconsin* had refueled destroyers over 250 times in eight months. The vessel presented cakes to numbers 100 and 200.[4]

The battleships also provided the smaller craft with medical assistance. The standard complement of physicians in 1945 stood at four medical officers per battleship. With their well-equipped sick bays and operating room,

The battleships were able to fuel two destroyers at once through the 10-inch lines. Here, the *Missouri* tops off the high-speed minesweepers *Thomson* (DMS-38) and *Carmice* (DMS-33) during the early part of the Korean War. [NARS]

The *Missouri* and a carrier pull alongside a stores ship to replenish during the summer of 1945. The relaxed attitude of the sailors and the covered anti-aircraft guns show that these are either safe waters or that the war has ended. Note the battleship's after main and secondary directors (at top right). The former is topped by the FH fire control radar; the latter by the Mk 12. Attached to the right hand side of the Mk 12 is a Mk 22 'orange peel'—a parabolic height-finder to pick up low-flying aircraft just above the horizon. [USN]

the doctors could give attention beyond the capability of most other ships. In her first two weeks with the fleet, the *Wisconsin* treated nine men and one officer from other ships. On 21 January, she took aboard 17 battle casualties from the destroyer *Maddox*. The navy doctors were confronted with a wide range of problems from appendectomies (three performed aboard the *Missouri* in February) to fractures (a target drone turned aggressive, crashed into the *Wisconsin* on 1 August, sending a man to the sick bay with a fracture of the left humerus).[5]

Rare, but not unknown, were the mental cases. During the bombardment of Okinawa, a sailor from the *Wisconsin* jumped over the side. He was rescued by a destroyer and admitted to sick bay as was another man suffering from 'extreme anxiety and nervous condition'.[6] Given the time the sailors spent at sea in very crowded quarters and under the constant threat of enemy action, it is surprising that many more men did not break down.

Some officers concluded that good morale was largely dependent on good food, mail from home and movies. Navy food usually boasted of as good a reputation as service food could have, and officers generally saw that the crew was well fed. For instance, when the anti-aircraft batteries required continuous manning aboard the *Missouri*, individual gun stations were secured in rotation for meals. When the *Wisconsin* bombarded Okinawa, the crews ate at their weapons and found the K rations 'adequate and appetizing', at least according to the action report which also noted that the K ration containers presented a serious fire hazard. At times, fresh food was in short supply. During the Okinawa campaign, the *Wisconsin* sailors went without fresh fruit or vegetables for 33 days.[7]

Mail arrived with regularity. Since the carrier task groups met with the replenishment groups—the tankers, supply, ammunition and hospital ships—about twice weekly, corre-

spondence travelled both ways quickly. Letters from the States reached the combat ships in ten days in the remotest areas, and 'even the censors looked forward to mail'.[8] Some men also took solace in the religious services. On the *Missouri* on Easter Sunday, several hundred men, dog-tired from the day's bombardment of Okinawa, filled the mess compartment and sang traditional hymns 'with much gusto and enthusiasm'.[9]

Movies, potentially one of the greatest morale builders, presented continual problems. By navy regulations, a ship was allowed only four prints at once. With 2,800 anxious viewers aboard the battleships, four shows ran simultaneously in different parts of the ship. And with the Fleet at sea for such lengthy periods of time, movies wore out. One battleship complained that 'new' films were often water-soaked and missing, on occasion, entire reels. Despite these irritants, the captain of the *Wisconsin* concluded in May that his crew could stay in the combat area for at least four months with proper replenishment. Having come close to meeting just that goal by late August, he decided instead that his battleship could remain operational 'indefinitely'. As he put it, 'There is no lowering of morale, discontent or operational fatigue at any time.'[10]

The equipment often faltered before the men. In the space of five weeks at sea, the *Wisconsin* reported six machinery failures of note. Among them were two air compressors down for a total of 29 days and a main feed booster pump which took five days to fix. Most serious, on two occasions tubes failed in No. 4 main condenser. The shaft had to be locked, a procedure that required slowing the ship and, thus, the entire task group.

Storms sometimes hurt the battleships despite their great size and seaworthiness. Exposed supplementary anti-aircraft mounts suffered the most frequent damage. The February storms that covered Spruance's Fifth Fleet on its run toward the Japanese coast bent or broke the ring sights of all the quadruple 40 mm mounts Nos 1, 2, 16 and 17 on the *Missouri*, dished in their shields, bent their flash hiders and caused minor electrical grounds. The same storm sheered the training wheels off two 40 mm mounts on the *Wisconsin*. Even the heavy ordnance was vulnerable at times. The optics of turret No. 1 in the *Missouri* were slightly damaged when heavy seas smashed into its rangefinder shutter. On 18 January, the forward 16-inch magazine cooling system of the *Wisconsin* and the ship's main distilling plant had to be shut down for 24 hours when spray entered exhaust ducts and shorted the load-center switchboard.[11]

Collision posed another danger to ships operating in large numbers in close formation. The destroyer *Franks*, changing station at night in foul weather on 2 April, ran almost head on into the port bow of the *New Jersey*. Damage to the battleship proved negligible, but the ship's huge anchor crushed the destroyer's captain in the bridge wing, demolished 40 mm gun mounts and directors, and buckled the stacks. On an earlier occasion, the destroyer *Welles*, passing mail to the *New Jersey*, damaged an OS2U Kingfisher beyond repair. Sailors stripped the plane and tossed it overboard.[12]

In fact, some officers began to question the worth of the aviation units. The planes and their catapults took up valuable quarterdeck space where they were vulnerable to storm as

Ships of TG.58.4 under *Kamikaze* attack off Okinawa on 11 April 1945. Somewhere in that forest of anti-aircraft bursts is a low-flying Mitsubishi *Zero* headed straight for the *Missouri*. Note the cordite smoke pouring off the battleship's starboard side, the intense flash from the 5″/38 on the destroyer preceding her and the numerous shell splashes in the water. [NARS]

A gout of black smoke
erupts from the
starboard side of the
battleship as the *Zeke* hits its target. The
picture was made from
the *Intrepid*. [NARS]

One of the most famous
action photographs of
World War Two and of
all time: the Japanese
fighter's wing is actually
at the moment of
contact with the
Missouri's side. Some
gunners see the aircraft;
others are unaware of it.
The barrels of the 5″/38
mounts are depressed,
as are the Bofors in
mounts Nos 11 and 15.
Mount No 9 cannot bear
on the aircraft. Note the
directors for the 40-mm
guns. The photo-
grapher's identity is
unfortunately unknown.
[NARS]

well as collision damage. Handling them
proved tricky, as the pilot of an SC-1 Seahawk
found out. Transferred from the *Guam* to the
Missouri, his propeller fouled the crane cable of
the battleship. The brand-new plane capsized,
and its carcass was sunk by destroyer gunfire.
That unlucky aircraft had been intended as a
replacement for an SC-1 last seen trailing
smoke in a steep glide off Iwo Jima.

Two missions kept the clumsy planes
aboard. They were sometimes able to rescue
downed carrier pilots, often in tight circumstances. For instance, during the Saipan invasion, an OS2U from the *New Jersey* picked up
three aviators under fire from Guam and taxied
them 15 miles to safety. On 18 March, two

Kingfishers from that ship landed near
Kyushu to rescue a *Bunker Hill* pilot. Three
months later, one of the *Wisconsin*'s planes
saved a *Shangri-La* pilot from the same waters.

The floatplanes also continued to fly spotting missions for the big guns. On 24 March,
aircraft from the *Missouri*, *New Jersey* and
Wisconsin called fire for a bombardment of
Okinawa. The operation was designed to draw
Japanese attention away from the intended
point of assault and to give the battleships an
opportunity to exercise their main batteries
against enemy targets. The *New Jersey* had last
shot 16-inch shells at the Japanese on Saipan,
nine months earlier. For the *Missouri* and
Wisconsin, of course, Okinawa would consti-
tute the first test for their shore bombardment
techniques. Preparation was thorough. Officers of the *Missouri* built a scale terrain model
which, to the surprise of all concerned, looked
very much like the real thing. The air spotters
spent two days in briefing. When the ships
opened fire at 0845, they found that their only
problem lay in identifying a target.[13]

The *Missouri* did find an ammunition dump
whose explosion sent yellowish brown flames
boiling 1,000 ft into the air. However, spotters
for the *New Jersey* were bothered by haze, and
that vessel opened fire simply in hopes of
stripping away Japanese camouflage. But nothing of military importance was exposed, and
the *New Jersey* could only claim damage to
several small structures, a trench system and a
section of road. The *Wisconsin*, after firing 155
rounds of 16-inch, concluded that for the
expenditure of main battery ammunition she
had destroyed a grounded hulk and started
brush fires. Admiral E. W. Hanson, commander of BatDiv 9, wrote to Ernie King that the
bombardment would not assist the capture of
the island, although Hanson did note that the
action gave a valuable morale boost to the two
newest ships.[14]

The *Missouri* got another chance to repeat
her success against the Japanese on Okinawa
when, on 27 May, she conducted a shoot
against Japanese caves believed to be sheltering suicide boats. Results were problematical,
although observers saw flames and smoke

belch from the mouths of several of the caves hit directly by 5-inch shellfire.[15]

The Fleet was threatened far more seriously by Kamikaze aircraft which made their greatest effort of the war during the Okinawa campaign. Officers of the *New Jersey*, ultimately filing a voluminous action report, remarked, '... the anti-aircraft action that occurred from 18–20 March was the most intense experienced by this vessel since the attacks on 25 November 1944'.[16] In a little over three weeks, the ship expended 738 rounds of 5-inch, 2,025 40 mm, and 3,754 20 mm. Often, an action would last four to five seconds; that is, the plane would be identified as hostile and fired upon, either successfully or not, before it crashed or flew out of range—all within that short span of time.

Part of the problem lay in the fact that Japanese planes flying above 25,000 ft would be lost to the SK radar at 30 miles. They would then appear suddenly in a steep suicide dive. *New Jersey* officers noted, 'More enemy planes got over the formation undetected than was thought probable with search radar gear in operation.' Rapid detection by the anti-aircraft gunners provided the only immediate remedy, but both the *New Jersey* and *Wisconsin* strongly recommended the deployment of an overhead search radar set.

This deficiency notwithstanding, the battleships provided valuable assistance to the hard pressed carriers. For instance, the *New Jersey* on 19 March with her light anti-aircraft guns winged a Judy diving at over 300 knots out of cloud cover on the *Essex*. Hit, the plane crashed off the carrier's bow. Half an hour later, another Judy in a similar attack against the *Bunker Hill* met the same fate. That afternoon, the ship fired proximity fused 5-inch shells at two Zekes and downed both. The next night, the *New Jersey* claimed a night intruder at over 10,000 yards in 40 seconds with the 5-inch guns. As the ship noted in its action report, because several vessels fired on all of these planes, the exact allocation of credit was impossible. However, from 19 March to 11 April, the *New Jersey* listed as 'sure assists' 11 Japanese aircraft.

A grim photograph of the remains of the Japanese *Kamikaze* pilot on the *Missouri*. When his aircraft hit the ship, the top half of his body was apparently catapulted through the windshield onto the battleship's deck. He was given a military funeral. [NARS]

A one-in-a-million occurrence: a machine gun from the suicide plane jammed down the muzzle of one of the *Missouri*'s 40-mm guns. The slight damage was repaired by the ship's force. [NARS]

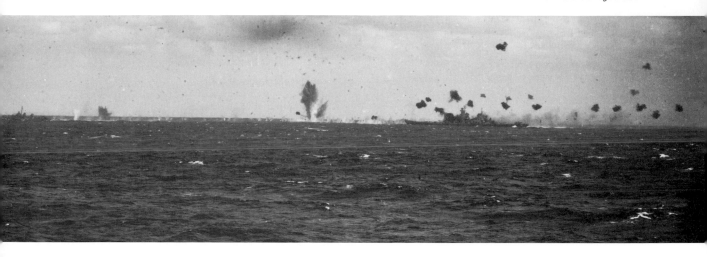

A busy day, 11 April 1945, for the *Missouri*. Shortly after being crashed, the battleship is narrowly missed just ahead by another *Kamikaze*. The sky is peppered with flak bursts and the battleship is shrouded in her own cordite smoke. [NARS]

The *Missouri* and *Wisconsin* shared in the action. For the Okinawa campaign, the latter ship submitted an action report of 68 pages with analyses of combat against 22 separate planes. Also, the *Wisconsin* took on the job of controlling some of the American fighters when the carriers were swamped with too many individual actions or when the flat top's radars were malfunctioning.

The *Missouri* concluded that the period was one of constant action, radar contacts and alarms; yet of the three battleships, only that one suffered damage. On 11 April, a Zeke crashed into the ship on the starboard side about three feet below the main deck level. Had the plan flown only a few feet higher, it would have done substantial damage to the anti-aircraft batteries amidships. As it was, the Zeke's fuselage disintegrated against the *Missouri*'s side. Blazing gasoline set several deck fires, quickly extinguished, under the 5-inch battery. The starboard wing of the aircraft was thrown forward to the first superstructure level causing freakish, but minor, damage to the No. 17 quad 40 mm mount. The next day, the ship's crew gave a military funeral to the young Japanese pilot, only 18 or 19 years old.[17]

The Kamikaze threat at Okinawa tested crews and equipment to the fullest. Aboard the *Wisconsin*, for instance, the crew fully manned the anti-aircraft batteries from before dawn to after sunset. The constant jarring of the 5-inchers put many of the 40 mm and 20 mm sights out of action on that ship. With 'an entirely inadequate' allowance of spares, the *Wisconsin* was relying on open sights for 17 20 mm guns and two of the more potent 40 mm quad mounts by the end of the campaign.

The Japanese attempted to blind American radar with 'window', although the battleships generally had little trouble seeing through it. When the *Missouri* anchored off Okinawa in May, she played the same game by using one of her boats to lay a smokescreen so thick that defending fighters radioed, 'We can't see anything but a forest fire . . . down there.'[19]

Still, the whole situation was nerve-racking. An action report filed by the *Wisconsin* candidly admitted that the suicide attacks made the crew jumpy and that fire discipline presented a serious problem. At times, her men shot at planes when ships lay in the line of fire; on other occasions, the gunners failed to obey the cease-fire signal promptly. Less serious, anti-aircraft crews wasted ammunition by shooting at planes spinning out of control until they hit the water. Part of the problem rested in the fact that, with the Japanese using single engine planes for Kamikaze missions, quick recognition was very tough. When planes approached from head on, a difficult situation became that much harder. The *New Jersey* recommended that American engine cowlings be painted white. *Wisconsin* officers emphasized, '*Too much time is wasted in making certain that we do not shoot down a friend*, not to mention the strain on the nerves of all hands.'[20]

Tragically, just that accident occurred on 29 March. Three planes suddenly dived out of the clouds at over 300 knots on the *Yorktown*. The first was clearly a Judy, intent on suicide. All ships in the task group, including the *Missouri* and *New Jersey*, opened fire. The Judy was downed, but so were the two pursuing planes, F6F Hellcats. To top off a bad day, a 20 mm loader on the *Missouri* was wounded in the stomach by friendly 20 mm fire, and the ship was hit by 5-inch fragments.

Nonetheless, given the circumstances, the intensity and the duration of the Okinawa campaign, officers on the *New Jersey* noted with satisfaction that their ship had avoided, with that one exception, firing on friendly planes when other ships had done so. Throughout the attacks, enemy aircraft failed to do more than minor damage to any ship while the *New Jersey* was in company. Parenthetically, the 'Iowas' fired their guns at aircraft for the last time in their careers (to date) off Okinawa.[21]

A job well done earned the *New Jersey* a stateside trip. In the war zone for 15 months, she badly needed a refit. Providing her relief was the *Iowa*. She had been overhauled at San Francisco from 15 January to 19 March and arrived off Okinawa on 15 April. The *New Jersey* headed for Puget Sound the next day.

In one of the periodic changes of command, Admiral Halsey prepared to take over the carrier task force. The *Missouri* was therefore detached on 5 May from the main body off Okinawa, and was altered at Ulithi to make space for Halsey's staff of 60 officers and the supporting force of 300 enlisted men. Halsey then hoisted his flag aboard the new battleship on 18 May at Guam. He planned more aerial attacks against Japan, and the *Missouri*, *Iowa* and *Wisconsin* all escorted the carriers. The Japanese had shot their bolt at Okinawa, however, and the battleships saw no action except for another bout with a typhoon which did them no serious harm. From 28 May to 10 June, the *Missouri* travelled 6,014 miles on the raids. The three ships stepped up anti-aircraft practice because their next orders mandated a main battery shoot against the home islands.[22]

Leaving Leyte Gulf on 1 July, they headed for northern Honshu and Hokkaido, areas out of range of the B-29s and thus virgin territory. For the first time since the British, French and Dutch had bombarded Shimonoseki in 1864, hostile vessels were to shell Japan itself. On 14 July, a force of the 27-knot battleships bombarded Kamaishi. The next day, Rear Admiral Oscar Badger took the *Iowa*, *Missouri* and *Wisconsin* at 26 knots into the bay fronting Muroran, Hokkaido. The cruisers *Atlanta* and *Dayton* with two destroyer divisions made up the escorting force. Halsey, along for the ride in the *Missouri*, was most apprehensive and later wrote:

Not all Japanese aviators were ready to die for the emperor. This dramatic and unusual photograph taken from the *Wisconsin* on 18 March 1945 shows the flaming body of a single-engine Japanese plane, seemingly directly above the escorting destroyer. Following the aircraft's fuselage is the tail section and then two parachuting fliers. [NARS]

Right into the enemy's jaws. The chart justifies my metaphor; during the hour that we shelled ... Muroran ... we were landlocked on three sides. ... I kept one eye on the target and the other on the sky. Our three-hour approach had been in plain view, as would be our three-hour retirement, and I thought that every minute would bring an air attack. None came ... but those were the longest six hours of my life.[23]

To avoid blast damage to their floatplanes, the big ships detached them to cruisers of Task Force 38 for safekeeping. Carrier planes from that force would spot the bombardment, although the *Missouri* later complained that her spotter made no contact with the ship until an hour before the action started. And he then confessed that he had no grid chart, a serious matter had the ships encountered coast defense artillery. Fortunately, most of the targets were visible from Spot 1 on the ship.[24]

Streaming their paravanes against mines, Badger's battleships opened fire at 0936. The range was 31,800 yards; the targets, the Nihon Steel Company and the Wanishi Ironworks. The Captain of the *Missouri*, 'Sunshine' Mur-

The *New Jersey* with her
Ms 22 paint scheme
looking very worn
shortly before her first
stateside visit home in
well over a year. A
hospital ship and two
escort carriers ride at
anchor in the
background. [USN]

ray, remembered later that he watched his first
salvo of three shells land. For an instant,
nothing happened, and Murray thought, 'uh
oh, duds'.[25] Then, the earth jumped up, and
Murray realized that the crew of No. 1 turret
had fired three armor-piercing shells.

The three battleships expended 833 rounds
of 16-inch ammunition. Except for that first
blast from the *Missouri*, the vessels were shooting high capacity bombardment shells with
steel nose plugs and base detonating fuses to
destroy heavy industrial equipment. All three
ships inflicted substantial, indeed often spectacular damage, to the two steelworks. The *Iowa*
directed two salvos at the Nihon open hearth
furnaces. The air spotter radioed, 'Right in the
furnaces'.[26] After six *Iowa* salvos against Wanishi, the entire area was obscured by heavy

smoke plumes and clouds of escaping steam.
The *Missouri*, after bombarding Nihon, saw a
large explosion followed by flames shooting
300 ft in the air from the shops. The same
battleship, concentrating then on the Wanishi
coal liquefaction plant and coke ovens, toppled
four of their eight smokestacks. Of the
company's blast furnaces, the *Missouri*
wrecked all but one. Another juicy target, large
hammerhead cranes, attracted 27 rounds, but
by that point, the *Missouri* found it impossible
to spot results through the great clouds of
smoke.[27]

The *Wisconsin* ran into the same problem.
Starting strongly, the ship observed a 'terrific
explosion' in the center of the Nihon area after
her ninth salvo and subsequent numerous fires
in her area at Wanishi. However, the ship's

63

airborne observer quickly found his job impossible, and the gunnery officers relied completely on indirect fire with corrections figured at the plotting board. Fortunately, navigational fixes were easy to obtain from radar in light of the configuration of the harbor. Still, the *Wisconsin*'s action report concluded that concentrated fire be avoided in the future when aerial spotting was available and navigation certain. More deliberate, dispersed shellfire would lend itself to more accurate observation of the fall of shot and would also 'add to the discomfort of the enemy by prolonging the bombardment of each area'.[28]

The operation also revealed some equipment deficiencies. The *Iowa* suffered several radar failures. Her 25th salvo caved in the cover on the SCR-720 antenna; big-gun blasts broke six struts on the SK radar; and the SG set kicked out after every salvo, but could be fixed immediately.

Some of the main armament equipment gave trouble on all three ships. A gasket in a powder car hoist blew on the *Iowa*. The 32 gallons of oil drained out, and the hoist was immobilised. The ship's force made a new gasket after the action. The center gun in turret No. 1 on the *Missouri* missed four salvos when the breech operating lever latch jammed in the down position. The *Wisconsin* reported three misfires of an unspecified nature and concluded that training deficiencies were to blame. 'There is no substitute for actual loading of projectiles,' her action report added.[29]

The bombardment lasted less than one hour. The battleships ceased fire at 1025 and retired at 26 knots. Still on anti-aircraft alert, the crews ate K rations at their gun stations. A post-war evaluation revealed the extent of the damage these men had wrought in their short morning's work. The Wanishi Ironworks, Japan's second largest producer of coke and pig iron, lost the equivalent of 75 days of coke production. The factory could have turned out pig iron again after about 60 days of repair work. The Nihon Steel Company suffered similarly. The ships also did considerable damage to the city of Muroran.[30]

Two days later, Badger's ships returned, this time to Honshu. Their target, the industrial city of Hitachi Miro, lay in a very shallow bay on a featureless section of the island about 80 miles northeast of Tokyo. Several factories there turned out arms and ammunition. To close down those plants, the

'Tokyo Express.' This 16″/HC was fired on 14 July at Muroran, Hokkaido. The shell is fitted with a Mk 29 Point Detonating Fuze to give the quickest possible explosion. The sailor is holding a Mk 15 primer. Fired electrically or by percussion, the flash from this primer ignites the black powder quilted on the silk powder bags. Over the man's right shoulder is a hoist control indicator. [NARS]

Muroran raiders were reinforced by the *North Carolina* and *Alabama*. HMS *King George V* and two British destroyers also joined the task group, but maneuvered independently. Badger, flying his flag in the *Iowa*, intended to surprise the Japanese with a night strike. Consequently, as the force began its run toward the target at 24 knots, the ships used their radars only when absolutely necessary. To foil the two big Japanese radar stations behind Hitachi, the 'Iowas' employed their new jamming gear; to prevent air attack, the *Wisconsin* served as radar guard ship with a night intercept officer especially assigned. The *Bon Homme Richard* provided the two night fighters for top cover and two radar countermeasures picket planes. The *Wisconsin* did pick up several bogies at 58 miles, but these turned away when challenged on a VHF channel and when the combat air patrol moved to intercept, they fled.[31]

Despite this promising beginning, things began to go awry for Badger's force. As the ships closed in on the coast, so did rainsqualls. Winds gusted to 40 knots; the ceiling fell to 500 ft; rain fell continuously. Air spot was therefore out of the question. Radar would have to provide the navigational fixes, yet the coast was relatively unknown, and charts varied. Worse, the coastline, being quite smooth, offered very few distinctive tracking points, unlike the situation at Muroran two days earlier.

Navigators were able to take some fixes from

Loran during the approach, and the MK 8 radars were invaluable in determining position. Once the ships opened fire at 2314, the MK 13 radar on the *Iowa* was able to pick up clearly the fall of 16-inch shells deliberately dropped into the water just offshore. This excellent performance by some of the radar sets was counterbalanced by a distressing number of failures. On the *Iowa*, the SG continued to kick out on every salvo, only to be promptly reset. Blast pressure sheered several struts on the SK-4 and cracked its main supporting frame. The *Wisconsin* recorded a litany of radar complaints—all after every piece of equipment had been checked following the Muroran bombardment and found to be operating 'at peak performance'.[32] (See Appendix I.) On the other hand, the battleship ordnance performed perfectly.

In 51 minutes, the three *Iowa*s shot off 697 16-inch shells, mostly with point detonating fuses set on 'Super Quick', although the *Missouri* fired one armor-piercing projectile by mistake. Initial post-bombardment assessments were optimistic. Judging from aerial photographs, *Missouri* officers concluded the damage to be very severe. Evaluators on the spot after the war reached a very different conclusion. Only three of the nine industrial areas were hit, and even in those unlucky three, direct damage was slight. Offsetting these disappointing results, most of the population fled the area after the bombardment. Twenty-four hours later, a B-29 raid caught the city without fire-fighters and burned out 80 per cent of the built-up area.

In fact, battleship bombardments were terrifying, especially to civilians. Post-war interrogators discovered that the average person was more frightened by shelling than by high-explosive or incendiary bombing. After one plant at Hitachi was hit by only four shells, absenteeism stopped production for a month. Copper miners who suffered under the same bombardment refused to return because another shelling might wreck the pumps and drown them. Monthly copper production at Hitachi plummeted from 40,000 to 1,500 tons. Such a panic reaction did not always prevail; at Muroran's Wanishi Iron Works, the shelling of 15 July elicited a 'London Blitz' spirit.[33]

Whatever the results, shore bombardment was fast becoming the principal concern of the fast battleships. With the Imperial Fleet a memory and Japanese aviation beaten down, at least for the moment, the ships began the practice necessary to master the technique. The old, slow victims of Pearl Harbor had worked up the expertise; the *Iowa* now headed for the bombardment range at Kahoolawe island, south of Maui. In two days of careful shooting, 29–30 July, the *Iowa* received 'satisfactory' marks in gunnery, with the best, a 'superior'.[34]

The *New Jersey* put in practice shoots too. That ship, finished with her Puget Sound overhaul on 4 July, exercised at San Clemente and then completed the course at Kahoolawe. To perfect her skills, she returned to the Pacific war via Wake, still held by the Japanese. The unfortunate garrison there now regularly played the part of the clay pigeon. The *Pennsylvania*, a veteran of World War One, had just worked the island over with her 14-inchers and reported the destruction of two 8-inch coast defense guns on Peacock Point.

The *New Jersey* and the light cruiser *Biloxi*, escorted by four destroyers, planned a methodical bombardment. Floatplane spotters, briefed for two days ahead of time, completely controlled the shoot. On the morning of 8 August—a beautiful day with unlimited visibility—the ships opened fire at 0905 from the range of 16,000 yards. The aim was maximum training benefit, not damage to the Japanese. The *New Jersey* fired slow single gun salvos, many of which landed within 25 yards of the target. One shell made a direct hit on the main bridge on Wake, severely damaging the span.

For over an hour, the exercise proceeded routinely, but suddenly at 1032, a large splash erupted 600 yards off the starboard bow, followed three minutes later by a second miss. Viewing the size of the splashes, *New Jersey* officers decided that the Peacock Point 8-inchers silenced by the *Pennsylvania* had been resurrected. Anti-aircraft guns on the island also opened up a largely ineffectual fire on the seaplanes overhead, although a .50 caliber bullet did pierce one float. Consequently, the *New Jersey* shifted her guns to the offending Japanese weapons, although she kept to a very deliberate rate of fire.

Having completed the first phase of the training program at 1052, she broke off for lunch and then returned for two hours of afternoon practice. She caved in one side of the revetment at Peacock Point with a 16-inch shell, but a lone afternoon splash 200 yards off

the port bow led her to report that the 8-inchers were probably still in commission. Her silencing fire directed against the irritating anti-aircraft guns flushed about 50 of their crewmen from a bunker, and one of the float-planes got the unusual satisfaction of strafing its tormentors. In all, the *New Jersey* expended 106 big shells and 266 5-inchers on Wake. One 5-inch round exploded prematurely; there were no duds at all.[35]

These projectiles were the last rounds that her class would fire in World War Two. A radio flash at 0745 on 15 August notified Halsey aboard the *Missouri* that President Truman had announced acceptance of the Japanese surrender offer. In celebration, the ship sounded its whistle and siren for a minute and broke out the battle colors at the main-mast. Over the next few days, Halsey's task force waited 200 miles south of Tokyo while the details of the surrender ceremony were arranged. On 16 August, Admiral Bruce Fraser, RN, came aboard the *Missouri* to confer on Halsey the order Knight of the British Empire. The following day, all the ships of Task Force 38 closed up in compact formation for Operation Snapshot; shortly thereafter, the *Missouri* detached 215 sailors to the *Wisconsin* for shore duty with the leading occupation force that entered Tokyo on 29

August. The two vessels closed up to within 100 ft of each other, and the *Missouri*'s detachment crossed to the *Wisconsin* two or three at a time via cargo net. Halsey pointed out that had two battleships moved to within 500 yards of each other during the 1930s, the collision alarms would have been sounded. 'This is really something to see,' he exclaimed, 'two great big battleships alongside each other cruising … at 12 knots and more or less laughing and talking with each other. . . .'[36]

Far more exciting, the fleet received a message on 21 August from Gen. MacArthur, now wearing the hat of Supreme Commander of the Allied Powers, setting 31 August as the date for the formal surrender. MacArthur added that the ceremonies would 'take place aboard a US battleship'.[37] The carriers, which had done most of the fighting, were too vulnerable in the enclosed waters of Tokyo Bay in case of Japanese treachery.

Of the battleships, the *Washington* or *South Dakota* possessed the best combat records, but President Truman settled all arguments by designating the *Missouri* as the surrender ship. As the last battleship to join up, there could be no question as to battle record. The new President also had always taken a very close interest in his state's namesake. His daughter had launched the battleship, and he had given

'The Setting of the Rising Sun.' The Third Fleet off Honshu. A *South Dakota* class battleship is off to the right; the *Iowa* class dead center is either the *Missouri* or *Wisconsin*. This fine photograph was taken by the light cruiser *Duluth* on 15th August 1945, the day Japan capitulated. [USN]

The *Missouri* close alongside the *Iowa*, 20 August 1945. The newer ship can be distinguished by her round SK-2 air search radar (barely visible at the top of her fire control tower). The *Iowa* still sports the original rectangular SK, and atop her turret No 2 are three 20-mm Oerlikons, whereas the *Missouri* has a quad 40-mm mount in that location. The larger gun installation was never fitted to the *Iowa* because it would have blocked the lines of sight from the third and lowest level (the flag level) of her conning tower. [NARS]

the principal address at the ceremony. His nephew, John C. Truman, served aboard as a quartermaster. So Truman picked the *Missouri* and thereby virtually ensured her preservation as a memorial, making her within days the most famous ship in the world, a distinction that she still holds.

On 23 August, the Captain of the *Missouri*, 'Sunshine' Murray learned of his command's illustrious new status when the ship received mail. Murray's chief yeoman dashed up to bridge with a letter containing a clipping from the Santa Barbara paper detailing the news. Murray quickly opened a letter from his wife who complained, 'Why don't you tell me about these things instead of letting me read it in the newspaper.'[38] Soon thereafter, a dispatch confirmed the reports.

Some of the other battleship commanders heaved a sigh of relief when they learned of Truman's decision. Captain Murray found himself in the shoes of the fictional Horatio Hornblower arranging the funeral of Lord Nelson; that is, Murray had the heavy responsibility of ordering all the details of a most public ceremony with a high potential for mishaps great and small. Immediately, Murray set to work to make his ship presentable. Patches of paint were peeling from the *Missouri*; she had left Leyte on 1 July. Because of the fire hazard, paint was not supposed to be aboard ships in the war zone, but Murray's bo'sun 'found' 15 gallons. The *Missouri*'s decks were holystoned for the first time to remove their wartime paint.

To handle the large number of correspondents and radio broadcasters, the *Iowa* provided them quarters and communication facilities. She transmitted their reports 12 hours a day by a very long range, high powered radio. When its transmitter warmed up, the set radiated enough energy to flood the radar screens. With blinded sets, the battleships had to revert to pre-radar station-keeping at night. Also, the signals, of course, fixed the Fleet's position for the Japanese.

The possibility of Japanese treachery was taken very seriously. The *Missouri* kept her anti-aircraft batteries fully manned from one hour after sunset until she reached Guam a week after the surrender ceremonies. On 27 August, the *Missouri* and *Iowa* put into Sagami Bay with all hands at battle stations and with all watertight doors closed. As the Japanese naval officers delegated to surrender the Yokosuka naval district boarded the *Missouri*, they were stripped of their Samurai swords under the eyes of Marines armed with sub-machine guns. To guard against mines in Sagami Bay, Capt. Murray ordered the Japanese destroyer

which had brought out the delegation to lead the *Missouri* and accompanying ships to their anchorage. When the destroyer was slow to move, Murray trained the starboard 5-inch broadside at her, whereupon the destroyer '... took off at full speed. You could see that ship jump when those guns got down on him'.[39] Murray then ordered the destroyer to search with sonar for any rogue submarines. Because the destroyer also disregarded these instructions, Murray trained the two forward 16-inch turrets at the Japanese ship. Before the turrets even got around, '... he started pinging. You could hear him through the hull of the *Missouri*, he was pinging so hard!'[40]

After spending 28 August in Sagami Bay, the *Missouri* and *Iowa* entered Tokyo Bay the following day. As the two ships headed towards Yokohama, personnel could see large coast defense guns elevated at a 45° angle. The American ships kept their guns on the Japan-

ese artillery pieces until they were safely passed. As the vessels rounded a bend in the channel, the last Japanese battleship, the *Nagato*, came into view, tied up at the dock at Yokosuka. Her guns were also at maximum elevation, but trained down the channel at the American ships. Murray aimed his forward guns at the *Nagato*, but breathed a sigh of relief when he saw that the Japanese turrets did not follow his vessel. In fact, the Japanese battleship was not even manned.

The *Missouri* anchored deliberately at the spot where Commodore Matthew Perry had anchored in 1853. The ships kept half their boilers on line, to be able to move at a moment's notice. Boats and UDT swimmers patrolled the floodlit waters at night; a constant combat air patrol from the carriers offshore plus manned anti-aircraft guns guarded against a possible Kamikaze attack. On the surrender day, pushed back to 2 September

because of the uncertain track of a typhoon, a double patrol of fighters covered Tokyo Bay, for a suicide attack on the *Missouri* could have killed most of the Allied brass in the Pacific.

One of the more exasperating problems facing Capt. Murray was to allocate vantage spots to the 225 correspondents and 75 photographers who would cover the ceremony. To avoid a mob scene, Murray had his sailors mark off and number places on the deck with chalk. The reporters and cameramen drew lots and blue jacket escorts whose job it was to ensure that the newsmen remained in their assigned locations. The sole Japanese photographer was closely watched by two Marines armed with Colt .45 pistols. Perhaps the most unusual vantage point went to the senior aviator of the *Missouri*. Chosen because he was skinny, this officer crouched in the cramped right hood aperture of turret No. 2's rangefinder. Stationed directly above the surrender

The *Missouri* jammed with photographers and spectators. Commodore Perry's flag is in the case on the right. Note the Japanese photographer at left and the vessel's victory and bombardment claims painted on the ship's structure at center right. [USN]

Douglas MacArthur and Chester Nimitz, with Halsey behind them, arrive on the *Missouri* for the surrender ceremony. The battleship officer stationed in the rangefinder hood is just out of the picture to the top left. Visible though on the turret are the hoods for the right sight pointer and the right sight trainer (the latter farthest from the camera). [USN]

table, he had a superb view of the proceedings but soon ran out of film for his 16 mm camera.

For this obviously historic occasion, the *Missouri*'s printshop made up a commemorative card given to each person aboard the ship during the capitulation. Murray then destroyed the die. Commodore Perry's flag was brought by plane from the Naval Academy Museum and hung facing the surrender desk. Despite later tales that the national flag flown at the mainmast was the same one that had flown over the White House or the Capitol on 7 December 1941, in fact, it was a new regulation flag issued probably at Guam in May. At 0805, Admiral Nimitz boarded the ship; Halsey's four-star flag was hauled down and Nimitz' five-stars broken out. Half an hour later, a second five-star flag went up as MacArthur came aboard.[41]

The Japanese delegation boarded the battleship from boats, because American officers feared some sort of perfidy if the Imperial destroyer was allowed directly alongside. The ceremony went quickly and smoothly, although the Soviet newsmen presented minor problems. Their correspondent attempted to line up with the signers, and when Marines tried to remove him, he dashed through the ranks of the dignitaries before he was caught. The Russian photographer who had drawn one of the less desirable locations, tried to climb a

ladder to a better position, and was grabbed by the pants by Capt. Murray and his bo'sun. The Soviet's suspenders snapped, the trousers dropped to his knees, and the two Americans carried the unhappy Russian back to his original place.

The only other unpleasant moment for the *Missouri*'s officers was brought on by the surrender table itself. Admiral Fraser had volunteered a beautiful mahogany table from his flagship. It looked entirely adequate until the surrender documents arrived on board only 15 minutes before the Japanese delegation. Because the papers were too large for the British table, Murray and four sailors rushed to the wardroom and found the officers' tables bolted to the deck. They then dashed into the crew's mess compartment and snatched one of the folding tables. On the way back through the wardroom, Murray yanked a green felt cloth from the closest table. The Naval Academy Museum later asked Murray why the cloth was speckled with coffee stains. During the signing, as Japanese Foreign Minister Mamoru Shigemitsu sat down in front of the documents, his wooden leg hit the diagonal tie rod and almost collapsed the table into his lap.

Following the signing and the departure of the top officials, Capt. Murray and his staff were relaxing in his cabin when someone mentioned that they should save the surrender furniture for the Naval Academy Museum. When the officers returned to the quarterdeck, they found the cloth crumpled alongside the bulkhead. The table had disappeared. Heaving the cloth inside his cabin, Capt. Murray hurried below deck to find the table back in its original spot with the mess crew setting it for lunch. The mess cook lost it for the second time that morning. Later, the ship received a permanent plaque to mark the spot on the deck where the surrender had taken place. Teak planks removed from that area were turned into memorial cigarette boxes, and Capt. Murray received well-earned congratulatory messages from MacArthur and Nimitz on his handling of the proceedings.

So, the war had ended on an 'Iowa'-class battleship. With massive demobilization in the offing, the question facing black-shoe officers in the Fleet was whether any place existed in the post-war Navy for the fast battleship. Perhaps in a drastically reduced peacetime force, carrier aviation, clearly dominant, would consume all the available resources.

On V-J Day, the US Navy listed the *Missouri* as one of 23 active battleships. By 1950, she was the only one—and more visible than ever as a result of a much publicised grounding outside Norfolk. In the meantime, her three sisters had been retired from active service and were resting in the 'mothball fleet'.

Not that the Navy had failed to get useful service from them in the meantime. All four carried home returning military personnel as part of Operation *Magic Carpet*. The *Iowa*, for instance, picked up 1,500 Seabee construction workers at Buckner Bay, Okinawa. Crowding was severe. Designed for a crew of 1,900, the *Iowa* by 1945 had 2,700 navy men aboard. With the Seabees added, men ate and slept in shifts. The Seabees, never a very disciplined bunch anyhow, relieved their boredom by fighting each other. With the ship too crowded for the usual deck sports, the *Iowa* officers tried to diffuse tension with monumental bouts of tug-of-war and races around the weather deck.

With startling rapidity, however, the battleship went from the overflowing to seriously undermanned. Capt. Murray, on the *Missouri*, predicted accurately that his ship would lose about 30 per cent of her permanent crew as soon as she reached the United States. Consequently, as the *Missouri* brought Admiral Nimitz' files from Guam, he began an extensive training program so that the 'newly caught' ensigns aboard could benefit from the expertise of the retiring veterans. Many of the vacancies lay in critical posts. Typically, all three of her turret officers were released from active duty by the end of the year. By November, the *Iowa* had lost so many people that her captain regarded her condition as hazardous.[1]

The *Missouri*, on Truman's instructions, headed for New York City as the Navy Day representative of the Fleet. She first put into Norfolk to allow workers to install her commemorative plaque and to remove most of her 20 mm guns. She reached New York on 23 October in an extremely heavy fog which veiled her from the hundreds of small craft waiting to give her a rousing welcome.

On Navy Day, 27 October, the *Missouri*, anchored now in the Hudson River, welcomed aboard President Truman, his family and a host of distinguished guests including Governor Thomas E. Dewey and Admiral of the Fleet William Leahy. Truman spoke to all the sailors from Missouri and inquired particularly about his nephew who had insisted on leaving the ship at Norfolk. Truman then retired to the Captain's cabin, declared the ship 'wet' for one hour, and drank some bourbon.

The following day, Katherine Hepburn and Frederic March broadcast a bond drive from the ship which then moved to the *Queen Mary*'s dock. Admiral Jonas Ingram hoisted his flag aboard the *Missouri* as commander-in-chief, Atlantic Fleet. The public was invited to board the ship, although only the main deck was open to visitors. The ship's company stripped the deck of everything loose, but the flood of guests managed to make off with souvenirs anyhow. People prised loose name plates from hatches and machinery covers. They managed to open portholes which had been dogged down with wrenches. Keepsake

The *Missouri* became a symbol of the triumph of the United States. When Chester Nimitz returned to Washington, DC for a parade in his honor on 6 October 1945, he stood before a highly stylized mock-up of that battleship's fore turrets and fire control tower. [USN]

hunters then would reach in and grab whatever they could. They stole Capt. Murray's hat from his desk and took all of his pencils and papers. Incredulous officers watched people drag their hands in the muzzles of the 16-inch guns to pack grease under their fingernails. And when the battleship went into the New York Naval Shipyard for an overhaul, movable supplies and equipment disappeared, even medical implements and chronometers. The ship's chaplain, after noting that the yard had a bad reputation, still sadly remarked that the experience was 'disillusioning'.[2]

By early 1946, the *Wisconsin* had joined the *Missouri* in the Atlantic; the *Iowa* and *New Jersey* remained in Pacific waters. The four ships settled down to a routine of training cruises broken by maintenance in the dockyards. Crew morale often suffered when the ships were undermanned. The *Wisconsin* in mid-1946 was down to 600 sailors, so few that the ship could not get underway. On the *Missouri*, an ambitious supply officer hoping to make captain, added fuel to the flames by scrimping on the crew's mess in early 1946. The chaplain's protests did no good, but some of the sailors got word of their plight to the President. Truman personally ordered improvements in the *Missouri*'s food; a bright new supply officer earned superb fitness reports by spending all the savings that his predecessor had accumulated. The latter found himself passed over for captain.[3]

In the years immediately after the war, the training of reserves became the primary mission of the battleships. The *Wisconsin,* for example, carried out in 1947 two-week cruises for reserves. To make room for the 900 part-time sailors, the permanent crew of the battleship was set at 1,100 people, on the edge of the safety of operation. Theoretically, the reserve seamen could take up some of the slack, but as officers on the *Wisconsin* discovered, many of the 'sailors' had never even been to sea. In one case, the ship received a detail of 100 newly signed reserves, none of whom had gone through boot camp, and some of whom were still in civilian clothes. In another episode, 18 mailmen reported aboard for the 14 day cruise during which period not one piece of mail reached the ship. The executive officer of the battleship complained, 'How does one intelligently employ 18 mailmen for two weeks?'[4]

The training round was broken on occasion by the dispatch of the battleships on good will, show-the-flag trips. With increasing Cold War tensions and Soviet threats towards the Balkans, the *Missouri* went to the Mediterranean in 1946. Leaving New York on 22 March with the Turkish ambassador's remains, she reached Istanbul on 5 April, the first American warship to visit the city in 24 years. The American colony had gone to great pains to welcome the vessel with USO shows and sightseeing trips. The head of the Socony-Vacuum Oil Company told the startled chaplain of the *Missouri* of his arrangements for the crew's recreation. The well-intentioned oil

The *Missouri* anchored by the Turkish battlecruiser *Yavuz,* ex-SMS *Goeben* of World War One fame. This ship survived well into the 1960s and was then broken up by the Turks despite efforts of the West German government to save her. At the left lies an American destroyer; a Turkish destroyer is near the *Yavuz.* [NARS]

executive had convinced the police to close the red light district a week before the ship's arrival, '. . . so that', as he said, 'the girls would be well rested when we got there'.[5]

Of greater professional interest was the Turkish flagship, the *Yavuz*. Some *Missouri* officers dined aboard this ex-German veteran of World War One. The Turks also honored the American battleship in an unusual manner by issuing a set of postage stamps showing the ship painted in her striking measure 32/22D camouflage scheme of 1944.

Leaving Istanbul on 9 April, the *Missouri* docked at Piraeus to indicate American support for the hard-pressed Greek government. She next visited Naples, and her Roman Catholic chaplain arranged for all three duty sections to travel by special trains for audiences with Pope Pius XII. Before leaving the Mediterranean the battleship put into Algiers where Captain Roscoe Hillenkoetter displayed his ship-handling prowess by backing his 57,000-ton vessel to the pier unaided by tugs. Twenty *Missouri* officers flew in an aged Ju 52 to Sidi-bel-Abbes, the headquarters of the French Foreign Legion, for a high proof luncheon. The *Missouri* then reached Norfolk without incident on 9 May.

Later in that year, the *Wisconsin* made a similar lengthy cruise to Latin America. The battleship was chosen to transport Truman's representative, Fleet Admiral William Leahy, to the inauguration of the new president of Chile. Desperately shorthanded at the beginning of October, the battleship received 1,600 crewmen within two weeks. A carrier, two destroyers, an oiler and an amphibious ship to ferry sailors ashore on leave made up the *Wisconsin*'s escort. For Admiral Leahy's personal use, the *Wisconsin* carried his big black Packard on the deck by No. 3 turret. During the month-long voyage, the flotilla visited Chile, Peru and Venezuela. The presidents of all three countries came aboard the *Wisconsin*.

In 1947, the *New Jersey* joined the *Wisconsin* in taking Annapolis midshipmen on their first post-war cruise. Fittingly, the two battleships also paid the first courtesy call by American vessels to northern Europe since the end of the conflict. The navymen were overwhelmed by their reception. So many invitations poured into the ships at the first port-of-call, Edinburgh, that midshipmen and the sailors eventually had to be ordered to attend functions. Also at the Scottish capital, Admiral Richard L. Conolly, commander of US naval forces in Europe, broke his flag in the *New Jersey* for the duration of the cruise.

The battleships touched at Oslo, where King Haakon VII gave a dinner for top officers. At Portsmouth, the *Wisconsin*'s executive officer was handed a social events schedule two inches thick. He said later, '. . . it was an outpouring, an expression of symbolic appreciation, really, to the United States. Families were seeking Americans to come to their houses'.[6] At the English base, Admiral Bruce Fraser invited a number of the American officers to dinner in Lord Nelson's mess aboard HMS *Victory*. Leaving Portsmouth on 18 July, the *New Jersey* that fall hoisted the flag of Rear Admiral Herbert H. McClean, commander of Battleship Division One, in New York.

Meanwhile, the *Missouri* drew the plum assignment of returning President Truman to the United States from Brazil where he had signed the Rio Treaty. When the battleship

A fine view of the *Missouri* at Piraeus, Greece, on 10 April 1946. She has already lost some light anti-aircraft guns: for instance, the 20-mm alongside turret No. 2. Her floatplanes are the modern Curtiss SC-1 Seahawk. [USN]

reached the Brazilian port on 29 August 1947, the harbor pilot told the American officer conning the ship to anchor in a very crowded area. The officer questioned the choice of spots, but the Brazilian was adamant. 'They'll move,' he said, and they did.[7] The rest of the visit went as smoothly. Sailors found no trouble ashore because the police had jailed in advance over 1,000 suspected thieves and pickpockets. The battleship welcomed aboard both Presidents Truman and Eurico Dutra of Brazil, 'innumerable' generals and admirals, and by actual count, 17 ambassadors.

When the *Missouri* left Rio de Janeiro on 7 September, she was 'absolutely packed' with the presidential party which included Secret Service agents plus 40 reporters. The President slept in the captain's cabin, and his wife and daughter took over the flag cabin which had been specially fitted with twin beds. Despite the crowding, the voyage home proved pleasant enough. The weather co-operated with 12 days of flat calm, and the ship's company put on an elaborate crossing-the-line ceremony. Inquiry revealed that the oldest shellback aboard was Admiral Leahy, who had been initiated on the *Oregon* during her run from the West Coast to Santiago in 1898. The President also watched the shooting of the big guns, the downing of an anti-aircraft drone and the catapulting of the floatplanes.

Truman kept in constant touch with the State Department via his own personal code, to which only the commanding and communications officers of the *Missouri* held the key. Most reports were routine, but one evening, the Captain, R. L. Dennison, brought into Truman's cabin a message that Tito was threatening the invasion of Trieste. Truman, who was playing poker with aides, read the note to himself and said to Dennison, 'Tell the SOB he's going to have to shoot his way in.'[8]

As Dennison left the cabin, he noticed that Truman's staff looked utterly dumbfounded.

Upon arriving in Norfolk, the presidential party disembarked, and the *Missouri* went on to New York for a minor refit. Here, Capt. Dennison soon found secret orders to report without delay to Washington, D.C. to serve as the President's naval aide. With one day to give up his command and reach the White House, Dennison turned over the *Missouri* to his executive officer, Commander J. B. Colwell. When Colwell notified fleet headquarters in Norfolk, the immediate reaction there was '... what in the world has happened to Dennison and who in the hell is Colwell?'[9] Once the dust settled, Commander Colwell retained his exalted post for a month before being relieved by Capt. Jimmy Thach.

Truman's interest in the *Missouri* not only affected her personnel but kept her in commission when her sisters were leaving the service. In 1947, the six 27-knot 'North Carolinas' and 'South Dakotas' went into the reserve fleet. In short order, the *New Jersey* followed, hauling down her pennant at Bayonne on 30 June 1948. The next day, the *Wisconsin* was removed from the list of active warships at Norfolk. The *Iowa* continued her training duties on the West Coast, until she too was placed in mothballs on 24 March 1949 at San Francisco. Only the *Missouri* remained. The preceding fall, she had embarked on a three-week cold weather training cruise above the Arctic Circle to the Davis Strait between Baffin Island and Greenland. She spent 1949 on Atlantic command exercises interrupted by two midshipman training cruises. On the first, she visited Portsmouth, and like her sisters two years earlier, was deluged with guests. The second trip, to France this time, found her at sea on the fourth anniversary of V-J Day. The cadets assembled on the quarterdeck to hear a radioed message from Douglas MacArthur. On her return, the last active battleship put into Norfolk for a three month overhaul.

While in the yard, the *Missouri* underwent a change in command. Capt. William D. Brown, an officer with a fine war record in submarines, took over on 10 December. Most of his peers thought Brown destined for flag rank, although some regarded him as a bit of a martinet. Others considered him flamboyant. Since the end of the war, Brown had been engaged in oceanographic research. He had never commanded a big ship and was not accustomed to

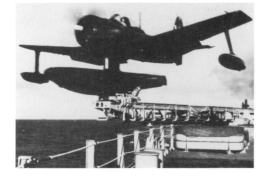

An SC-1 Seahawk catapulted from the *Missouri* on 27 February 1948. Piloted by Ensign F. H. Gilkie, this aircraft is almost certainly making the last floatplane flight from a battleship. The SC-1, although it had a much superior performance to the OS2U, was prone to mechanical failure and, more damning, initially had no second seat for rescue work. [NARS]

the handling of a battleship nor to the greater navigating precision that such a vessel required.[10] On 23 December 1949, Brown took the *Missouri* out for his first time and brought her back without incident the next evening. A lengthier cruise to Guantanamo was scheduled beginning on 17 January 1950. Before sailing, Brown received an envelope asking him to make a calibration run on the acoustical range as he left port. Brown paid little attention to the critical matter of buoy markers and, in the press of last minute details, turned the packet of information over to his operations officer who handed it to the navigator—like Brown, new aboard. Brown would later claim that his chief subordinates failed him at a critical moment. In fact, after the brief pre-Christmas shake-down cruise, Brown had pointedly rejected some well-intentioned advice from his executive officer whose job, Brown said, was to see that the captain's orders were executed. Brown had always run his submarines this way, and successfully too.

Consequently, when the *Missouri* headed out of Norfolk on the morning of 17 January, Brown, high in the fire control tower, took the con himself. Sighting what he believed to be the buoys marking the acoustical range, Brown ordered the ship's speed increased to 15 knots. In fact, the markers were spar buoys: stakes driven into the sand delimiting a shallow fishing channel through Thimble Shoals. As the battleship accelerated, some of Brown's uneasy officers diffidently suggested a change in course. Brown brusquely rejected these misgivings. The navigator, thoroughly alarmed, waved his arms at the captain and shouted, 'Come right! There's shoal water ahead.'[11] Brown dismissed the warning with the caustic comment that the navigator was lost. Meanwhile the executive officer, plotting the ship's course four levels below the captain, sent increasingly urgent warnings to Brown. In this comedy of errors, the seaman 'talker' who relayed these messages proved almost inarticulate when examined by the court of inquiry. In any event, Brown paid no attention to the alarms of the executive officer as muttered by the 'talker'.

Watching on his chart the *Missouri* speeding toward disaster, the frantic executive officer sent a last message which dispensed with all formality, 'Come right immediately! Twist ship!'[12] Had the latter maneuver been adopted, the *Missouri* would have reversed the starboard engines, gone to full ahead on the port engines, and swung the rudder hard right, thus making the sharpest possible turn to starboard. In any event, Brown gave no sign that he heard this last warning. No matter; it was far too late. The *Missouri*, still gaining speed, was already riding up on the sand. Brown finally realised his plight when he heard from, of all people, his chief engineer who reported the engines slowing as the propellers bit into the bottom. Brown at last ordered full speed astern, but the chief engineer had already shut down the engines to avoid the total destruction of his machinery from the sand and mud flooding in through the intakes. With her huge size and $12\frac{1}{2}$ knot speed, the *Missouri* continued to glide up the shelving bottom for almost a half mile. When she at last came to a stop, the battleship was stuck fast, and in a most public way.

Within plain view of the thousands of residents of the Norfolk area, the battleship lay close to the important army installation at Fort Monroe. Since her name was known to virtually all Americans and her situation was so visible, her plight received nationwide attention. Dozens of bad jokes made the rounds: for the first time, a battleship had hit a bar that the sailors didn't like; the crew's time was now counted as shore leave; 'Join the navy and see Thimble Shoals.' The official Soviet naval publication caustically commented that the grounding demonstrated the low level of American naval proficiency.

American naval officers were humiliated. Although a few later professed sympathy for Brown's position, most expressed bewilderment or outrage. One officer commented, 'Having been in and out of Norfolk ever since I was a midshipman, you just didn't go over where she was because that was all shallow water.'[13] Others used phrases like 'absolutely inexcusable', and 'shocking'. A destroyer captain who went by the *Missouri* several times over the next two weeks sardonically remarked, 'she was a good reminder to all of us that it didn't pay to get outside of the line of buoys'.[14]

Captain Brown stood court martial, as did the operations officer, navigator and the combat intelligence center officer. All were found guilty and set so far down the promotion lists that their careers were finished. Brown unsuccessfully attempted suicide and his wife suffered a nervous breakdown.[15]

The job of getting the *Missouri* off the beach fell to Admiral H. P. Smith, commander of

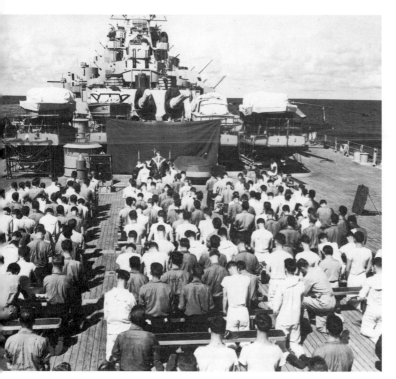

Helicopters had replaced the catapult planes on the *Missouri* by 1949. This picture, taken August of that year, shows the ship's complement of two HO3S-1 Dragonflys. Note the large number of boats carried in peacetime. [NARS]

cruisers and battleships in the Atlantic. He and his staff lived aboard the *Missouri* for the duration of the job. They pumped out of her 8,000 tons of oil fuel, took off her anchors and chains and put ashore all of her ammunition. In fact, all removable fluids and weights, except for the crew members, were taken off the ship. An army dredge, the *Comber*, dug a channel around the ship and astern to deep water. Divers with high pressure air lances softened the sand, compacted almost to the consistency of concrete by the *Missouri*'s weight. To break the suction of the mud on the hull, three destroyers made high speed runs at 27 knots up the channel. This stratagem proved counter-productive when the tremendous waves created raised havoc with the tugs stationed to pull her off. Finally, at high tide, on 1 February, the *Missouri* slipped free. Admiral Smith broke out her battle flags and signalled 'Reporting for Duty'.[16]

In fact, she was not fit for duty; the grounding had hurt her severely enough to require a trip to drydock. The extent of the damage has been the subject of a great deal of speculation ever since 1950, and when the Reagan administration proposed re-commissioning the 'Iowas', the debate resurfaced. The US *Naval Institute Proceedings* published some very categorical statements from writers that the *Missouri* had suffered a cracked barbette and a bent keelson—both basic structural problems that would be extremely difficult and expensive to fix. Another contributor to the same journal maintained that the ship's speed had permanently to be limited to 15 knots.[17] Two experts on naval architecture wrote that the *Missouri* was a poor candidate for reactivation in 1967 because '... a speed limitation had been imposed on the ship after her grounding in 1950'.[18] This assertion has even found its way into official naval publications, such as the narrative history of the *New Jersey*'s tour in Vietnam.[19] One prolific author on warships stated in 1980 that the *Missouri* 'had suffered considerable hull damage'.[20]

In blunt fact, the ship had suffered remarkably *little* damage considering the speed at which she had been run into the sand. Most of the damage to her bottom was done by one old anchor stuck in the mud. This relic from an earlier wreck did rupture the hull between frames 99 and 114. The other injuries were slight (for a complete list, see Appendix K). The ship's damage report summarised:

All damage incurred in the grounding and salvage operations has been repaired by Norfolk Naval Shipyard and by the ship's force of this vessel. On 8 February 1950, a fully successful post repair trial was conducted at sea.[21]

Indeed, the damage to the *Missouri* was inconsequential compared to the great tears ripped in the hull of *Iowa* when she ran onto the rocks at Casco Bay on 16 July 1943. Wartime security had shrouded that incident from the press and public. Thimble Shoals could hardly be beaten as a stage; the *Missouri*, the last battleship on active service, could hardly have been more famous.

Inevitably, calls came to ring down the curtain, to retire the last of the 'dinosaurs'. But the Navy won a half-way victory. The *Missouri* would remain in commission filling the training slot as she had done for the past four years. Within six months, the outbreak of the Korean War gave the ship an ideal opportunity to demonstrate the usefulness of the big gun in the jet age.

On 25 June 1950, as the *Missouri* steamed for Panama on another midshipman cruise, communist North Korea struck across the 38th parallel. The surprise attack gained almost complete success, and the *Missouri* was hurried across the Pacific to provide fire support for the hard-pressed defenders. Her big guns proved so valuable that all three of her sisters were recommissioned as well. In terms of main battery rounds fired, the four battleships saw more action over the next three years than in the rest of their careers put together.

In the seven weeks following the communist invasion, the South Koreans and their allies were pushed back into the south-eastern part of the peninsula. To recoup, Gen. MacArthur, the commander of all United Nations forces, called for reinforcements and began preparations for one of the most daring amphibious assaults in history—the landings at Inchon. The Korean peninsula, being only 150 miles wide, offered excellent opportunities for the UN forces to exercise their overwhelmingly superior naval forces in support of the hard-pressed ground troops. Accordingly, on 13 August, the *Missouri* received orders to proceed to the Far East.

The battleship spent five days at Norfolk taking on ammunition and supplies. Although the vessel was ready to leave on 18 August, a hurricane moving along the eastern coast threatened to hold her up. Admiral 'Jimmy' Holloway, the hard charger who had run the *Iowa* into the drydock without tugs back in December 1944, proved that he had lost none of his drive when he ordered the *Missouri* to sea despite the storm. The battleship steamed at 25 knots through enormous seas to clear the hurricane center, the eye of which she passed at 117 miles.

Holloway's 'calculated risk' may have paid off, but the ship also paid certain costs. Six of her boats were utterly demolished. Seas thundering aboard sprang four watertight doors on the main deck and tore a 24-inch searchlight from its pedestal on the Flag Bridge! One of the 40 mm mounts was damaged beyond repair, numerous electrical circuits shorted out, and both HO3S-1 helicopters were swept overboard. The only trace of the two aircraft was a single landing strut, with wheel still attached, dangling forlornly at the end of its tie-down line. Although her combat effectiveness was relatively unimpaired, the damage was severe enough that her Captain, Irving T. Duke, deviated by two days from his scheduled course to avoid another tropical storm east of Hawaii.[1]

The *Missouri* reached Pearl Harbor on 31 August and spent the next five days making good the hurricane casualties and adding 14 20 mm guns to her anti-aircraft arsenal. She reached Korean waters in the evening of 14 September, just 24 hours before the Marines would cross the sea walls at Inchon. To draw North Korean attention from the invasion site on the west coast, the *Missouri* opened fire the next day in support of South Korean (ROK) troops advancing on the east coast city of Samchok. Using both of her helicopters for air spot, the battleship knocked down half of a railroad bridge with 52 16-inch shells. She also covered the rescue of 725 men from the ROK *LST 667*, aground close to the city.

On 16 September, the *Missouri* moved down the coast to Pohang just as the 3rd ROK Division prepared to ford the Hyong-san River. Because the north bank was strongly held by two North Korean divisions, American advisors attached to the ROK formation called for naval gunfire support. As the heavy cruiser *Helena* moved into position, she was interrupted by a radio message from the arriving *Missouri*, 'Hello Cliffdweller, this is Battle Ax. We will take that mission.'[2]

Nine miles offshore, the *Missouri* opened fire. The first shells landed 2,000 yards from the American observers who quickly brought the shells right down on the river bank only 300 yards away. One of the army officers later reported, 'I didn't know it could be done. ... The *Missouri*'s fire was really demoralizing to those Red troops. We practically waded across that river standing up.'[3] In total, the battleship

The *Missouri* at sea, June 1950. The only battleship still in service, she would shortly be rejoined by her three sisters. Note her large mainmast stepped on her after funnel. The tripod mast that seems to grow out of turret No 3 belongs to a destroyer on the far side of the battleship. The catapults have been removed, but the crane remains on the stern. [USN]

expended 300 rounds of 16-inch and 62 of 5-inch in this very effective bombardment. Not surprisingly, certain problems manifested themselves: with inadequate hydrographic data and poor charts, positioning the ship accurately had been difficult. Radio communication with the army spotter ashore was spotty because of terrain shielding. A large number of 5-inch tracers had proven faulty, and one 16-inch shell burst only 50 ft from the muzzle, probably due to a fuse malfunction. Nonetheless, the *Missouri*'s work after a five year layoff was gratifying to her officers.[4]

From Pohang, the *Missouri* moved around to the western side of the peninsula to back up the Inchon invaders. When the battleship reported for duty, the cruiser *Toledo* needled her, 'Found a mudbank to sit on, Mac?' The *Missouri* retorted, 'Go home, small fry. We brought the real guns.'[5] To use them, the *Missouri* moved as close as possible to the coast and fired long-range shots at the Seoul-Wonsan Road. However, the situation at the front was so fluid that the ship expended only 11 ranging rounds in four days. During that period, Douglas MacArthur paid the ship a visit—his first since the Japanese surrender.[6]

For the next several weeks, the *Missouri* screened the *Valley Forge* which was giving air support to the UN troops pursuing the fleeing communists into North Korea. Then, in a dramatic demonstration of the potency of UN seapower, the *Missouri*, with the commander of the 7th Fleet—Vice Admiral A. D. Struble—aboard, headed a multi-national bombardment force made up of the cruisers *Worcester*, *Helena* and HMS *Ceylon*. Destroyers

from Canada, Australia and Britain provided the anti-submarine protection while planes from the *Valley Forge* flew top cover. The target was Chongjin, a city only 40 miles from Red China and 50 miles from the Soviet border. Located in this far northern enemy city was the Mitsubishi Ironworks.

With all the ships flying UN flags from their foretrunks, Admiral Struble's force concentrated their fire on the steel yard and on the docks. The *Missouri* put 96 16-inch shells into the former which was soon covered with violent fires. The docks received 41 of the big projectiles which 'devastated' the area. The hour's work, Admiral Struble told the press as the ships retired southward, was to demonstrate to the enemy that the UN had plenty of sea power and was prepared to use it. Some planners hoped that the bombardment might persuade the demoralised North Koreans to surrender. Another major objective was to dissuade Red China from intervention. On their withdrawal, the force punctuated its arguments with a shelling of the railroad marshalling yards at Tanchon, a city about 120 miles down the coast.[7]

Although the bombardments were tactically successful, the broader strategic intentions were not realised. The North Koreans kept fighting, and the Communist Chinese prepared a massive army of 'volunteers' to throw into the fray. In late November, these fresh troops intervened with terrible effect. Portions of the Eighth Army were surrounded at the Chosin Reservoir and had to fight their way to the coast at Hungnam. As their field artillery was loaded aboard cargo ships 22–24 December, naval gunfire took over the task of holding back the enemy troops.

The *Missouri* expanded 162 of her big shells and 699 of her 5-inch projectiles. With the help of spotting planes from the *Leyte*, she zeroed in on enemy soldiers in Hamhung. She hit an enemy troop shelter, and the spotter reported Chinese Communists running out of it in all directions. She killed perhaps 100 enemy soldiers and covered the withdrawal of the last units from the beach with 5-inch illuminating and harassing fire. Army observers rated her assistance as 'very effective', and one verse from an improvised Marine Corps song ran 'Bless the old Battleax, "Mudflat Maru" '.[8]

A month later, the *Missouri* took part in Operation Ascendant—an amphibious feint in the Kansong-Kosong area. The battleship was placed in the unusual position of taking orders from a task force commander flying his flag in a destroyer tender, the *Dixie*. That auxiliary took part in the bombardment as did the light cruiser *Manchester*, but the *Missouri* provided most of the punch. Shooting at highway and railroad bridges, the ship expended 382 16-inch and 3,002 5-inch shells. The latter guns were worked so rapidly that 12 men suffered minor hand injuries while handling ammunition. Six of the 5-inch shells burst prematurely well along their trajectories. Although the faulty projectiles represented only a tiny fraction of the total number of rounds fired, they caused concern for the other ships operating in close proximity to the *Missouri*.[9]

Putting quickly into Sasebo, Japan, to replenish, the ship was back on station by 5 February. She assisted the ROK Capital Division near Kangnung and then participated in another fake landing three days later at Inchon. The communists, naturally wary of UN amphibious prowess, rapidly withdrew from the area. Bouncing back to the east coast, the battleship fired an extensive series of bombardments on Tanchon and Songjin. One elusive railroad bridge took 171 16-inch shells before it was wrecked. A second was the victim of better shooting or weaker construction when it collapsed after only 13 'bullets', whereas the third in the area went down on the 29th round. A warehouse storing explosives spewed flames 100 ft into the air when hit, but a hotel-barrack perched on the edge of a cliff lived a charmed life when correcting the fall of shot turned out to be remarkably difficult. As the *Missouri* left the Tanchon area on 23 February, the hotel

still stood, but every bridge in the area was unusable. In the midst of all of this activity, the battleship welcomed such distinguished guests as Syngman Rhee, the South Korean strongman, and General Matthew Ridgway. Her doctors also performed an appendectomy on a destroyerman from the *John A. Bole*.[10]

After two weeks of maintenance at Yokosuka, the *Missouri* returned for five more days

The *Missouri* in action off Chongjin, only a short distance from Soviet and Red Chinese territory. She suffered seven 16-inch HC premature bursts during her first Korean tour. She is still carrying some 20-mm guns, including the two in her eyes. This particular photograph was widely published ... and was used for this recruiting poster seen around the United States in the summer of 1951. [Both USN]

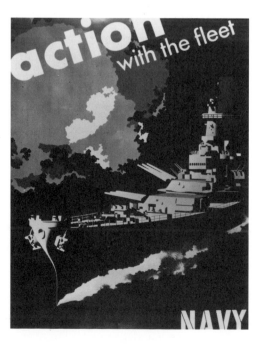

of action in mid-March. Aiming mainly at the transportation network from Wonsan to Song-jin, she usually operated at the edge of the 100-fathom curve to avoid enemy mines. By her own count, she destroyed or damaged 15 bridges, two tunnel entrances, 33 railroad cars, a fuel dump, gun positions and storage areas. She even fired on fishing craft with her 5-inchers. Her helicopter got a work-out when it attempted unsuccessfully to rescue an F–51 pilot shot down in Wonsan harbor. The heli-copter proved extremely effective at spotting, although it was quite vulnerable to anti-aircraft fire and thus did not venture inland. This task fell then to the faster, but less capable fighters from the off-shore carriers.

By far the most difficult target for the battleship was the railroad 'bridge' at Chaho. Not really a bridge at all, the structure, made of heavily reinforced concrete fill, ran along the shore at the base of a mountain. When ten hits with 16-inch HC shells caused only superficial damage to the 'bridge', the *Missouri* moved in to the 50-fathom curve in swept water and fired AP shells at 10,000 yards. Direct hits des-troyed the center portion of the structure and 'overs' exploding in the mountainside buried much of the rest of the 'bridge' with landslides. The ship's action report concluded, 'This target was an excellent test of the accuracy and hitting power of 16-inch guns.'[11]

The Chaho affair also tested the resilience of

The *New Jersey* on 3 November 1950, at Bayonne, New Jersey, 18 days before her recommissioning. She will carry the two 20-mm on her first trip to Korea, but not the rangefinder in turret No 1. [USN]

the North Korean repair crews. Within three weeks, they had one of the two tracks back in service. Admiral Allan E. Smith, the head of the UN Blockading and Escort Force, noted, '... the same thing happens to all bridges whether broken by air or ship since the enemy is very good at improvisation'.[12] These words were prophetic.

Also pointing the road to future develop-ments was the *Missouri*'s last day of action during this initial tour. On 19 March, she supported allied forces at Wonsan—the first battleship to take part in this siege that would last as long as the war lasted. Then she left Korea, put into Yokohama, and headed for Long Beach. The crowds gave her a rousing welcome when she arrived on 12 April. During her first Korean deployment, the *Missouri* had travelled 62,100 miles and fired 2,895 16-inch and 8,043 5-inch shells.[13]

For two months, UN forces carried on without a battleship in the combat zone until the *New Jersey* arrived on 17 May. Recommis-sioned on 21 November 1950, that vessel worked up in the Caribbean. When she reached Korea, Vice Admiral Harold M. Mar-tin made her the flagship of the Seventh Fleet for the next six months. She fired her first missions since Wake in August 1945 in the Kansong and Wonsan areas.

As in that last World War Two bombard-ment, the battleship scored a direct hit on a bridge. This time, the support collapsed, as did the two spans that it supported. She also hit an ammunition dump and halted a truck convoy at a road junction. However, not all was smooth sailing. As the *New Jersey* shelled Wonsan on 21 May, hot particles from a 16-inch discharge ignited oil in an open can on a 40mm mount. The blazing oil set fire to life jackets and canvas ammunition covers. One 40mm shell exploded; gunners heaved the rest overboard. Although no one was injured, the flames took 17 minutes to extinguish.

Six hours later at 0930, the ship was not so fortunate. A North Korean shore battery on Kalma Gak, the peninsula jutting into the bay fronting Wonsan, bracketed the *New Jersey*, and then hit No. 1 turret. The small shell destroyed the forward ammunition handling boom and mangled an access ladder. Frag-ments from an air burst killed one sailor, R. H. Osterwind, and wounded three others. These men were the only combat casualties suffered by the *New Jersey* in her four wars to date. The

The *New Jersey* off Korea. Note the rugged coastline that was so characteristic of the eastern side of the peninsula. The ship is still carrying the SK-2 on her fire control tower and an SP on her mainmast. [NARS]

The *New Jersey* fires a two-gun salvo: deliberate shooting was usually the order of the day during the Korean conflict. It allowed for more accuracy and saved ammunition. [NARS]

battleship turned its guns on the offending battery and silenced it within 13 minutes.[14]

In June, the *New Jersey* operated in the Kangnung and Wonsan areas. The CNO, Forrest Sherman, and the commander of naval forces in the Far East, Turner Joy, were aboard on 28 June to view the latter bombardment. Wonsan turned feisty again as Communist coast defense artillery took the *New Jersey* under fire for a second time. Although the guns scored no more hits, several shells landed uncomfortably close to the ship's port side. The *New Jersey* took evasive maneuvers and put several of the offending weapons out of commission with her counterbattery fire.[15]

Shortly thereafter, the ship backed up a limited UN offensive near Kansong. Aboard for the fireworks on 4 July was the commander of the Eighth Army, General James Van Fleet. After watching the shoot, which proceeded as uneventfully as such a drama could, the General left the ship by his helicopter. That aircraft blundered into a mountain, and the *New Jersey* sent a medical officer by helicopter, piloted by a lieutenant (junior grade), G. T. Tuffanelli. The doctor found the crash victims suffering from shock but only minor injuries.

The 5-inch guns saw plenty of action, the 40-mm much less. By 1951, the 40-mm were too slow to take on jet aircraft; the guns also suffered from frequent electrical grounds. Fortunately, they were never challenged. The 5″/38, however, remained a most useful weapon. Reliable, accurate, and quick firing, it proved its worth again in the shore bombardment role. Here, the *New Jersey* fires against Kosong on 13 September 1951. [NARS]

The battleship continued its support of the Allied push over the next several days. Her fire often drew accolades from observers ashore. On 6 July, one spotter reported that entrenched enemy troops fled after the *New Jersey*'s first salvo had inflicted casualties as high as 65 per cent upon them. Similarly, the big guns often hit point targets such as mortar positions and battalion emplacements 'on the nose'. On 17 July at Wonsan, the *New Jersey* came to the rescue of American destroyers which had endured over 500 rounds from North Korean batteries in the so-called Battle of the Buzz Saw. And the next day, the battleship put on a marksmanship demonstration by scoring five direct hits on five of the offending gun emplacements.[16]

The *New Jersey* was limping slightly at this point, because she had lost No. 3 main engine two days earlier while covering carrier flight operations. A drop in lubricating oil pressure caused sufficient damage to send the vessel to Yokosuka. There she was repaired from 23 July to 12 August by the *Ajax* which replaced some turbine bearings with their attendant oil seals and carbon packing.[17]

The battleship was soon back in action. On 18 August, for instance, she fired 483 16-inch shells to drive off two counterattacks on ROK troops near Kansong. Prisoners subsequently admitted that the ship's gunfire had caused havoc in their regiment. The commanding general of the Tenth Corps radioed that the battleship's assistance had been 'decisive' and that '... future support by the *New Jersey* is anticipated with keen interest by this entire command'.[18]

For the following ten week period, the *New Jersey* lived up to her high standard with some of the most effective battleship gunnery ever exhibited. In September, she destroyed a bridge and breached a dam. In early October, a ground spotter reported, 'Fire for effect was excellent—best coverage we have seen— reverse slope firing perfect'.[19] On 5 October, she hit more bridges and an oil refinery. When communist shore batteries at Hamhung forced mine-sweepers to retire and straddled her a number of times, she silenced them with 5-inch shellfire. The next day, she shot up a locomotive at Tanchon and then headed for Japan to replenish her depleted magazines.

She returned quickly—now in a task force commanded by Admiral A. K. Scott-Moncrief, RN, in HMS *Belfast*. For the first

A 5-inch white phosphorus (WP) smoke round from the *New Jersey* explodes near Hungnam. The projectiles were developed to lay smoke screens in distant areas (at a maximum effective range of 8000 yards), but they did not perform reliably. The *Iowa* fired WP airbursts at Wonsan on 5 July 1952 to hinder North Korean firefighting efforts, but she reported that about 25 percent of the shells failed to burst or gave off very little smoke. [NARS]

The *New Jersey* fires a nine-gun broadside, probably near Hungnam in October 1951. The official US Navy caption to this photograph says, 'Notice the terrific push effect firing of all nine guns has on ship.' That statement, of course, is quite in error: to imagine that the recoil from nine 1900 lb shells could thrust a 57,000 ton ship 50 feet sideways through the water is to presuppose a suspension of the laws of physics. The ruffled water surface is, instead, caused by the blast pressure from the 16-inch guns. [NARS]

time, the *New Jersey* operated under a non-American officer. Australian pilots from HMAS *Sydney* flew the spotting missions, and the whole arrangement worked out very well. The *New Jersey* found the pilots to be most competent. Firing against Kansong, the *New Jersey* in five hours blasted artillery positions, troop concentrations and an ammunition dump. The latter went up in tremendous smoke clouds lit occasionally by secondary explosions. The Australian spotter radioed, 'Enemy troops running and falling. Beautiful shooting—every shot on target—most beautiful shooting I have seen in five years.'[20]

In November, the *New Jersey* cut railroad traffic by shooting on tracks, bridges and marshalling yards at Wonsan and Hungnam. To discourage repair parties, the ship, screened by the Dutch destroyer *Van Galen*, fired illuminating rounds from the 5-inchers by night. With the commander of the First ROK Corps observing aboard, the big guns of the *New Jersey* uprooted several communist gun positions and killed or wounded about 250 enemy soldiers near Kansong on 11 November. Two days later, as she fired the last bombardment of her tour, she passed the 3,000 mark for 16-inch shells expended.

As the ship's officers concluded, much of her success was due to the excellent spotting assistance received on occasion from carrier pilots but more often from her own helicopters. Lt (jg) Tuffanelli also made a daring rescue of a *Bon Homme Richard* flier shot down in a river ten miles south of Wonsan. For braving heavy small arms fire to accomplish his mission, Tuffanelli was commended by the commander of the Seventh Fleet.[21] After six months of combat, the *New Jersey* deserved a rest. She headed home. During her transit of the Panama Canal, she helped test its defenses, and then she put into Norfolk for a six-month overhaul.

Filling in for her was the *Wisconsin*. That ship had re-entered service on 3 March 1951. During the summer, she took midshipmen to Europe and to Cuba. She now relieved the *New Jersey* at Yokohama where Admiral Martin transferred his Seventh Fleet flag to the newcomer. Commanding the *Wisconsin* was Capt. Thomas Burrowes; one of his division officers aboard was Lcdr E. R. Zumwalt, a future CNO.

The battleship fired her big guns in anger for the first time since World War Two on 3 December. Operating in support of the ROK 11th Division near Kansong, the *Wisconsin* destroyed an enemy tank and two 76 mm guns. She then helped the First Marine Division by killing an estimated 75 communist soldiers and provided illumination to First ROK Corps enabling troops from that unit to repulse an enemy night assault with hand grenades.

Over the month of December, the *Wisconsin* cruised off the 'bombline', or the front, shoot-

The *Wisconsin* relieved the *New Jersey*. Naturally nicknamed the *Wisky* by her crew, she was the only 'Iowa' to go out to Korea with her No 1 turret rangefinder still in place. She carries the new SPS-6 air search radar on her foremast and an older SC on her mainmast. [NARS]

ing at targets as diverse as command posts, troops in the open and oxcarts loaded with ammunition. She also ranged up to Wonsan where she fired at camouflaged boats along the shore. The North Koreans were readying these craft to assault the UN held islands off the harbor. The battleship targeted flak batteries in the area to such good effect that Allied planes met with very little anti-aircraft fire over the city later that month. The ship also helped the aviators by rescuing with her helicopter a pilot from the *Antietam* three days before Christmas. For the smaller ships, *Wisconsin* physicians treated injured and sick personnel from destroyers *Kyes*, *Eversole* and *Higbee*. A badly wounded North Korean was also transferred aboard for care, but he died and was buried at sea. Covering what bases they could, the ship's crewmen gave the enemy soldier conditional Protestant and Roman Catholic services.[22]

After a year-end trip to Japan, the *Wisconsin* returned to action. Shuttling between the bombline and targets farther north, the vessel gave emergency aid to ROK troops. Shooting at an average range of 16 miles, the battleship fired 100 rounds of 16-inch HC at the Chinese 45th Division. Aerial photographs of the results showed 29 caves sealed off and a number of dead soldiers lying in the open. Just one shell striking an enemy group wounded an estimated 35 enemy infantrymen and killed ten.[23]

Testimony to the effectiveness of the *Wisconsin*'s gunfire came from prisoner interrogations in addition to the photographic evidence. One POW reported that a 16-inch shell striking the divisional command post where he had been stationed had killed or wounded half of the personnel in it. Another prisoner said that the size of a 16-inch dud convinced him that the time to surrender had come. A third captive stated that the political officer of his battalion explained the size of the 16-inch shell craters as having been caused by atomic artillery.[24]

However, in bombarding the railroad facilities at Wonsan, the *Wisconsin* experienced substantial problems with the spotting planes provided by the carriers. The fighters carried bombs, and often loitered over the area looking for worthwhile targets. In the meantime, the battleship was forced to hold her fire. During one scheduled four-hour gun strike, the vessel lost over an hour to the circling aviator. Additionally, the ship complained that damage assessment by the fighter pilots was too often inaccurate. For instance, when the *Wisconsin* shot up the roundhouse at Wonsan on 30 January, the spotter declared that the facility was completely destroyed. Photo reconnaissance later showed it standing but damaged. Results like these mitigated the flier's remarks that 'he had spotted for many other ships, and this was by far the best shooting he had seen'.[25]

85

The *Wisconsin* in foul weather, 8 February 1952. Her helicopter four days earlier had attempted the rescue of a *Valley Forge* pilot in the mountains of North Korea. Hit by heavy flak, the aircraft was forced to abandon the attempt. By this point night had fallen, and the pilot radioed the *Wisconsin* that he was running low on fuel. The battleship altered course to meet the helicopter, increased speed to 28 knots, and turned on her searchlight as a beacon. When the helicopter was finally recovered, it had three gallons of fuel in its tanks. To the left sits the wheeled launcher for the ship's drone. [NARS]

Transportation targets remained the focal point for the remainder of the *Wisconsin*'s tour. On 4 February, she entered the bay at Wonsan, stopped all her engines, and lay off Hodo Pando, a peninsula jutting south into the bay. She slowly and deliberately fired at marshalling yards, a roundhouse and even a large coal pile (with WP 5-inch rounds). Toward the end of the month, she destroyed an estimated 50 per cent of Kosong with over 300 16-inch shells. Although the exact results were obscured by a blowing snowstorm, spotters could make out three large secondary explosions.

The *Wisconsin* took part the next month in the major operations—known as 'Package' and 'Derail'— designed to break the railroad line running down the eastern coast of North Korea. The battleship would also use the opportunity to conduct fuse tests on the 16-inch shells. The ship got off to a hot start when she caught a train outside a tunnel and blasted it with her 40 mm battery on 15 March. To employ the light weapons, the battleship closed the shore perhaps to a dangerous degree. That afternoon, she received the only enemy damage of her career when a communist 155 mm shell tore a 24″ × 30″ hole through her steel deck at the 02 level. Three men were wounded by metal fragments. The ship's surgeons were able to patch up two of the sailors, but the third, with shrapnel in his right eye, was sent to the hospital ship *Consolation* for care. The *Wisconsin* turned on the enemy guns and scored two direct hits on the battery (of nine shells fired).[26]

As for the fuse test, the results were inconclusive. The *Wisconsin*, using a PDF 16-inch shell, scored a direct hit on a steam engine with terminal consequences for the locomotive. Then firing BDF shells, the ship penetrated the side wall of a tunnel where a train was

On her way home, the *Wisconsin* tested the navy's largest floating drydock, the *AFDB-1*, at Apra harbor, Guam. Big as the dock is, the *Wisconsin* overhangs by the bow. [USN]

Shell damage to the *Wisconsin* off Songjin, 15 March 1952. The damage control officer inspects the hole through the wooden planking and steel deck between frames Nos 144 and 145. Fragments injured three sailors. [NARS]

hiding. Ten minutes after the initial blasts, officers observed large secondary explosions and great volumes of smoke pouring from both tunnel entrances. The railroad was blocked for five days as a result of this action, and the commander of Task Force 77 reported to the CNO, 'The versatility of the 16″/50 caliber is well demonstrated. ... The ability to inflict major damage upon the enemy is most gratifying.'[27] As to the fuse matter, the *Wisconsin* recommended that her replacement, the *Iowa*, continue the tests.

The two ships met at Yokosuka on 1 April. On her way home, the *Wisconsin* stopped in at Guam and successfully tested the largest floating drydock in the Navy. In all, the *Wisconsin* served only a little over four months off Korea. To some of her crew, the tour seemed an eternity, and the ship had, in fact, spent prolonged periods buttoned up for action. Sailors in No. 1 turret jokingly compiled a list of round-shouldered men able to sleep in the gun barrels and another of flat-headed individuals who could rest upside down in the projectile hoists.[28]

The *Iowa*'s stay was destined to be two months longer than the *Wisconsin*'s. Capt. William R. Smedberg III, the officer charged with returning the *Iowa* to service, found his mothballed battleship in good condition, but he lacked personnel familiar with the 16-inch turrets. In order to get the ship to sea in a hurry, enlisted men who had trained for heavy cruiser duty were transferred aboard. In barely three weeks, the *Iowa* was ready for trials. Smedberg's first orders were to test her machinery at 20 knots in San Francisco Bay. Capt. Smedberg was most reluctant, because the bay is treacherous with its strong currents and shifting mud flats. Smedberg and his navigator worked out a course around Alcatraz and close to the Golden Gate bridge. After circling the prison island twice, the ship was almost shoved by the current onto that hostile shore. Smedberg later confessed that he probably missed grounding only by a few feet. Admiral of the Fleet Chester Nimitz, living in retirement overlooking the bay, telephoned Smedberg the next day and admonished the *Iowa*'s captain, 'Smedberg, I saw you taking the *Iowa* around that bay yesterday, and I've never seen such a foolhardy stunt in my life. Why did you do it?' Smedberg pleaded superior orders. Nimitz retorted, 'You've got to think about the safety of that ship. You shouldn't have done it.'[29]

Shortly thereafter, Smedberg followed Nimitz's advice when Admiral Thomas Sprague ordered him to anchor the *Iowa* inside the San Diego harbor. Smedberg knew that part of the channel was only 36 ft deep and was afraid that the *Iowa* might touch bottom. He therefore requested permission to anchor outside in Coronado Roads. Sprague, with whom Smedberg had argued before, preemptorily ordered the *Iowa* in anyway. When Smedberg dropped anchor outside the harbor, a furious interview followed during which Sprague insisted that the *Iowa* could move in any waters that carriers could use. Smedberg retorted that the flat-tops often drew a critical four or five feet less water than a fully laden battleship. Smedberg stuck by his guns, knowing that he could appeal to Admiral Nimitz for backing if need be.[30]

In March 1952, the *Iowa* left West Coast waters for Korea. She relieved the *Wisconsin* and went into action, firing her first rounds on 8 April near Chaho. After filling in tunnel entrances and covering tracks with dirt slides up to 20 ft deep, the battleship hurried south to support I ROK Corps the next day. Her action report admitted later that the 38 rounds she expended to back up the South Koreans had negligible results. On 10 April, her fire proved more effective as she blasted several enemy bunkers, although she drew one enemy shell that splashed 250 yards off the starboard quarter. The cautious enemy battery then escaped retribution by lying low: On 11 April, the *Iowa*, after at-sea replenishment, was back in action supporting the US X Corps. Firing at the long range of 18 miles, the battleship's fire so damaged enemy mortar positions, command posts and bunkers that all communist action against X Corps ceased by the conclusion of the bombardment.[31]

Until 16 April, the *Iowa* basically followed this same schedule, shuttling from the 'bomb-line' to targets along the North Korean coast. At night, the ship would fire harassment missions at enemy troops and supply areas. Generally, the *Iowa* shot 5-inchers on these missions, but Capt. Smedberg would 'just for the hell of it ..., fire a 16-inch shell in'.[32] Generally, Smedberg would wait for the ship's nightly movie to end and then warn the crew to stand by for the 16-inch. Smedberg avoided any pattern; on occasion, he fired two or three rounds at an interval of 20 minutes. At other times, he would wait an hour between single

The *Iowa* on her first day of action in the Korean theater, 7 April 1952. The ship's helicopter caught the North Korean mountains behind the battleship as she headed down the coast from Chaho to the bombline. Her aircraft crane is pointed aft (contrary to World War Two practice) to make it easier for her helicopter to operate. [USN]

salvos. He imagined the effect to be that of 'waiting for the other shoe to drop'.[33]

During the daylight hours of 13 April, the battleship provided especially effective help to I ROK Corps. In the judgment of the American army liaison officer who spotted the mission, the *Iowa* killed almost 100 communist soldiers, destroyed six gun emplacements and disrupted a divisional headquarters. She turned in a similar performance the following day up at Wonsan when she scored at least three direct hits on guns from 76 mm to 122 mm in size, buried two observation posts, and damaged a warehouse and the railroad marshalling yards. By evening, she was back at the bombline, ready to support UN troops.

In fact, the *Iowa* was putting on a most convincing demonstration of the virtues of her class: mobility and firepower. Able to race from one area to another, the ship could take quick advantage of juicy targets and disrupt both the enemy's logistical arrangements and his tactical operations. Admiral Earl E. Stone, commander of CRUDIV 1, passed his assessment of the *Iowa*'s performance to the CNO:

The destruction and damage caused by 16-inch gunfire was particularly gratifying. Continued use of battleship main battery fire on MSR [main supply route] targets and deeply embedded gun positions is recommended.[34]

The *Iowa* had compiled this excellent record despite being seriously short of certain ratings.

Especially scarce were such specialists as radiomen, electronics technicians and quartermasters. The engineering department was unable to operate all boilers except on a killing watch-and-watch basis. Thus, the *Iowa* was restricted to a maximum speed of 27 knots except in an emergency. In what was certainly a futile protest, the *Iowa*'s officers also complained about the heavy burden of routine paperwork and asked for its reduction. Vice Admiral J. J. 'Jocko' Clark noted that this recommendation called for a separate report with specific recommendations.

In any case, the battleship, having expended 549 main battery projectiles (and 1,486 5-inchers) in just nine days, spent four days away from the action filling her magazines. She put in her next appearance well north of the 38th parallel. With her helicopter calling fire, she sealed up four railroad tunnels near Tanchon on 20 April. Two days later, she counted the splashes of 17 misses from communist coast defence artillery; in turn, she missed a lighthouse with her big guns. Then Admiral Arthur Radford, CINCPAC, arrived aboard the ship by helicopter from the *Boxer* and spent a day observing operations. Shortly after his departure, on 25 April, the *Iowa* destroyed the village of Chindong, sheltering enemy troops, by burning the houses with 5-inch WP shells. The next day, 26 April, the battleship demolished at Kosong a dwelling which was reported inhabited by a T-34 tank. The obvious problem of avoiding the death of civilians challenged the battleship officers, and, as Smedberg said, 'We tried very hard not to let shells burst in the area of just civilian housing.'[35]

Back at Wonsan shortly thereafter, the *Iowa* concentrated on a locomotive shop which was soon in ruins. She then destroyed or derailed 16 cars. Having shot off more than half her 16-inch ammunition, she cancelled a strike at Kojo and retired on 30 April. Admiral Stone praised the ship again by calling special attention to her performance against rail targets. In her action report, the *Iowa* noted that many of her missions were fired at ranges of 16 or 17 miles. 'An initial spot of 200 yards or less was frequently received. This is considered excellent shooting.'[36]

One of the most dramatic bombardments ever fired by any of the class came on 25 May when the *Iowa* attacked Chongjin. Only once before, when the *Missouri* raided the same city in November 1950 in very different circumstances, had a battleship operated so far north. Escorted by the destroyers *McCoy Reynolds*, *Duncan* and HMAS *Warramunga*, the *Iowa* received top cover on request from the carriers of Task Force 77 which also provided two F4U Corsairs to supplement the battleship's helicopter spot. As the bombardment group approached at 0500, the *Iowa* picked up on her radar three bogies near the Manchurian border. These planes were quickly joined by ten more. Probably Russian, the aircraft caused intense concern on the *Iowa* until four F9F fighters from the CAP arrived at which point the bogies backed off.

Apart from this threat, the operation went extraordinarily well. As Capt. Smedberg remembered the scene:

We arrived and fired the first shot at 0530 in the most beautiful dawn you can imagine. The sea was flat calm—mirror like—and the temperature a balmy 68°. The sun was bright, there was not a cloud in the sky, and a soft breeze was just sufficient to move the dust and smoke away from our targets and our line of fire.[37]

The *Iowa* settled down to an all day shoot. Moving at an easy 10 knots just outside the 100-fathom curve, she fired—single salvos, usually—for the next 11 hours. Periodically, she would break off for carrier strikes 50 planes strong. Some 200 aircraft dropped 230 tons of bombs. The *Iowa* virtually matched that figure with 202 16-inch HC rounds—192 tons.

The *Iowa*'s guns pound Wonsan, 27 April 1952. Using her helicopter to spot, the battleship carved up a locomotive shop, artillery emplacements and a number of railroad cars. The forward 40-mm mounts have been secured for the duration of the bombardment; no human could stand 16-inch blast pressures at such a close distance. [USN]

Shooting deliberately, the battleship carried out enormous execution. She ravaged a roundhouse, an iron works and a rayon factory. She started a huge fire at the boat works and put a shell right into a gas storage area. The latter '... went up like an atomic explosion', said Smedberg. 'It was the most spectacular thing you ever saw in your life.'[38] The *Iowa* also destroyed three transformer and power stations. Her 5-inchers scored a direct hit on a radio tower, and her big guns toppled two gantry cranes and damaged three more.

About midday, radio operators intercepted a Peking broadcast which stated that American ships were deliberately shelling civilians at Chongjin. Three hours later, the same station reported that three of the four intruding Yankee ships had been sunk.

As a matter of fact, none of the vessels had been damaged or even fired upon by the time that they retired in the evening. However, in the action report, *Iowa* officers did voice concern about the aerial threat. With Red Chinese and Soviet airfields so nearby, battleship officers worried, with reason, about a sudden enemy attack. Against jet aircraft, the ship's anti-aircraft battery would have been woefully inadequate. The 40 mm Bofors were clearly not up to the danger: in fact, the navy had developed the 3-inch rapid fire gun when the Swedish weapon had proved too light to defeat the Kamikaze threat. Moreover, the 40-mm battery was showing its age with frequent malfunctions mainly caused by electrical

The *Iowa*, shooting either at Wonsan, 27 June, or at Chodo, 11 July 1952. She has anchored for better shooting, a practice which drew admonishments from the commander of TF 77 and CINCPAC. [USN]

more time on the bombline, the *Iowa* sailed for Sasebo and a well-earned rest on 1 June.[40]

The crew's morale seemed high to the officers. The men contributed heavily to the Navy Relief Drive in early June and worked with a will to put the ship back on station in less than a week. She revisited on 10 June the Mayang Do area where she had cut a bridge on 27 May. To the amazement of the Americans, communist labor battalions had completely replaced the structure, so the *Iowa* completely destroyed it again. The next month, when the vessel raided the Chaho area, she found one bridge that had been thoroughly wrecked now rebuilt with a heavy rock formation. The persistence of the North Koreans elicited grudging admiration from battleship officers; the feeling must have been mutual.

In June, the *Iowa* paid two visits to Wonsan. On the ninth, the battleship covered the off-loading of *LST-692* at Yodo Island. On the 27th, Capt. Smedberg eased the *Iowa* completely into the hostile port. Photo interpreters estimated that the enemy had more than 1,000 artillery pieces, mortars and machine guns hidden in the caves and hills surrounding the landlocked harbor. Although most of these communist guns were anti-aircraft pieces, perhaps 160 were large enough to pose a threat to UN ships. In fact, they often took mine-sweepers and other light craft under fire.

In the middle of this hornet's nest, Smedberg anchored the *Iowa*. He admitted later that he was somewhat concerned about floating mines which occasionally damaged UN vessels and about a motor torpedo boat attack in the dark. Especially bothersome to him was the fear that a Soviet submarine masquerading as a North Korean would put a torpedo into his side. However, the coast defense artillery posed the most immediate threat. A fog closed in on the *Iowa*. The ship was blanketed except for the tops of the masts, and Smedberg always wondered why the North Koreans failed to take advantage of his situation. When the air cleared, she conducted some 'extremely accurate shooting' against an electric sub-station and an underground ammunition factory.[41]

During the next week of cruising along the North Korean coast, including two more visits to Chongjin, the *Iowa* repeated her latest *modus operandi* by anchoring off Chodo Island at the entrance to Chinnampo harbor on the western side of North Korea. The battleships rarely operated on the west coast because of shallow

troubles. For instance, in August 1952, the *Iowa* lost to shorts and grounding 15 of her 19 40-mm mounts when water seeped into the electrical motors and controllers. To counter the communist air threat, the *Iowa* recommended continuous air cover for any UN ships operating as far north as Chongjin.[39]

Leaving the industrial sections of that city in ashes, the *Iowa* headed back down the coast. On the way, she indulged in some more railroad work, cutting track, sliding rock over tunnel entrances, caving in a seawall and catching one unfortunate train in the open. Back on the bombline by 28 May, she supported X Corps again. One observer counted 95 communist soldiers killed in shelters by her 16-inch shellfire and watched the giant projectiles slam into two squads that attempted to flee the carnage. After another trip to Wonsan and

waters. HMS *Ocean* provided the observation planes. The *Iowa*'s action report noted that the ship had never before worked with British aircraft and concluded, 'It is considered that the spotting was excellent and the co-ordination and teamwork between the spotters and the ship were outstanding.'[42] Lending weight to the *Iowa*'s efforts was HMS *Belfast*. Together the two gun ships concentrated on enemy anti-aircraft and coastal guns. The *Iowa* put one of the latter permanently out of the war by collapsing a cliff on it. But effective as the new technique of fighting at anchor was, it drew criticism from superior officers who argued that prudence dictated a moving battleship in waters where submarine or aircraft attacks were possible. Chodo was terribly close

to enemy airfields. CINCPAC concurred with these objections, and the experiment was not repeated.

The six weeks from the middle of June to the end of August saw the ship visit her old haunts. The *Iowa* proudly noted of her work along the bombline, 'Spotters ashore commented time after time on the destructiveness and accuracy of the *Iowa*'s fire.[43] She travelled up the coast again to Songjin where she scored 15 direct hits on an unlucky factory. She also hunted a shore battery that had hit the destroyer *Thompson*. Ten of that ship's sailors required medical attention aboard the *Iowa*, and they were cheated of revenge when the miserable visibility ushered in by Hurricane Karen conspired to hide the offending weapon.[44]

In the fall of 1952, the *Iowa* is still at work. Note how her muzzle flash is reflected off the anchor chains in the foreground; the temperature of the propellant gasses exceeds 700° F. The 20-mm guns that had been mounted in the tub atop turret No 2 are long gone.

The battleship helped other navy men in trouble with her helicopter. On 26 May, the *Iowa*'s aircraft had tried to extricate an aviator from rugged and high terrain. That attempt had come to nothing, but on 9 June, the helicopter did rescue a *Princeton* pilot. An F4U of VF 193 from that same ship was downed on 16 July, 35 miles northwest of Hungnam. Hiding in the same hills crossed by marines 19 months earlier on their desperate retreat from the Chosin Reservoir, the American flier killed with his pistol two enemy soldiers out searching for him. Into this inhospitable situation flew Lt Robert Dolton in the *Iowa*'s helicopter. Dolton managed to find the pilot and to fly him to safety. The successful and risky mission earned Dolton a Distinguished Flying Cross.[45]

While all this action was going on, the *Iowa* served as a meeting place for the famous and powerful. Admiral Sir Guy Russell, RN, visited, as did John Muccio, the US ambassador to South Korea. Mark Clark, the commanding general of all UN forces, met Vice Admiral Briscoe aboard the ship on 24 September. Welcoming these notables was Jocko Clark, a most gregarious officer who had taken command of the Seventh Fleet when Admiral Briscoe was elevated to head the US Navy in the Far East in early June. Keeping track of this steady stream of visitors was the ship's radio officer Sam Gravely, later the first black admiral in the Navy. Because the VIPs occupied the captain's cabin, Capt. Smedberg rarely saw his official quarters.[46]

Jocko Clark proved a peculiar problem for Smedberg. Under the direct orders of COMCRUDIV, Admiral Earl Stone, the *Iowa* spent most of her time on bombardment missions. Clark, a devoted aviator, wanted to be out with the carriers, but as Commander of the Seventh Fleet, he had to ride the fleet flagship. Unlike Admiral Briscoe, Clark appeared to be bored with the shooting and would spend most of his time in his cabin. Unfortunately for him, that area of the ship was severely shaken by the blast of turrets Nos 1 and 2. Eventually, Clark ordered Smedberg to use only turret No. 3, and the sailors were forced to shift ammunition from the two fore turrets to the after one—'a terrible job', according to Smedberg. At every opportunity, Clark would whip out to spend time with the carriers, generally stationed about 80 miles off the coast. In fact, Clark told Smedberg that he would rather go duck hunting at Pusan than continue the shore bombardments.[47]

In July, Joshua Cooper replaced Smedberg. Clark continued his somewhat eccentric behavior. He loved to fly and would insist on being taken up in the *Iowa*'s helicopter in all sorts of weather. At one point he was almost lost in the pitch dark before his pilot miraculously found the battleship.

In late September, after a visit to Japan, the *Iowa* worked over Wonsan again on the 23rd. She scored her greatest success there with a hit on an ammunition dump for a gun emplacement. Smoke from the secondary explosion boiled several thousand feet in the air. Two days later, she caught a train stopped by the destroyer HMS *Charity*. The *Iowa* hammered the locomotive and 30 box cars with 45 16-inch shells. Next came missions to Kojo, Songjin, and Wonsan. Off Tanchon, she arranged the rescue of a number of refugees waving white flags from small craft. Early October brought her back to the bombline, providing threatened UN soldiers with illuminating fire.[48]

Before returning home, the *Iowa* took part in Operation Decoy—an amphibious feint at Kojo on 14 October. Planners hoped that the communist command would react to the fake landings by withdrawing troops from their front line bunkers. As the reinforcements rushed in the open toward Kojo, they could be pounded by UN ships and aircraft. Together with the heavy cruiser *Toledo*, the *Iowa* fired a heavy 'pre-invasion' bombardment. She complained that a number of lucrative targets were denied her for fear that her shells would interfere with air attacks. The operation was therefore less than satisfactory for the *Iowa*, especially as the signs of communist response were minimal. Moreover, the left gun in turret No. 2 suffered a ruptured hydraulic line and was out of action for two hours. Her helicopter did pluck a *Bon Homme Richard* pilot from the waters off Kojo, and on 16 October, the *Iowa* moved close to the *Mount McKinley* to provide that ship with anti-aircraft support in case Migs opposing Task Force 77 planes over Kojo turned on the ships. That action rang down the curtain for the *Iowa*. She departed Yokosuka for Norfolk on 19 October.[49]

Thus, by the end of 1952, all four 'Iowas' had seen action in Korea. They had demonstrated forcefully their great utility in a limited war where circumstances favored their employment. In the atomic age, the battleship could still play a part.

As the 'police action' in Korea continued its seemingly interminable course, the battleships made ready for another round of combat. Two of the big vessels fought for a second time, but the uneasy truce of July 1953 left their role in a shrinking peacetime navy uncertain. Despite modernisation proposals, one by one, they were decommissioned. When the *Wisconsin* hauled down her flag on 8 March 1958, not a single battleship remained in service. Their day had surely passed.

Before that unhappy time arrived, a final spurt of action awaited the *Missouri* and *New Jersey*. Having been the first battleship to fight off Korea, the *Missouri* was the logical ship to replace the *Iowa* in October 1952. During the intervening 19-month period, the *Missouri* had conducted three midshipman cruises and flown the flag of Jimmy Holloway, commander of Cruiser Force, Atlantic Fleet. Now, as she lay at Yokosuka, Admiral Jocko Clark moved his staff aboard on 19 October. The top ship in the Seventh Fleet, the *Missouri*, six days later was shelling communist positions near Tanchon. Until March 1953, the battleship followed the well-established routine of support for UN troops at the bombline, interdiction of enemy railroads, and bombardment of strategic targets. For example, the vessel ran in swiftly to the Chaho area, conducted a shoot, and retired at high speed on 2 November. Three days later, she repeated the exercise and left a railroad bridge with one span twisted and another knocked into the ravine below. In mid-November, she attacked Wonsan and Chongjin. In December, she fired hundreds of rounds at targets up and down the coast. The only untoward event occurred when her spotting helicopter crashed four days before Christmas off Hungnam. The pilot and both Marine spotters drowned.[1]

The new year, 1953, found the ship punishing with all her ordnance, from the 16-inch rifles to the 40-mm anti-aircraft guns, enemy coast defence guns emplaced in caves. She paid several visits to Wonsan which, by the end of February, was entering its third year of siege by UN naval forces—certainly one of the longest such operations in modern times. For her bombardment of 6–7 February, the *Missouri* welcomed aboard the commander of the South Korean Navy, Admiral Sohn Won Yil, General James Van Fleet and Lieutenant General Maxwell Taylor. She put on a good show for them by destroying seven bunkers and damaging 49. Vice Admiral Briscoe watched her performance in the same area in early March, and Lt Col R. D. Heinl of the Marine Corps also observed her gunnery. Heinl would later become one of the foremost proponents of returning the 'Iowas' to service in the 1960s and 1970s.[2]

In March, the *Missouri* subjected Kojo, Chaho, Hungnam and Wonsan to more damage. At the last port, with one 16-inch shell she scored a '... direct hit which took a big chunk out of a bridge'.[3] In turn, 12 enemy rounds were aimed at her, but the nearest splashed 500 yards away. On 25 March, the *Missouri* fired her last mission near Kojo and departed for Japan. The only casualty of this relatively short tour of four months came as Capt. Warner R. Edsall maneuvered his ship in the narrow waters of Sasebo. He suffered a massive heart attack and died on the bridge.[4]

At Yokosuka, the *Missouri* relinquished her status of flagship of the Seventh Fleet to the

A most unusual sight: two active 'Iowas' moored to the same buoy. Here at Yokosuka, the *Missouri* prepares for her second tour in Korea while the *Iowa* gets ready for the journey home. In comparing the battleships, their bow tubs are obviously of a different shape, and the *Iowa* is equipped with the Mk 12/22 radars on her Mk 37 directors, while the *Missouri* mounts the newer Mk 25 on her Mk 37s. Otherwise, the two vessels look almost identical from this angle. [USN]

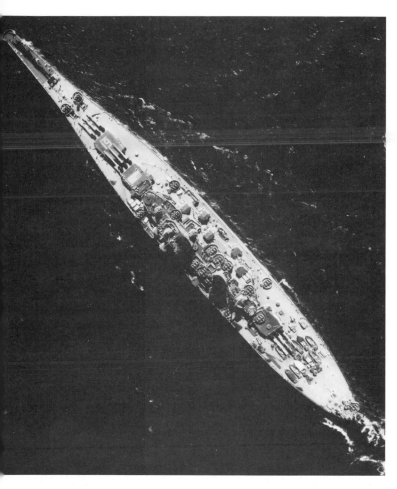

A very fine overhead view of the *Iowa* as she heads for home from Korea. Painted on her No 1 turret is her type number; a large American flag 'flies' on turret No 2. She was the only one of the battleships to be dressed out in this fashion during the Korean conflict. The date of the picture is 28 October 1952, and the *Iowa* is approaching Pearl Harbor. [USN]

New Jersey, freshly arrived from the United States. The latter vessel had spent the 16 months since she had left the Far East undergoing a half year refit at Norfolk and conducting various exercises, including the NROTC midshipman training cruise to France, Portugal and the Caribbean during the summer of 1952. Under the command of Charles L. Melson, the *New Jersey* reached Yokosuka 5 April. Tugboats brought her alongside the *Missouri*. For the next two days, staff officers from the Seventh Fleet inspected their new staterooms and transferred their files. On the seventh, Jocko Clark moved aboard. Capt. Melson greeted the admiral with some trepidation, since scuttlebutt about Clark's peculiarities had made its way throughout the fleet. However, Melson was surprised and pleased to find Clark easy to work for, although the captain often worried about his superior's proclivity for flying to his beloved carriers at all hours and in any sort of weather.[5]

Within five days, the *New Jersey* was back in action. For the first time, she struck the far northern city of Chongjin. Steaming at a leisurely seven knots, she aimed at the telephone exchange and a weather station from a position 11 miles out to sea. Her positioning so far offshore was calculated to avoid mines, but she narrowly escaped damage from just that menace. A crewman sighted a contact mine in the bow wave of the ship. Although disaster looked imminent, the mine washed down the battleship's side and was sunk by rifle fire from the destroyer *Laws*. Altogether, the results of the Chongjin bombardment proved disappointing, as did an attack the next day on a convoy of 30 trucks near Kojo. Despite shooting 15 rounds at the vehicles, the battleship had to report 'no damage observed'.[6]

Perhaps the *New Jersey* was just warming up, because she did better work against the railroad between Hungnam and Songjin. Standing four miles off the coast and using her helicopter to spot, the *New Jersey* scaled a tunnel with 46 16-inch shells and destroyed the center span of the nearby highway bridge. She then began a bombardment of Wonsan on 19 April. Two minutes after she opened fire, the communist shore batteries, so strangely silent when the *Iowa* sat shrouded in fog, replied with 76-mm to 105-mm rounds. The *New Jersey*'s 5-inchers immediately engaged the enemy weapons, but it took 30 minutes before they were silenced. The ship counted 28 enemy shell splashes, the closest of which hit only 10 yards from the vessel's side, and showered the deck with water and splinters. Fortunately, no one was hurt.[7]

The *New Jersey* returned to the Songjin area on 23 April and then left the war zone for resupply. Beginning on May Day, the battleship started a busy schedule of bombardments which lasted for a week. In Wonsan harbor, she fired eight salvos at a Red four-gun 155-mm battery stationed on Hodo Pando island. The communist artillery lapsed into temporary silence until the *New Jersey* left harbor heading north that evening. Over the next two days, the battleship blew away completely two bridges and an electrical power station near Hungnam. Then, the ship returned to Wonsan to settle accounts with the stubborn Hodo Pando pieces. This time, she thoroughly plastered their positions with 115 HC rounds which shut them up for over three weeks. She also fired a flak suppression mission to assist Task Force

A drone launched from its special catapult on the *Missouri* in Korean waters. There were two types of such targets: one with a jet engine and the second—the type here—with a propeller. Controlled by radio, the drone could make 200 knots. Such a launch was not an everyday affair, as the large number of onlookers on a cold day will confirm. Note the vice-admiral's flag on the foremast and the SPS-6 air search set slightly above it. The ship still carries the Mark 13 fire control radar on her after main battery director. Attached to the side of the 40-mm gun tub on turret No 3 is a rack holding helmets for ready use. [NARS]

77 aircraft. Watching all this action was Gen. Mark Clark, Maj.-Gen. G. L. Eberle and 45 War College students.[8]

The *New Jersey* celebrated the tenth anniversary of her commissioning on 23 May by welcoming aboard at Inchon a party of dignitaries including Lt Gen. Maxwell Taylor and President Syngman Rhee with his wife. Two days later, the battleship combined with the British cruiser *Newcastle* to suppress communist gun emplacements near Chinampo. Then, the *New Jersey* swung back around the peninsula in a vivid demonstration of her mobility to attack Wonsan again on 27 May. The Hodo Pando guns, quiet since their last encounter with the goliath *New Jersey* on 5 May, played their David role again. The plucky communist artillerymen fired 12 shells at the battleship, although the closest landed 500 yards away. The *New Jersey*, assisted by the cruisers *Bremerton* and *Manchester*, settled down to a methodical coverage of the enemy positions. Over the next several days, the gunnery vessels belabored Hodo Pando. On 30 May alone, the *New Jersey* fired for nine hours. Not surprisingly, this pounding put the enemy pieces out

of action again, and they remained quiet throughout June.[9]

During that month, the *New Jersey* made several trips to the bombline to render direct support of UN forces near Kosong. As usual in such an assignment, she fired at communist bunkers, tunnels and caves. On 15 June, large secondary detonations coming from one of these targets were spotted by Army observers correcting the fall of shot from a light plane. On the same day, the ship's helicopter rescued a TF 77 flier.[10]

After a stint at Wonsan where she did some excellent shooting, the *New Jersey* returned to Kosong and the bombline. Despite the persistent bad weather, she managed to celebrate Independence Day by blasting off 251 of her big shells. Results were gratifying. The ship's observers counted during the course of the bombardment nine impressive explosions issuing from enemy dugouts.

The *New Jersey* spent most of mid and late July operating against Wonsan. Bad weather cancelled air strikes scheduled for 11 July, and the clouds kept the battleship's spotting plane down as well. As the rains hung on the *New*

The *New Jersey* makes a wide turn about 12 miles off the coast near Chongjin, 12 April 1953. She is starting her second Korean deployment and flies the flag of Jocko Clark, commander of the Seventh Fleet. On the last full day of the war, 26 July, she fired 912 16-inch shells into Wonsan—the most intensive bombardment ever conducted in one day by any battleship in history. Unlike the *Iowa*, the *New Jersey* carries neither hull number nor national flag on her turret tops. [USN]

Jersey went ahead with her gunfire program anyway by correcting the fall of shot with direct observation. In fact, the *New Jersey* fired one of her most concentrated bombardments of the Korean struggle here. For three days, the ship steamed slowly offshore shooting at bridges, radar control facilities and enemy batteries. She completely demolished a radar antenna tower. When the Hodo Pando batteries showed signs of life for the first time in six weeks, the *New Jersey* put them out of action for the rest of the war. Four direct hits completely smashed one 90-mm piece, and 16-inch shells hitting a cliff behind a four gun position totally buried it in a rock avalanche. In all, the battleship expended in three days 549 large shells and 106 5-inch rounds.[11]

On 23 July, she was back at the bombline supporting South Korean troops. Her gunfire shut down an observation post by closing the large cave in which it was housed. United Nations forces had been trying to eradicate this particular installation for a month. She then headed north to try to catch a train in the open near Wonsan. Four volunteer officers went ashore by whaleboat at night to signal its approach. The ship was then to fire a prearranged salvo into a tunnel destroying the train and blocking the route. After many tense minutes of waiting, the signal came from shore,

the ship fired her six gun salvo, and the officers returned safely. Whether this so-called 'rat-trap' mission bagged its quarry has remained an unresolved question.[12]

The *New Jersey* fired her last Korean War shells at that perennial target: Wonsan. On 26 July, in the most concentrated single effort of the entire conflict, the battleship shot off 912 16-inch shells and a lesser number of 5-inchers. Targets included an artillery blockhouse, guns, tunnels, trenches, oil tanks and assorted strong points. Combat tanks attracted the *New Jersey*'s attention, as did an infantry patrol which received two 16-inch shells. Not unexpectedly, the *New Jersey* reported the patrol 'dispersed'.[13]

The next day, 27 July, an uneasy truce settled on the peninsula after more than 37 months of fighting. The *New Jersey* sent 13 officers and men to help represent the UN at the truce signing. Admiral Clark also attended. To most of the battleship sailors, the results of the war seemed curiously inconclusive. With the armistice line roughly following the 38th parallel where the fighting had erupted earlier, many Americans accustomed to the total victories of World War Two wondered what had gone wrong. Consequently, the Navy began an extensive *post bellum* examination of its equipment and operating techniques. The 'Iowas' received their share of the attention.

Certainly many naval aviators had been initially sceptical of the value of the battleships. Until the *Missouri* shelled Chonjin in October 1950, some of these officers had anticipated that the ship would be most useful as a conference site for President Truman and General MacArthur. When the *Missouri* finished her first tour in March 1951, some analysts, while admitting the accuracy and value of her gunfire, questioned whether her employment was not a form of overkill. The cheaper 8-inch rifle in the heavy cruisers, they said, could perform many of the *Missouri*'s missions at a cheaper price in men and money.[14]

The *New Jersey*, on her first tour, put such arguments to rest. Almost half of her missions were beyond the range of the cruiser gun, and the destructive effects of her heavy shells more than compensated for the added expense. Subsequent battleship tours simply drove this lesson home. Pacific Fleet staffers calculated after the war that the four 'Iowas' had fired 20,424 16-inch projectiles at a cost, in shells

alone, of $27,613,248 (figured on an average of $1,352 per shell). Of all the naval shells fired during the Korean conflict, 16-inchers made up about two per cent of the number. Yet they did a disproportionate amount of damage. For instance, the First Marine Division kept careful records of the gunfire support that it received in the first three months of 1952. It concluded that battleship artillery was both more flexible and more destructive than any other type (See Appendix M).[15]

Two naval officers and students of the Korean conflict concluded of the 16-inch guns, '. . . pound for pound they were the most efficient rifles in the ... war'.[16] Part of their effectiveness lay, of course, in their great range; part in the powerful explosive punch packed by a 16-inch HC shell. Pacific Fleet evaluators concluded, 'There were no enemy fortifications known which could withstand the fire of 16-inch guns.'[17] Coupled with that destructive effect was the terrific accuracy of the big pieces. They routinely fired at long ranges to within 300 yards of friendly units— support as close or closer than aircraft could provide. This pinpoint accuracy contrasted sharply with most of the World War Two experience of the fast battleships and could be partially ascribed to careful single shots rather than the earlier nine gun salvos. Contributing to accuracy was helicopter or ground spotting, when they could be used.

Some evaluators strongly emphasised the value of the battleships in the bad weather or night interdiction of enemy supply lines. The lack of UN night aviation capabilities presented strategists with a serious problem that battleship gunfire did much to set right. In-deed, the 16-inch gun was often the only weapon that could reliably pierce enemy tunnels or destroy the stronger bridge foundations. Pacific Fleet evaluators noted, 'Usually after a visit to a target area by a battleship, enemy transportation along the eastern MSR ceased almost altogether for several days.'[18]

These same analysts concluded that one of the significant lessons of Korea was '. . . that 5-inch and 6-inch guns are inadequate and 8-inch barely satisfactory to neutralize gun emplacements when these guns are well camouflaged in caves and can be brought out and retracted at will'.[19] The 5"/38 weapons aboard the battleships certainly did have their virtues, though. With reasonable accuracy out to 17,000 yards, a high rate of fire, and a projectile that fragmented into many small pieces, the 5-incher proved very effective against troops in the open. The Iowa concluded after one bombardment to allocate to the 16-inch artillery all hardened targets and to reserve for the 5-inch, interdiction fire and buildings. When all was said and done, the battleships had compiled for themselves an enviable record. (For the results of the New Jersey's second cruise, see Appendix L.)

Problems had surfaced, to be sure. Co-operation with the ground troops had sometimes been difficult. Only the First Marine Division had organic personnel and communications trained for ship gun links. Spotting was rarely fully satisfactory, especially when fighter pilots flew the missions. The helicopters attached to the battleships generally turned in a more professional performance. Army and marine officers late in the war were demonstrating great ability, either calling fire

BatDiv 2 on 7 June 1954 off Norfolk. This was the only time the four battleships operated together. The *Iowa* is closest to the camera, then the *Wisconsin*, the *Missouri* and the *New Jersey*. At this time, the *Missouri* was the flagship of Rear Admiral R. E. Kirby, commander of Battleships-Cruisers, Atlantic Fleet. The vessels steamed together for only a few hours. [NARS]

from the ground or from light aircraft. Surprisingly, reliable damage assessment by aerial photographs was seldom employed.[21]

The inadequacy of the battleships' anti-aircraft defenses nagged many officers. The 40-mm armament was hopelessly outdated and subject to numerous malfunctions, to boot. Fire control equipment for the 5-inchers was showing its age as well and simply could not keep up with jet aircraft. In 1955, the Bureau of Ships proposed to replace every 40-mm gun with the 3″/50 just entering service. Plans called for 16 twin mounts; alternatively, the experimental 3″/70 might prove a better choice, the Bureau said.

But with most of defense money in the mid-1950s going to support the 'massive retaliation' policy of the Eisenhower administration, the upgraded anti-aircraft armament fell to the budget cutters.[22]

Some naval planners saw a role for the 'Iowas' in the nuclear age. The army was working with success on an atomic shell for a long range 280-mm cannon. The Navy therefore found it relatively simple to develop an atomic 16-inch projectile. Called Katie, or the Mk 23, the device apparently gave an explosive yield similar to the Hiroshima bomb (or slightly less than 20 kilotons). The *Iowa*, *New Jersey* and *Wisconsin* were modified in 1956 to carry nine shells each (the *Missouri* was already in reserve). All the projectiles were stowed in No. 2 barbette, although they could be transferred by the overhead monorail to either of the

other magazines. It is still unclear whether any of the ships operated with the nuclear weapons.[23]

For the most part, the four battleships lived an uneventful existence after the Korean War ended. All served as flagships at one point or another: the *Wisconsin* relieved the *New Jersey* at the head of the Seventh Fleet in the fall of 1953. Before the latter vessel returned home, President Rhee personally awarded the *New Jersey* the Korean Presidential Unit Citation. She served three years later as flagship for the Second Fleet in northern European waters. The *Wisconsin* was the last to hoist an admiral's pennant when she served as host to Rear Admiral L. S. Parks as Commander, Battleship Division 2 in the summer of 1957.

All also took part in midshipman training cruises. The battleships were often shorthanded, and the prospective officers were most welcome as supplements to the ship's force. In June 1954, all the 'Iowas' took midshipmen to Guantanamo Bay and, for a few hours, operated as one unit. In 1955, the *New Jersey* undertook a typical cruise to Europe. She visited Valencia, Spain and Portsmouth and Weymouth, England. Some of her personnel came down with gastro-enteritis from the Spanish food. Of the 594 midshipmen embarked, 70 per cent suffered from the malady. This unpleasantness aside, both the Spanish and British hosts rolled out the red carpet. At Portsmouth, the Royal Navy provided small vessels to ferry sizeable batches of men ashore and gave cocktail parties for American officers aboard HMS *Maidstone*. The next year, the *New Jersey* visited Lisbon, Greenock and Oslo. The Scots put on a dance for some of the enlisted men at the Women's Prison; the *New Jersey* reciprocated by giving a tour of the ship to '50 unwanted children'. The most remarkable facet of the Norwegian stay was that not one single case of gonorrhea surfaced—something that could not be said of the other two ports.[24]

The battleships also took part in various exercises. The *Iowa*, for instance, participated in NATO Operation Strikeback in September 1957, and the *Wisconsin* spent part of April that year off Turkey and followed her summer cruise with visits to France and Britain on NATO maneuvers. All of this travelling after Korea was marred by only two accidents of note—both involving the *Wisconsin*. As she was operating in Japanese waters in January 1954 as flagship of the Seventh Fleet, a fire

The *Wisconsin* after colliding with the *Eaton* (DDE-510) in a heavy fog. A slightly different view of the *Wisconsin* in this condition went the rounds in navy circles with a quotation from Thucydides: 'A collision at sea can ruin your entire day.' [USN]

main burst, flooding the radar console room with two feet of water. It took the crew 'three days of almost continuous work' to put the equipment back in order.[25]

More serious, on 6 May 1956, the *Wisconsin* rammed the destroyer *Eaton* in a heavy fog off Virginia. The destroyer was badly damaged, although finally towed stern first to harbor. The collision mangled the battleship's bow, and she entered drydock for repairs at Norfolk. To hurry the job, the bow of the *Kentucky*, lying incomplete across Hampton Roads at Newport News, was amputated in a 68 ft long, 120-ton section and carried in one piece to Norfolk by barge. Dockyard workers and the *Wisconsin*'s crew worked 24 hours a day to graft the new bow on the older ship. On 28 June, the *Wisconsin* was ready for sea—a remarkable feat.[26]

For vessels that appeared to most knowledgeable people to be at the end of their careers, the Navy was taking a lot of trouble to keep them ship-shape. The *Iowa*, for example, was re-gunned for the first and only time in December 1955. Her nine barrels had fired, in practice and in combat, during her 12 years afloat 8,279 rounds. By this time, one of her sisters had already left service. With Harry Truman back in Independence, the *Missouri* was the first to decommission. She entered Puget Sound Naval Shipyard on 18 September 1954 for the necessary work preparatory to her deactivation. On 26 February 1955, she hauled down her flag and became officially part of the Pacific Reserve Fleet at Bremerton. Here she

To repair the *Wisconsin*, the bow of the *Kentucky* was snipped off and towed from Newport News to Norfolk. The 68-foot long section weighed 120 tons. [NARS]

would sit for almost 30 years, albeit as a major tourist attraction drawing approximately 100,000 visitors a year.[27]

On 14 December 1956, the *New Jersey*, returning from Norway, put into New York and was carefully laid up at Bayonne, New Jersey, on 21 August 1957. The *Iowa* followed quickly, with her official deactivation on 24 February 1958 at Philadelphia. Hardly a week later, the *Wisconsin*, on 8 March 1958, went through the decommissioning ritual at Bayonne. For the first time since 1895, the United States Navy had no battleship on active duty. Subsequently, the *Wisconsin* and the

Another bow shot of the *Wisconsin*. This time, the Soviet tanker *Komsomol* cuts in front of her, most probably during the NATO exercise RED PIVOT held off Turkey in April 1957. Following Suez and Hungary in 1956, the eastern Mediterranean was a tense sea. [USN]

The *Iowa*, seemingly at the end of her career, hosts the International Naval Review, Norfolk, on 11 June 1957. A long line of warships from many nations stretches far out to sea. A blimp floats over the harbor, and near Fort Monroe are anchored the carriers *Saratoga* and HMS *Ark Royal* (nearer the camera). [USN]

The *Wisconsin*, *New Jersey*, and *Iowa* looking forlorn at Philadelphia, April 1967. The two outboard ships have had their light anti-aircraft guns removed; the 40-mm mounts on the *New Jersey* are under cocoons. Their sister, the *Missouri*, sits a continent away at Bremerton, Washington. [USN]

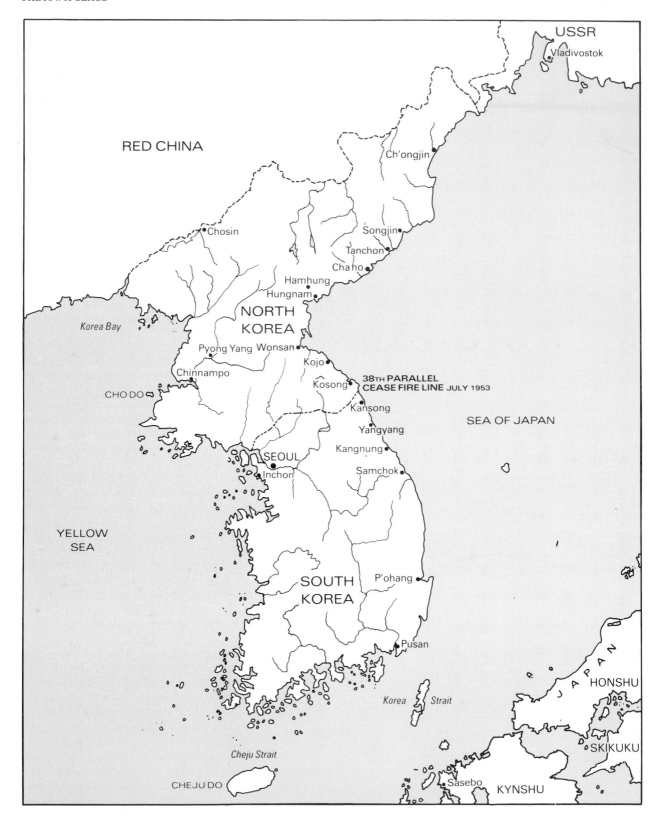

New Jersey were towed to Philadelphia where they joined the *Iowa* when the Bayonne facility closed.

Many people outside the Navy, and even a few inside, regard a ship in reserve as little better than a floating rust bucket. Such a misperception would later serve to undermine the case of the proponents of battleship reactivation. Actually, the 'mothballing' process involved much more than simply tying a ship to a pier. Central to the preservation of a battleship was the control of humidity; rusting would indeed turn a ship into a hulk. Therefore, all openings but one in the vessel's hull were sealed, and the interior humidity kept at an ideal 40 per cent. Aluminum 'igloos' enclosed the 40-mm mounts. The 5-inch turrets were secured from outside air by an elastic compound, and the 16-inch rifles were packed with grease. The exterior of the ship was painted, and hull fitted with cathodic protection to defeat electrolysis. Additionally, the bilges and other spaces below the waterline were equipped with flooding alarms. Radars and communications equipment were removed; some pieces were stored inside the ship, others ashore. The ship's records remained aboard, as did all spare parts.[28] The entire process of preparing a battleship for mothballs took from four to eight months. The work was done in large part by the ship's company, and for most of them it was a sad time. 'Disheartening', said one of the *Wisconsin*'s officers. Once cocooned, the battleships were maintained by personnel from the Reserve Fleet, who chipped and painted, listened for the alarms, and often added their own pragmatic warnings of trouble. A nail suspended on a line in a deckhouse would give an early indication of rust, for example.

Even as the 'Iowas' were being removed from service, some planners expressed an interest in modifying them for further use. Their relatively short active life, high speed, large size, good protection and great range all made them attractive for alternate missions. Proposals spanned the gamut from relatively minor upgrading to almost total reconstruction.[29]

For several years, the *Kentucky* seemed the prime candidate. Her construction had continued fitfully for several years after World War Two. Some thought was given to turning her into a prototype anti-aircraft battleship, or BB (AA). Under the plan, her armament would

The greatest efforts were made to keep the ships from rusting. Note the special ductwork under the rangefinder of turret No 3 on the *Wisconsin*, 28 June 1979. [Robert J. Cressman]

Work proceeded at a rapid pace on the *Kentucky* for about a year after the war. She was well along when this photograph was taken on 11 September 1946. Note the large transverse armored bulkhead ahead of barbette No 1. [NARS]

The *Kentucky* departs for the breakers, 31 October 1958. Parts of the *Wisconsin*'s bow rest atop her hull. So do two anchors, four 5-inch mounts, and two sections of the ship's thick conning tower tube. Her barbettes have been covered over for a decade. [Boston Metals Co.]

The *Kentucky* was not a total loss: Boston Metals of Baltimore paid $1,176,666 for her. Her engines went into the fast replenishment ships *Sacramento* and *Camden*. Both were large vessels (53,600 tons at full load; 792 × 107 × 39 feet). The 100,000 shp plants from the *Kentucky* drove them to 27 knots—almost exactly the speed that the 'Iowas' attained on four boilers. [USN]

have included anti-aircraft missiles launched from turrets and 8"/55 anti-aircraft guns in triple or quadruple mountings. She was floated out of her building dock on 20 January 1950 to free it for the *Missouri* after that ship's Thimble Shoals accident. The *Kentucky* was 73 per cent complete at that time. In 1955, the Ship Characteristics Board (SCB) moved that the vessel be finished as a missile battleship retaining two 16-inch turrets and mounting the new 5"/54 and 3"/50. Her anti-aircraft defense would be bolstered by Terrier, Talos or Tartar missiles, and the Regulus II winged missile would give the ship long range punch. Interestingly, this last concept was a key factor in reviving the 'Iowa' class in the 1980s. The SCB projected costs at $130 million. A similar, but more expensive plan in 1956 called for the Polaris ballistic missile in place of the Regulus II. By this time, however, the costs hovered around $200 million. Moreover, the *Kentucky* had been disfigured to fix the *Wisconsin*, and thus plans to use her were dropped and she was towed to Boston Metals Co., Baltimore for scrapping 31 October 1958.

The four remaining 'Iowas', however, continued to attract interest as missile ships. One

1958 SCB scheme proposed ripping out all the guns but four 5"/38; another kept the two forward 16-inch turrets. Polaris appeared in some sketches; Regulus in others. Also floated was a proposal to turn one of the battleships into a specialised satellite-launching vessel. Other officers argued that the 'Iowas' could be converted into perfect support vessels for the fast carrier task forces. The Second Fleet initiated the idea of rebuilding an 'Iowa' as a combination fleet flagship and combat oiler. Receiving more detailed consideration was the suggestion by the Amphibious Warfare Board in 1961 that an 'Iowa' be remade into a commando ship (CS). The project, designed to beef up the Navy's declining amphibious capabilities, envisioned the substitution of No. 3 turret with a helicopter hanger and troop quarters.[30]

All of these radical conversion projects foundered on the rocks of fiscal realities. Despite the increases in money for conventional forces in the Kennedy administration, the Polaris submarine program consumed prodigious chunks of cash. Thus, the four battleships languished through the first part of the 1960s in the mothball fleet.

8 VIETNAM

As the struggle in South-East Asia intensified during the mid-1960s, some policymakers seriously proposed returning the 'Iowas' to active duty. Intense opposition to battleship reactivation, particularly by the naval aviation community, kept all but the *New Jersey* in reserve. After an austere overhaul, she went out to Vietnam where her missions, as in Korea 15 years earlier, were to interdict enemy supplies and troop movements from the north in addition to supporting friendly forces in the south. She did these jobs well—indeed, too well. As her crew was preparing for a second tour of duty in 1969, top officials in the Nixon administration, viewing her power as destabilising, sent her back to mothballs rather than to war. For the third time, the *New Jersey* was decommissioned.

The genesis of her Vietnam deployment can be traced to the peculiar military realities of that war. The sinuous coastal land was divided along the 17th parallel by a supposedly neutral strip called the DMZ (demilitarised zone). Across this border, the communist North Vietnamese sent forces to assist the Viet Cong,

The *New Jersey* heads for the open sea once again, 26 March 1968. [USN]

South Vietnamese rebelling against their American-backed government. Because the Saigon regimes had shown themselves incapable of dealing with the insurgency, the Kennedy and Johnson administrations committed increasingly substantial American forces.

With this expanding commitment in which the US Navy played an increasingly significant role, some officers became seriously concerned about the decline of their gunfire capabilities. The only new gun deployed in the decade after Korea was the 5″/54 which possessed a good rate of fire but little weight and penetrating power. The four heavy cruisers still in commission carried the largest rifles at sea: the 8″/55 firing a 355-lb shell.

In November 1964, Vice Admiral Edwin B. Hooper, one of the Navy's top gunnery experts, headed a commission to remedy this problem. The group recommended the activation of two 'Iowas' and two heavy cruisers. Had the proposal been promptly implemented, the US Navy would almost certainly have saved many planes and pilots lost to North Vietnamese anti-aircraft fire over the next four years. Ironically, some top aviators managed to block the Hooper panel recommendations. Admiral Roy L. Johnson, commander of the Pacific Fleet from 1965–67, opposed battleship reactivation. He defended his stand with the erroneous assertions that the 8-inch guns possessed the same range and effectiveness as the 16-incher and that the reserve stocks of battleship projectiles had been exhausted. The CNO, Admiral David L. MacDonald, was also an aviator, and his opposition helped stymie the project until 1967.[1]

Despite this resistance at the top, battleship advocates both within the Defense Department and Congress studied the matter with increasing urgency. The United States by 1967 was losing, on average, one aircraft per day in Vietnam. Putting aside all but fiscal considerations, the air campaign was most expensive. Aircraft cost about $2 million each, and pilots cost $1 million to train. One of the 'Iowas' could be returned to service with a

reduced complement and austere updating for perhaps $25 million. This sum therefore represented little more than one week's toll of aircraft—or 25 B-52 strikes. Given figures like these, Senator Richard Russell pushed strongly for a battleship, as did Gen. Wallace M. Greene, Jr., the Marine Corps Commandant.

Those big gun advocates won out in the end. One day after MacDonald retired on 31 July 1967, the Defense Department announced that the *New Jersey* would be returned to service. Of the four 'Iowas', she was chosen in part because she had been regunned shortly before leaving service in 1957, and also because her deactivation had been performed with unusual care. The plan attracted nationwide attention. Critics derided the expense as outlandish; they claimed that the ship was terribly vulnerable to enemy attack. One Congressman, William E. Minshall, warned against an attempt by the Viet Cong or the North Vietnamese to capture the *New Jersey*. 'The battleship', he said,

'presents an attractive target not only from the loss of the ship itself but the propaganda value. I anticipate they [the communists] will use every trick in the book to try to get her.'[2]

More menacing in actuality were the budget trimmers. The reactivation, ruled the Defense Department, would be paid for out of the Navy's operating and maintenance funds. Accordingly, one navy proposal called for the reactivation of the ship's 16-inch battery only. She would be towed along the Vietnamese coast as an artillery hulk. A more generous plan would have brought to life two shafts, two fire rooms and two engines, but no 5-inchers. The Philadelphia Naval Shipyard estimated that for $24 million, it could deliver in nine months the *New Jersey* with the full power plant and all main and secondary turrets operational. The Navy selected this configuration. The ship's 'sole' mission was shore bombardment; there would be no missiles, no height-finding radar, and only limited upgrading of electronics and communications equipment. This 'austere'

The *Wisconsin* stirs, very briefly, in her sleep at Philadelphia. The tugs push her out so that the *New Jersey* can be moved to Pier 4 for sandblasting. The carrier *Antietam* of the 'Essex' class lies just ahead of the battleships. Even the stacks on the *Wisconsin* are sealed tight. [USN]

The *New Jersey* on the blocks, Philadelphia Naval Shipyard. She entered this drydock (No 3) on 20 September 1967 and left it on 13 January 1968. [USN]

which had developed cracks. The packing for both 5-inch and 16-inch recoil mechanisms had to be renewed. An inspection of No. 1 turret revealed an especially serious—and totally unexpected—flaw. Two of the Navy Yard's officers described the problem:

One of the most serious discrepancies . . . was that, at some unknown time, the port 16-inch gun of No. 1 turret had locked with the No. 2 turret. This had sprung the outboard deck lug and cracked the trunnion bearing of the port gun (No. 1 turret). The deck lug was straightened out by applying heat from induction coils and jacking with hydraulic jacks. This process took almost two weeks. When the shipyard went to order a replacement trunnion bearing, it was found that none were available in the Naval Supply System. A bearing was finally borrowed from the U.S. Army at the Aberdeen Proving Grounds. It is fortunate indeed that the heating and jacking method corrected the situation. One only has to imagine the work involved with replacing a 16-inch deck lug![3]

conversion—the term 'austere' was never defined and thus was the subject of much bickering—was intended to provide a useful service life of three years.

On 20 September, the *New Jersey* entered drydock. Yard workers found her to be in generally fine condition. Her boilers, for example, required relatively little attention. However, a number of unanticipated problems came to light. Records showed that the timing on one set of reduction gears was suspect; on closer inspection, all four needed retiming—an expensive and lengthy proposition. A number of bearings in pumps, turbines and generators required replacement, as did all four propellers

Replacement items for much of the equipment proved difficult to find, in part because the vessel was 25 years old and also because no battleship had been in service for almost 10 years. For example, the seals for the air conditioning compressors in the 16-inch powder handling rooms had deteriorated badly. The original supplier no longer made the seals; the expense of re-tooling to produce them was prohibitive. The shipyard found it cheaper to replace the entire compressor units.

Many of the parts records had been lost, but exhaustive searches by dockyard personnel managed to uncover a *New Jersey* rangefinder at the Picatinny Arsenal in New Jersey, 16-inch receiver regulators at Hawthorne, Nevada, and equipment from the never-finished *Kentucky* and *Illinois* at the Washington Navy Yard. Some materials, however, could not be tracked down, so shipyard workers cannibalised the *Iowa* and *Wisconsin* in order to get the *New Jersey* to sea on schedule. The items taken from these two ships, such as old valve parts and stores handling equipment, were then manufactured at leisure.

Work also started on assuring the *New Jersey* a first-class main battery. Beginning in August, the 16-inch rifles were cleaned and reworked at the rate of three monthly. Projectiles were also refurbished: 1,200 per month. For the first

The *New Jersey* in February 1968. The base for her prominent conical-monopole communications antenna is in place on the bow. The 40-mm gun tub on turret No 2 is soon to go, but the other two emplacements forward of turret No 1 would stay aboard until after her trials. [USN]

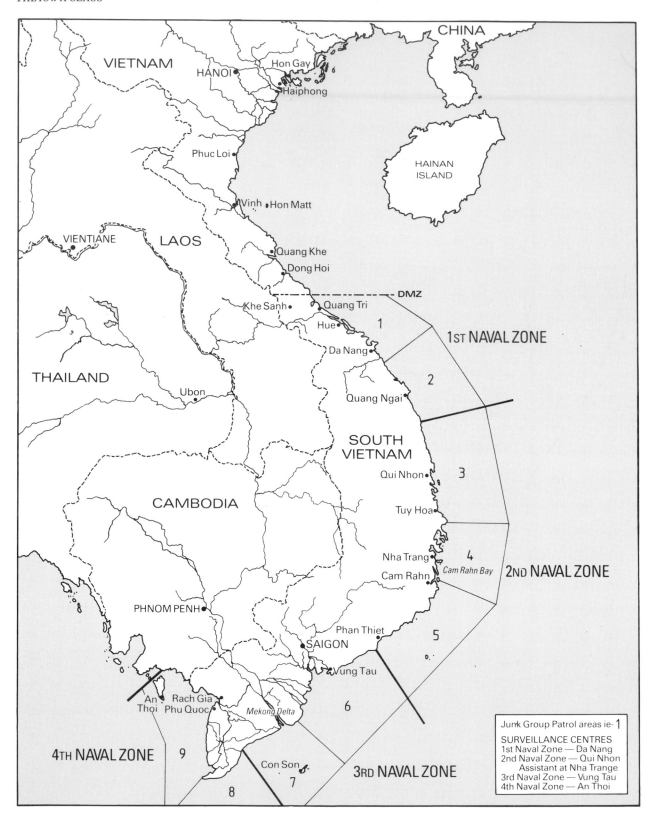

CHINA

VIETNAM

HANOI

Hon Gay

Haiphong

Phuc Loi

Vinh • Hon Matt

VIENTIANE

LAOS

HAINAN
ISLAND

Quang Khe

Dong Hoi

DMZ

Khe Sanh • • Quang Tri

Hue •

1

1ST NAVAL ZONE

THAILAND

Da Nang •

2

Ubon

Quang Ngai •

SOUTH
VIETNAM

CAMBODIA

Qui Nhon •

3

Tuy Hoa •

Nha Trang •

4

PHNOM PENH •

Cam Rahn •

Cam Rahn Bay

2ND NAVAL ZONE

Phan Thiet •

SAIGON

5

Vung Tau

An
Thoi

Rach Gia

Phu Quoc

Mekong Delta

6

Junk Group Patrol areas ie- 1

SURVEILLANCE CENTRES
1st Naval Zone — Da Nang
2nd Naval Zone — Qui Nhon
    Assistant at Nha Trange
3rd Naval Zone — Vung Tau
4th Naval Zone — An Thoi

4TH NAVAL ZONE

9

Con Son

7

3RD NAVAL ZONE

8

The *New Jersey* on
trials. She carries a
variety of new ECM and
IFF devices on her two
masts, but her aft main
battery director looks
familiar, as does the
Mark 13 fire control
radar atop it. New whip
aerials have been
attached to her fantail.
[USN]

time, spare 16-inch barrels were stocked west
of Pearl Harbor. At that base, three rifles were
put aboard a barge which was floated into the
well of the LSD *Gunston Hall*. The landing ship
transported barge and barrels to Subic Bay in
the Philippines.[4]

Other gunnery improvements included
Swedish additive, or a titanium dioxide wax
jacket, available for the first time to reduce
bore erosion. To help the crew handle ammunition, two fork lifts were stationed aboard. To
assist the gunners with the complex main
battery manual, its schematics were color-
coded. The main battery fire control system
was upgraded by the addition of two Mk 48
computers and a target-designation system.
Concern over sea-skimming missiles such as
the Soviet Styx which sank the Israeli destroyer *Eilat* in 1967 led to the provision of the
prominent ULQ-6B jammer atop the *New
Jersey*'s foremast. To decoy such missiles chaff
launchers were added. This new equipment
did not prove completely reliable—exacerba-
ted by the jarring shock from the main battery.

Communications gear was also upgraded
with on-line automatic encryption and decryp-
tion gear, 100-word-a-minute teletypes, and
receivers and transmitters for infra-red, HF,
VHF and UHF bands. New support facilities
for helicopters included two 1,000-gallon JP5
tanks, a grounding system, fire fighting gear
and a 1,600 square ft landing platform with tie
downs and safety nets.[5]

The crew's comfort was enhanced by such
improvements as toilets in place of troughs,
better lighting, roomier berthing spaces and
spot-type air conditioning. The ship's booster
society in New Jersey donated a closed circuit
color TV system.

Vestiges of an earlier navy lingered. The
crew still holystoned the teak decks to a
gleaming white with broom handles, boiler
firebricks, bleach, acid, soap and scouring
powder. A bugler played during underway
replenishment. His tune, the William Tell
Overture, reminded everyone that the *New
Jersey* was the Lone Ranger. With their own
time and money, crewmen refurbished the flag

quarters in memory of top officers, such as Lee, Spruance and Halsey, all of whom had lived there.[6]

In the interests of economy, planners ordered the size of the crew to be kept as small as possible. The Defense Department originally set the maximum figure at 1,400 enlisted men and 70 officers—about one-half of the *New Jersey*'s original complement. Savings were made by stripping from the ship all flag facilities and all 40-mm mounts. Numerous sailors had been required earlier to man the guns, directors and magazines of those weapons. Irritating to many traditionalists, a Marine Corps detachment was omitted for the first time from a US battleship. Nonetheless, the 1,400 men proved inadequate to work the ship safely, and the Defense Department reluctantly increased the allocation to 1,556.

Although many navymen were most interested in serving aboard the *New Jersey*, the press of time demanded that the ship be manned through the usual channels. Thus, despite later reports that most of the sailors were volunteers, the actual figure was less than 10 per cent, according to her CO, Capt. J. Edward Snyder, Jr. That the *New Jersey* was known as

a happy ship is all the more remarkable, then. Despite having the lowest manpower/ton ratio of any combat ship off Vietnam, in other words, despite having the most overworked crew, the *New Jersey* was unique among larger ships in not having *one* sailor desert when she sailed for the war.[7]

She did lose her first captain, though. Picked for this top assignment was Capt. Richard G. Alexander. However, this officer chose to involve himself in the defense of Marcus Aurelius Arnheiter, relieved of his command of the destroyer *Vance* for his erratic behavior during a Vietnam tour. Alexander's vehement and well-publicised stand cost him the *New Jersey* on 15 January 1968 after five months in billet. He was reassigned to the Boston Naval District as assistant chief of staff for operations, and Capt. Snyder took his place.

Right on time, 26 March 1968, the *New Jersey* headed down the Delaware River for her engineering trials. The next day she began a full power run off the Virginia Capes. The ship's pitometer log indicated a speed of 35.2 knots at 207 rpm. At the end of this six hour high-speed run, Snyder went to emergency power astern. This radical maneuver showed

The *New Jersey* moves down the Delaware River on 26 March 1968 for sea trials. Her large antenna forward spoils, just a bit, her classic profile. There are no light guns aboard at all, but her main and secondary turrets are fully reactivated. [USN]

Returning on 28 March from her successful machinery trials, the *New Jersey* shows off her new electronic suite. Beneath her main battery director is the large rectangular box containing the ULQ-6B jammer with its antennae projecting out both sides. It was designed to confuse the guidance equipment of the early cruise missiles like the *Styx*. Chaff rocket launchers of the Zuni type located in the old 40-mm emplacements between the funnels were designed to decoy any missiles that got by ULQ-6B. [USN]

The *New Jersey* approaches the Thacher Bridge on her transit through the Panama Canal, 4 June 1968. She travelled at about 15 knots between the locks. [USN]

On 5 September, she headed for the war. Few deployments in history have been so public. Interest in the ship was so intense that one of her first orders required daily, not weekly, combat reports. To greet her in the western Pacific, the Soviets sent two Tu95D Bear long range reconnaissance aircraft. The destroyer *Towers*, escorting the *New Jersey*, picked up the planes at 200 miles. The huge aircraft made three passes, the lowest at 1,000 ft.

Shortly after the battleship threaded San Bernardino Straits, she steamed over the grave of IJN *Musashi* and briefly visited Subic Bay. On 29 September, the *New Jersey* arrived off the DMZ, and the next day she fired her first rounds, with 32 reporters watching, at a fortified storage area in the DMZ. She destroyed five enemy bunkers, plowed up 300 meters of trench line, and silenced anti-aircraft guns shooting at her marine spotting aircraft. This plane, an A-4, buzzed the *New Jersey* at nearly supersonic speeds and transmitted, 'Welcome to the war'.[9]

The ship soon settled into a routine, supplying call fire to friendly units ashore, shooting at identifiable enemy strong points, and interfering with communist logistical efforts. For instance, on 1 October, the vessel blasted six bunkers, a flak site and a truck. The following day, her 5-inchers touched off 18 secondary explosions in enemy ammunition caches. Over the next week, she destroyed a variety of targets including a concrete observation post, a troop concentration and more bunkers. Especially noteworthy was her attack on a group of enemy supply boats off the Song Giang River on 7 October. Together with the de-

The *New Jersey* nears the Vietnamese war zone. Note that her forward 40-mm gun tubs are gone in front of turret No 1. The remaining four were painted white and used as swimming pools by the crew. [USN]

the ship's plant to be in top working order. The battleship returned to Philadelphia with a broom run up the halyard.[8]

On 6 April, the *New Jersey* recommissioned for the third time on schedule and under budget at $21.5 million. After inspection and survey, she took aboard supplies and departed for the West Coast on 16 May. Following gunnery practice at San Clemente—a citizen 50 miles away complained that the shock broke his windows—the vessel sharpened up her air defense skills by shooting at drones and by using her ECM gear to break the radar lock of an F-4 Phantom simulating as a cruise missile.

stroyer *Towers*, she demolished 11 of these craft before the remainder beached themselves in desperation.[10]

The need to replenish the ship's magazines frequently drew the *New Jersey* away from the gun line for short periods. During the month of October, the ship four times received ammunition and other necessities from such supply vessels as the *Mount Katmai, Mars, Rainier* and *Vesuvius*. The *New Jersey* also welcomed aboard a remarkable array of top brass. During her Vietnam tour, she was visited by Secretary of the Navy Paul R. Ignatius, the commander of the Seventh Fleet, and assorted top officers from the United States marines, army and air force as well as military leaders from South Vietnam, South Korea and the Philippines. Eventually the bemused crew painted on the helicopter deck in large white letters 'NEW JERSEY INTERNATIONAL'.[11]

The ship also made a concerted effort to play host to some of her regular customers: the ground troops whom she supported. In late October, for example, 50 Marines arrived aboard where they showered for the first time in a month. The ship's company did their laundry and gave them haircuts, a cake and head-of-the-line privileges at meals. 'Operation Hilton,' the crew named it. Later beneficiaries of the program included troopers from the 101st Airborne Division (Air Assault).[12]

Her principal goal, of course, was to hurt the enemy, and from the beginning, she found the accomplishment of this task hampered, not by operational problems, but rather by political constraints. As the ship was commissioning, President Johnson in April put off limits everything north of 19th parallel, a carrot to entice the enemy to the conference table and simultaneously a ploy to take some of the steam out of the antiwar movement. But Johnson thereby removed some of the juiciest targets in North Vietnam from the *New Jersey*'s list before the battleship ever had a crack at them.

Plenty of work remained, however. Near the DMZ the battleship shot up the heavily fortified Vinh caves, six trucks out of a convoy north of Nha Ky, and coastal artillery emplacements on Hon Matt island. The observer for the last mission (on 14 October) exclaimed as one battery was obliterated, 'You've blown away a large slice of the island. It's down in the ocean.'[13]

On 20 October, the battleship moved south

One of the early rounds fired in the fall of 1968. At the start of her Vietnam tour, the *New Jersey* carried in her magazines 1202 rounds of 16-inch ammunition, with 95 percent being HC and only 5 percent AP. [USN]

to the Nha Trang area to back up the Army's 173rd Airborne Brigade. She eased into the highly restricted waters of Baie de Van Fong to bombard Viet Cong command posts. Her coverage of the enemy area was excellent, but the thick jungle cover badly hampered damage assessors.

No such ambiguity existed about the *New Jersey*'s effectiveness in support of the Fifth Infantry Division in the Kinh Mon area. For five days, the *New Jersey* escorted by HMAS *Perth* fired at this Viet Cong stronghold. Earlier efforts to clean it out, even after B-52 strikes, had been both costly and unsuccessful. Now, as the Fifth Division swept through the enemy area, it lost seven soldiers. Enemy dead numbered 301. The *New Jersey* contributed directly to that casualty list. On the 25th, she shot 16-inch HC projectiles with mechanical time fuses which burst the shells at the optimum height of 75 ft directly over communist troops crouching in trenches. The next day, North Vietnamese artillery pieces tried to even the score, but of the 12 rounds directed against the *New Jersey*, the closest fell at least 500 meters away. The ship returned fire, but with no conclusive results.[14]

The *New Jersey* rounded out her first full month in combat by returning to the DMZ. There, she destroyed anti-aircraft batteries, bunkers and artillery positions. After six rounds directed against one hilltop battery, her spotter radioed, 'You've just lowered the mountain'.[15] Indeed, counterbattery fire

When the *New Jersey*'s secondary magazines were full, they held 10,050 5-inch rounds. In these containers are full charges for the semi-fixed ammunition. During her Vietnam tour, the *New Jersey* expended about 15,000 of the shells. [USN]

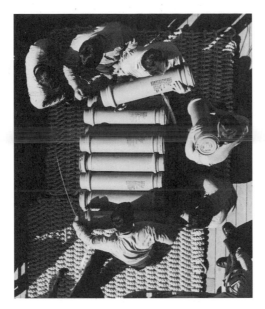

proved to be one of the ship's strong points throughout her entire deployment. One army officer said of North Vietnamese artillery pieces that so bedevilled American units on the other side of the DMZ, 'My 175mm guns couldn't hit them; B-52s couldn't take them out. The only thing that effectively shut them up was the *New Jersey*'.[16]

These North Vietnamese guns were suddenly put beyond the range of the *New Jersey*—as was everything else in North Vietnam on 1 November by President Johnson who ordered an end to offensive operations north of the DMZ. Accordingly, the battleship henceforth concentrated on support of friendly units in the south. For instance, she hurried at 25 knots to Phan Thiet on 2 November to back up the Second Corps. Three days later she fired night call missions for the 173rd Airborne Brigade. After she uprooted eight Viet Cong bunkers, the vessels rushed 180 miles north to help ROK troops operating in a strongly held enemy area. Her main batteries, shooting at the near maximum range of 23 miles the next day, set off three secondary explosions in Viet Cong caves.[17]

After more than a month of steady combat, the *New Jersey* spent the following two weeks giving the crew a rest and replenishing her depleted magazines and storerooms at Subic Bay. There, she offloaded 100 rounds of 16-inch AP. So far in Vietnam, the HC round had been amply destructive, and the heavier bombardment shell caused more barrel wear. The

battleship also took aboard her first 5-inch rocket assisted projectiles (RAP) which extended the range of the lighter weapon by at least one-third.

The battleship relieved the cruiser *Galveston* at Da Nang on 23 November. For two days she supported the Americal Division, but on the 25th she put in her best day's work of the tour so far. With General George S. Brown, commander of the Seventh Air Force, personally triggering some of the shots, the *New Jersey* hit two Viet Cong storage areas at Quang Ngai. She plowed up 32 bunkers and set off eight secondary explosions. Smoke and pieces of debris shot 1,000 ft into the air. Assessors later credited the ship with 40 communist soldiers killed. Her totals the next day were not quite as high, but impressive nonetheless: 19 Viet Cong dead, 66 structures and 22 bunkers destroyed during a bombardment which saw her fire the 5-inch RAP shells for the first time to a range of 23,000 yards.[18]

She next stood off the old imperial capital of Hue to render support for the 101st Airborne at Thanksgiving. Thirty of the battleship sailors traded places that day with the air assault soldiers. In early December, the *New Jersey* teamed with marine artillery to hit Viet Cong bunkers close to the DMZ. On 7 December, the battleship marked the 25th anniversary of her launch by a successful strike against Viet Cong bunkers and trench lines near Da Nang. Supporting Operation *Meade River* the following day, the battleship's shells left craters that to one awed army observer looked like 'the foundation of an eight-story building'.[19]

She then departed the gunline for reprovisioning at Subic Bay and spent four days for rest and recreation at Singapore where she welcomed aboard several top Royal Navy officers, including Rear Admiral Michael Kyrle-Pope. By 22 December, she was back on the gunline. Bop Hope and his troupe entertained the sailors on Christmas Day, but it was all business on the 26th when she supported the ARVN 47th Division. Striking at cave complexes and bunkers, her 16-inch shells sent massive logs tumbling several hundred feet into the air. She closed out the year by attacking communist bunkers placed in the supposedly neutral buffer zone at the DMZ. Turret No. 1 fired its 1,000th combat round in Vietnam, and the ship's shooting was so good that the spotter radioed after a large secondary explosion, 'Don't ever let anyone tell you can't put two bullets in the same hole. You can't miss. You must have a pair of magic tubes.'[20]

In the 71 days that she had spent in action since her arrival in September, the New Jersey had expended 3,017 16-inch shells and 6,949 5-inchers, of which 38 were rocket assisted. In return, assessors credited the ship with 345 enemy structures destroyed (231 damaged), 329 bunkers destroyed (142 damaged), 21 artillery sites neutralised, 111 secondary explosions and 136 confirmed enemy soldiers killed. The battleship also wrecked 38 cave and tunnel complexes and 9 supply boats, as well as interdicting 21 roads and caving in over 1,300 meters of enemy trench line. Most of this damage had been done after President Johnson placed the most sensitive enemy targets off limits.[21]

Bad weather plagued the ship early in the first week of 1969, but the New Jersey's crewmen managed to compensate for the problem. For instance, on 3 January when the ship needed to restock certain critical supply items, the First Marine Division at Da Nang asked for her assistance. In order to stay on station, the battleship replenished from the Mars by using two CH-53 helicopters despite a tropical downpour. Four days later, a Third Marine Division spotter called down 16-inch shells against Viet Cong bunkers in a fog so thick that the New Jersey could not even see the beach. Nonetheless, one of the ship's fire control radars locked onto the reference point, and the spotter was able to adjust the gunnery. The vessel fired simultaneous 16-inch and 5-inch salvos which destroyed four enemy bunkers.[22]

After standing by uneventfully in case she was needed to cover Operation Bold Mariner—the amphibious invasion of the Batangan peninsula, she replenished at Subic and then put into Yokosuka for upkeep. During her ten day stay there, 10,000 visitors came aboard, including Admiral S. Ibuki, the commander of the Japanese Self Defense Fleet. On her return trip to Vietnam, the battleship ran through a gale which did some slight damage to some of the vessel's fittings. After helping ROK marines near Da Nang, the New Jersey took up station off the DMZ. For over three weeks (from 14 February to 9 March), she coasted along in a small patrol area except for brief periods off the line to refuel and resupply. Most of the battleship's action was directed against communist attacks on the Third

Marine Division, and she fired on occasion into the DMZ itself when enemy activities justified such retaliation.

For instance, the New Jersey on her first day on station shot up automatic weapons positions which had fired at an American observation plane. The next day, a communist rocket site suffered her attentions. From the target area, seven fire balls flared 500 ft into the air; in all, observers counted 25 secondary explosions from the enemy position. Admiral John J. Hyland, the commander of the Pacific, told the crew during his visit aboard on 18 February:

We have admired your performance out here. You've had a long and hard cruise. Your clients ashore couldn't be more pleased with the way you're supporting them. Your whole performance has drawn the admiration of military and civilian authorities who have been watching what you do out here.[23]

The praise was vindicated in the most persuasive fashion five days later when the New Jersey saved an American outpost named Oceanview. Sited barely 1,000 meters from the DMZ, this position, defended by 20 marines, was attacked by an estimated 130 veteran North Vietnamese troops. In the busiest night of her entire Vietnamese deployment, the New Jersey fired 1,710 5-inch shells in support of the beleaguered garrison. Calling the shots was a marine lance corporal who also controlled the fire of the Coast Guard cutter Owasco and two marine artillery batteries. The commander of Oceanview summed up his feelings after the North Vietnamese had been repulsed, 'If it hadn't been for New Jersey, they would have zapped our ...!'[24]

Finally, on 10 March, the battleship moved south to Quang Ngai to support the ARVN Second Division. After destroying 22 enemy bunkers in that province, the vessel was relieved by the heavy cruiser Newport News and headed once again for Subic Bay. During her upkeep period there, the New Jersey played host to the Philippine—US Mutual Defense Board. Of the 65 staffers aboard on 19 March, 12 held flag rank. On the 21st, she made high speed run to Cam Ranh Bay to back up the ROK Ninth Division. After closing 11 caves, she spent the next week ranging up and down the coast between Phan Thiet and Tuy Hoa. Targeting Viet Cong base camps and supply dumps, the New Jersey destroyed 72 bunkers southwest of Phan Thiet on 26 March alone.

The center gun of turret No 2 fires a shell at maximum elevation. Shot at this angle, the shell will take about 53 seconds to reach its target over 22 miles down range. During her career, the *New Jersey* expended 771 16-inch shells in World War Two, 6671 in Korea and midshipman training cruises, and 5688 in Vietnam. [USN]

With her tour rapidly coming to an end, she fittingly returned on 28 March to the DMZ where she had done so much for the Third Marines over the preceding half year. On the last day of the month, she fired her last observed mission against an enemy complex northeast of Con Thien.[25]

From the beginning of the year, the *New Jersey* had silenced 14 weapons sites, caused 65 secondary explosions and destroyed 37 caves and tunnel complexes, 150 structures and 326 bunkers. She also damaged 120 structures and 181 bunkers. To accomplish this work, she had fired, in 641 missions, 2,658 16-inch and 8,093 5-inch rounds. When added to the projectiles shot off in the fall of 1968, her ammunition expenditure in Vietnam approximated her totals for World War Two and Korea.[26]

One gunnery expert who had seen the battleships at work in Korea concluded that the Vietnam deployment of the *New Jersey* shed '... no new light on the range, accuracy, lethality, or effectiveness' of the big guns as compared to their record established earlier.[27]

For those unused to working with 16-inch guns—that is, for most military personnel in Vietnam, the experience was something of a revelation. One soldier recalled that at night a 16-inch salvo from the battleship lit up the eastern sky like the sunrise and that the shell sounded like a train going by overhead. The sheer size of the shell craters, 50 ft across and 20 ft deep, impressed all who saw them. One driver from the 61st Infantry maneuvered his armored personnel carrier too close to the lip of a hole and slid in. Recovery of the vehicle took several hours. In fact, one HC round could create out of dense triple canopy jungle a helicopter landing zone 200 yards in diameter.[28]

Coupled with this destructive power was the extremely accurate fire of the battleship. Although much depended on the forward observer, Col Robert D. Heinl, USMC, said that the *New Jersey*'s accuracy and technical proficiency were among the finest ever exhibited by a big gun ship. He added that in quick response and in hitting on the opening salvo, the *New Jersey* equalled the best of the old slow battleships—the gunnery champions of World War Two. An army spotter praised the vessel for her 'extremely accurate' shooting. The only army artillery piece that came close, this officer felt, was the 8-inch howitzer, but most 16-inch missions were fired at ranges greater than 32,000 meters, that is, beyond the maximum range of the 8-inch weapon. The same army officer spotted for B-52s on many occasions. He regarded the 16-inch gun as 'much more effective'.[29] Two or three rounds would usually suffice for the average mission. Army airborne spotters particularly appreciated how the *New Jersey* suppressed enemy anti-aircraft batteries, not just directly, but often by her mere presence. One captain, a guest aboard the ship on Christmas Day 1968, remarked, 'As long as you are in the area and firing, the communists hole up with their flak machines and anti-aircraft weapons. This gives us more freedom in picking out better targets'.[30]

The Third Marine Division, which became intimately acquainted with the battleship, was enthusiastic from the beginning. One soldier wrote home, 'The *New Jersey* arrived here last week, and man, is she playing hell with Charlie [the Viet Cong]!'[31] A sergeant in the same outfit told of leading a platoon into a heavily fortified communist area:

We were ordered to pull back about 200 yards so that somebody, we didn't know who at the time, could start shooting at some communist bunkers and emplacements that had been giving us a lot of trouble. When we finally moved back about 500 yards, we heard what at first sounded like a subway train moving through a tunnel—a big rushing noise—then BANG! Later on when we went back into the area, there was nothing ... just nothing. It was like something had come along with a big eraser and wiped everything clean. And they were big, heavily fortified bunkers, targets our own artillery couldn't touch.[32]

A less impressionistic evaluation came from General R. G. Davis, commander of the marine division:

Accuracy. The 16″/50 ... has been consistently more accurate and more responsive to spots than any other naval gunfire control system used in Vietnam.

Penetration. The 16-inch projectile has a greater ability to penetrate hard targets than any other naval gun, artillery piece or air dropped weapon.

All-Weather Capability. Although there were many days when adverse weather prohibited air support of ground units, this weather did not restrict the use of naval gunfire support from the *New Jersey*.

Improved Morale. Since the arrival of the battleship in South-East Asia, the mere fact of its presence has had a noticeable effect on the morale of friendly troops.[33]

Given these overwhelmingly favorable report cards, the *New Jersey* headed in early April for Long Beach to exchange personnel and freshen equipment. Within 1,800 miles of the Califonia port, she received orders to reverse course and report for action at Yokosuka. The North Koreans had shot down an unarmed EC-121 reconnaissance plane over international waters. Steaming at 22 knots, the *New Jersey* arrived off Japan on 22 April. She took aboard 837 tons of ammunition from the *Paracutin*, the largest underway replenishment of her entire cruise. Thirty minutes after reaching her holding station, she was ordered to return to the United States. She finally docked at Long Beach on 5 May, more than two weeks late.[34]

Her schedule called for her to leave for her second Vietnam tour early in September. In the meantime, she undertook a cruise to train both the midshipmen and the replacements who had come aboard at Long Beach. For the cruise, the *New Jersey* became the flagship of Rear Admiral Lloyd Vasey who commanded a flotilla of 15 ships. The Admiral's presence caused problems for the battleship. Since she had not been fitted during her reactivation as a flagship, officers found their work spaces very crowded. The communications staff especially had their work load increased because all outgoing message traffic from the 15 ship force was sent to the *New Jersey* to be relayed ashore.

In any event, large crowds lined up at San Francisco, Tacoma, Pearl Harbor and San Diego to greet the battleship. One of the highlights for the midshipmen was a main battery practice shoot which sank the obsolete fleet minesweeper *Raven*. The *New Jersey* hit the target vessel on the second round. On 12 August, the battleship received the well-deserved Navy Unit Commendation 'for exceptionally meritorious service'.[35]

During the first three weeks of August, the *New Jersey*'s crew prepared for the next tour. She was to get a new CO, Capt. Robert C. Peniston who would take over from Capt.

Home to prepare for another trip to Southeast Asia, the *New Jersey* is pictured here underway near San Nicolas Island off California on 16 June 1969. Safety barricades have been erected on each side of her helicopter spot. [USN]

Snyder on 27 August. Her departure for Vietnam was scheduled from Long Beach on 5 September. With her pre-deployment ordnance review completed on 20 August, the crew was startled to hear the announcement the next day from the Defense Department that the *New Jersey* would be one of a hundred naval vessels deactivated during the fall. Secretary Laird cited budget tightening by Congress as the reason. Snyder's angry remarks reflected the reaction of most of the crew:

War is hell, and it is also expensive, and the American people have tired of the expense of defending freedom. And so this year when the winter monsoon comes to Vietnam and prevents the planes from accurately supporting our Allied ground forces, *New Jersey* will not be there. The ship that made the motto 'Firepower for Freedom' a reality will be abandoned in Bremerton and the American boys who looked to the 'Big J' for their very lives must look elsewhere.[36]

The bitterness of the Captain's tone was understandable precisely because the reason given for decommissioning the ship was so incomprehensible. Dollar for dollar, the *New Jersey* had shown herself the best bargain of any warship operating in South-East Asia.

Substantial funding had gone into preparing her for another tour, and now, just before departure, she was to be mothballed. It all made little sense until the truth emerged in a quite dramatic way during a Senate debate on 7 April 1981 over the Reagan administration proposal to reactivate the *New Jersey*.

On opposite sides stood two former secretaries of the Navy—Senator John Chafee from Rhode Island, who opposed reactivation, and Senator John Warner of Virginia who supported it. Their debate reached a climax over the ship's performance in Vietnam:

Mr Warner. Would the Senator from Rhode Island care to comment on the distinguished record of that ship during the time it was on active duty?

Mr Chafee. I certainly will. It was a very fine ship but we did not keep it.

Mr Warner. Does the Senator

Mr Chafee. Let me answer the question. You have opened the floodgate, and you will get the flood.

The ship proved ineffective in the mission for which it was designed—ineffective in the Vietnam war.

It was tremendously costly to operate. It required a very substantial number of crew. I would say over 1,500 men, and we deactivated it. It was not worth it. It was a fiasco, truly.

Mr Warner. Will the Senator yield?

Mr Chafee. And the Senator knows this well. We sent it back to mothballs.

Mr Warner. Mr President, if the Senator would yield, does he recall which watch it was sent back into mothballs under? Was it his or mine? It happened to have been my watch after he departed. And I will never forget the circumstances under which this ship was deactivated.

I respectfully contest the statements made by the distinguished Senator from Rhode Island. The ship was very effective. As a matter of fact, it was so effective that we were ordered to take it out of active service because its belligerency and its antagonism was [sic] impeding the progress of the peace talks at that time.

Mr Chafee. It was so effective, you sent it to Bremerton.

Mr Warner. I beg the Senator's pardon.

Mr Chafee. It was so effective, you sent it to Bremerton.

Mr Warner. Against my recommendations. I went down and personally saw the Secretary of Defense and was ordered from the White House that the ship should be deactivated because it was impeding the peace negotiations.[37]

At least Capt. Snyder was spared the sorrow of taking the ship out of service. That job fell to Peniston, an officer who felt a special affinity for the *New Jersey*, because in 1943 she had been the first ship on which he had set foot as a midshipman and then in 1946 the first ship to which he had been posted as an ensign. In his remarks at the change of command ceremony, Peniston declared that his goal was to lay up the *New Jersey* in the best possible shape. The only truly bright spot for the new CO over the next several months came on 5 September when the *New Jersey* received the coveted Battle Efficiency 'E' award. Her voyage to Bremerton was under a 'pall'. As her captain said, 'It was probably the last cruise for this battleship and thus for all battleships.' Having reached Puget Sound Navy Yard, the *New Jersey* tied up close to the *Missouri*.[38]

According to the 'book', the *New Jersey* should have taken four months to deactivate. Captain Peniston and his crew managed the feat in 100 days. When her ammunition was unloaded at Long Beach, it filled a 26-car train. Ultimately, she was retired with only one defect unrepaired—a problem on one boiler.

The Navy Department was determined to put the ship away as quickly and quietly as possible. Peniston invited Secretary Warner to speak at the decommissioning ceremony. He was told to refuse. The governor of Washington, an ex-*New Jersey* officer, was kind enough to make a few remarks at the 17 December function. Many in the audience were deeply touched by Peniston's address which ended:

The hour cometh and now is to say farewell. But, before doing so, my last order to you—Battleship *New Jersey*—is rest well, yet sleep lightly, and hear the call, if again sounded, to provide 'Firepower for Freedom.' She will hear the call and thanks to her magnificent crew, she is ready.[39]

The dignified ceremony was marred by the Navy Department's failure to send the 'Well Done' message normally dispatched to ships being decommissioned.[40]

For a brief time in 1972, it seemed that the *New Jersey* might be awakened to counter the North Vietnamese offensive in the spring of that year. White House aides queried Snyder, by this point a rear admiral, as to whether the *New Jersey* could be made ready for action in 30 days. Snyder felt such a timetable was impossible and said so. Consequently, the cruiser *Newport News* hurried out at her best possible speed, but she was, as one authority remarked, 'too little, too late'.[41] Certainly the Seventh Fleet commander, Vice Admiral William Mack, really missed the *New Jersey*, as he later testified.[42]

In certain respects, it could be argued that the *New Jersey* operated off Vietnam at the worst possible time in terms of fulfilling her potential there. Almost 85 per cent of Vietnam, both North and South, lay within range of the 16-inch guns. Had the battleship gone out prior to April 1968 (when President Johnson restricted operations above the 19th parallel), she could have saved valuable aircraft and aircrew by taking out crucial objectives in North Vietnam that were heavily defended against bombing raids. For instance, the United States lost 50 aircraft trying to destroy the Thanh Hoa bridge. The *New Jersey* undoubtedly could have wrecked that structure in one hour. Alternatively, had the battleship been in commission in 1972 when Nixon ordered attacks against previously untouchable targets in North Vietnam, the *New Jersey* could have performed the same sort of surgical strike on the port city of Haiphong that she carried out against Wonsan at the close of the Korean War. As it was, the retirement of the *New Jersey* in the last days of 1969 seemed to sound the final knell for her and for her type. The four 'Iowas' would sleep through the 1970s.

Following several close escapes from the scrapper's torch in the 1970s, the 'Iowas' became the center of controversy again when, late in the Carter term, an aviator and defense consultant began a single-handed crusade to reactivate the battleships. Despite the most vigorous opposition, the arguments for the vessels proved convincing to the in-coming Reagan administration. For a relatively modest investment, the battleships began to emerge from the yards with updated equipment and impressive new capabilities. By the end of 1983, the *New Jersey* was back in combat, this time in Mediterranean waters.

Their survival to that point, however, was by the narrowest of margins. In 1972, some top officers proposed that only the *New Jersey* be retained and the rest be disposed of. Had the Navy gone ahead with this scheme, the *Missouri* would certainly have been preserved as a museum ship, but the *Iowa* and *Wisconsin* would have gone to the breakers. Fortunately, the Marine Corps pressed strongly for the retention of the vessels; in fact, Col. Heinl

called in September 1972 in the *Naval Institute Proceedings* for their reactivation as 'Instant Sea-Control Ships'.

Indeed, over the next couple of years, the Navy conducted feasibility studies to see if the ships could accept the Aegis air defense system, Sea Sparrow and Harpoon missile launchers, and the CIWS 'gatling' gun. All of these weapons represented the latest technology, and planners were especially concerned about the effects of blast overpressure on them. The Navy contracted for a study by Gibbs and Cox, the respected naval engineering firm, who concluded that all the systems could be accommodated with few problems.[1]

Despite these promising studies, the Naval Ship System Command recommended in the spring of 1974 that the 'Iowas' be stricken from the navy list. The command argued that it seemed most unlikely the battleships would ever go to sea again, and therefore the money spent on their upkeep was being wasted. The command ordered a pre-strike inspection as the last step before their disposal. While this inspection was going on, a memo from the Vice Chief of Naval Operations stopped the process. One battleship authority, Howard W. Serig, Jr, maintains that the ships were saved by the personal intervention of Admiral Elmo Zumwalt, then the CNO. Whenever the scrapping of the 'Iowas' was suggested—and the idea was advanced numerous times—Zumwalt favored retention of the battleships on the grounds that their big guns were an irreplaceable asset for amphibious operations.[2]

Narrowly saved, the 'Iowas' still faced an uncertain future. In late 1976, talk started about appropriate sites for the *New Jersey* and *Missouri* as museum ships. A December *New York Times* article reported the Navy as offering the *New Jersey* to her name state if Trenton officials would raise the funds to maintain her. A group of volunteers banded together to form the Battleship *New Jersey* Historical Museum Society and began to raise funds, in part by the time-honored method of appealing to public-school children.

The 'Iowas' enter the 1970s. The photograph was taken by Robert E. Woods aboard the *Missouri* at Bremerton. [USN]

Another survey of the vessels' condition was taken in 1977. The PREINSURV team found all four battleships fit in hull, engineering plant and main battery, but ruled them unfit in habitability, command and control. The report concluded by recommending once again that the ships be stricken. And once again, the Marine Corps saved them. Marine fears were ably put forward in the Weller Report, issued in 1977 and drawing pointed attention to the pathetic state of the fleet's gunpower. A handful of 6-inch guns remained aboard light cruisers shortly to leave the service. The largest guns afloat would soon be the $5''/54$ if the 8-inch lightweight gun failed to materialise—as indeed it did. These Marine concerns were seconded by the commander of the Pacific Fleet who recommended to the CNO Jimmy Holloway that the battleships be retained in storage. The former skipper of the *Iowa* agreed.[3]

The decade closed with alarming developments for the United States. The fall of the Shah and the Soviet invasion of Afghanistan both boded ill for American interests. Moreover, the Soviet Navy was commissioning a number of potent vessels. On the stocks, for instance, was the *Kirov*, a nuclear-powered 'battlecruiser' armed with cruise missiles. Indeed, the *Kirov* was the largest warship, aside from carriers, built by any power since the end of World War Two.

Early in 1979, some Congressman began considering a plan to bolster American strength quickly by updating the 'Iowas'. The author of this proposal was Charles E. Myers, Jr, a defense consultant and, of all things, a former B-25 pilot for the Air Force. He had also flown jet fighters for the Navy. Myers, with first-hand experience in the strengths and weaknesses of tactical air power, worried especially about the problem of supporting an amphibious assault. In the spring of 1978, he began to read about battleships. Increasingly enthusiastic about the capabilities of the 'Iowas', Myers contacted Snyder and Peniston, the last COs of the *New Jersey*. From his research, Myers assembled a 40-page brief for battleship reactivation. Realising that no natural Congressional 'constituency' existed for the 'Iowas', that is, no legislator stood to gain a great deal from the reactivation of the ships, Myers particularly approached Congressmen such as Daniel Inouye and Strom Thurmond, men who had taken part in assaults like Salerno, Anzio and Normandy. Myers also condensed his arguments for the *Naval Institute Proceedings*. This article, headed by a dramatic photo of a *Missouri* broadside, appeared in the November 1979 issue just days after the seizure of the American embassy in Teheran. Myers proposed that the 'Iowas' be reactivated specifically to support land operations, and his arguments seemed compelling: the ships combined the best protection in existence with high speed, ample space and big guns. He pointed especially to the Thanh Hoa bridge—that North Vietnamese target which cost 50 American aircraft to destroy. Myers claimed that the battleships offered a unique combination of virtues at a minimal cost compared to other weapons systems (see Appendix O).[4]

In the meantime, the new CNO, Thomas B. Hayward, had become interested in the 'Iowas' as a quick fix for the increasing imbalance between the United States and Soviet fleets. Accordingly, he instructed his subordinates, shortly after Myers' article appeared, to brief Congressmen on the project. Two bills, one introduced by Thurmond, proposed added money to start the reactivation of the battleships. Hayward testified in their favor, although he clearly regarded increased funding for the carrier groups as a higher priority. Naturally, Marine Corps spokesmen were more enthusiastic. With this support, the plan edged closer to realisation. The House Armed Services Committee approved it by a comfortable margin. At this point, President Carter stepped into the argument. Reactivation of the battleships, he maintained, would merely 'resurrect 1940s technology', and he ordered top naval officers to cease lobbying for the project. When passage of the necessary legislation looked probable in spite of the presidential opposition, Carter offered at a 25 July 1980 cabinet meeting to involve himself personally in the lobbying process. The presidential initiative proved decisive—for the moment. The funding bill went down to a narrow defeat on the Senate floor.

Carter's victory was short-lived indeed. In November, Ronald Reagan won the presidency, in part, by promising a dramatic upgrading of America's defenses. To head the Navy Department, Reagan picked John Lehman, a former naval aviator who had chaired the Republican Party's committee on defense. Myers knew Lehman and was well aware that

An almost surreal view of the *New Jersey*'s bow at Long Beach (5 February 1982). [USN]

The ULQ-6B jammer equipment came out of the ECM box high on the foremast. The gear was replaced by the new SLQ-32 system. By the time she was back in service, the Navy would have spent over $300 million on her—approximately three times her building costs. [USN]

he had been an early advocate of the Tomahawk cruise missile. Consequently, Myers' arguments for Tomahawk-armed 'Iowas' fell on receptive ears. Lehman approached the president-elect in December about the matter and found Reagan to be 'very enthusiastic'.[5]

Winning the necessary funding still involved tumultuous debates in the Congress. The very term 'battleship' elicited hoots of derision. Senator William Proxmire jeered, 'I doubt if the Navy could find anything else as wasteful as reviving the battleship. The *battleship*. They have to be kidding.'[6] Dale Bumpers, a senator from Arkansas, attacked the *New Jersey* as '. . . an expensive, highly vulnerable vessel of questionable military utility which would simply siphon off very scarce Navy manpower. . . .' He added that the *Arkansas*, a totally unarmored ship, was 'perhaps' more survivable than the *New Jersey*, and concluded one of his numerous diatribes against the battleships by claiming that they were too slow to keep up with a carrier task force.[7]

These inaccurate statements were echoed by men who should have known better. Barry Goldwater, generally a staunch advocate of a powerful defense, argued, 'Reviving old battleships is like trying to revitalise the army by digging up old General Custer.'[8] Of course, Goldwater had always been an air power devotee. Almost incomprehensible, though, was the adamant opposition of Senator John Chafee, ex-Secretary of the Navy, 1969–72. Chafee criticised the reactivation plans on the grounds of manpower shortage—a legitimate concern, and then added the absurd statement, 'All the Russians have to do is lob a missile into one of those battleships, and they'd knock it out of commission.'[9] One recognised authority on naval affairs, Norman Polmar, the former US editor of *Jane's Fighting Ships*, characterised the 'Iowas' reactivation as 'ridiculous', principally because of the manning problem.'[10]

Other critics cited the age of the ships, the uncertain costs involved, or their supposedly unfit condition. The Thimble Shoals grounding weighed against the *Missouri* again; a minor electrical fire suffered by the *Wisconsin* during her deactivation was fanned to a major conflagration; and the *Iowa* was reported as stripped virtually bare in supporting the *New Jersey*'s 1968 recommissioning. One of the most peculiar arguments was advanced by the Kitsap County (Washington) Historical Society. 'Deploring' the plan to reactivate the

Missouri, the society pleaded with Secretary of Defense Casper Weinberger '... to eliminate the proposed desecration of a national historic treasure'.[11]

As a counterweight to these arguments, the Marine Corps strongly supported the ships, as expected. Vice Admiral Robert Walters, a surface warfare expert, fully endorsed the 'Iowas' before the House Subcommittee on Defense on 24 June 1981. Senator John Warner's testimony as to the effectiveness of the *New Jersey* in Vietnam proved telling. So did Senator Jeremiah Denton's plea for the ships. Denton had been one of the aviators shot down during the Thanh Hoa bridge strikes.

Most persuasive of all, however, was John Lehman. He fought vigorously for the ships by taking his case to both the Congress and the public. Appearing on the respected PBS program, the MacNeil/Lehrer Report, the Secretary debunked the contention of Stansfield Turner, ex-head of the CIA, that the bigger the ship, the easier it was to spot. Lehman explained that with modern electronic surveillance, a battleship was no more nor less visible to enemy sensors than a frigate one-tenth its tonnage. To Congressmen worried about uncontrollable costs, Lehman personally pledged that the *New Jersey* could be modernised for no more than $326 million. He summed up his assessment of the 'Iowas' by saying, '... the only real disadvantage to the battleships is that there are only four of them'.[12]

Lehman and other supporters of the vessels argued that battleships could fulfill a variety of tasks, and versatile the vessels are. By 1982, the Navy officially charged the ships with the following missions: (1) to operate offensively with carrier task forces in the highest threat areas, (2) to operate, backed by appropriate escorts, without carrier air cover in areas of lesser threat, (3) to support amphibious groups, (4) to conduct offensive operations against surface and shore targets, (5) to provide their own close-in defense against aircraft and anti-ship missiles, (6) to conduct naval gunfire strikes against hostile shores, (7) to control aircraft, (8) to operate and refuel all types of navy helicopters, (9) to refuel escorts, (10) to establish a naval presence, (11) to ease the severe pressure on carrier deployment cycles and thus to improve retention of personnel.[13] Indeed, the Congressional Budget Office eventually decided that the 'Iowas', modified

A stern view of the *New Jersey* at Long Beach. Her two inboard propellers have been removed for inspection. The sign on her stern cautions 'NO PHOTOGRAPHY'. [USN]

to carry V-STOL aircraft, could replace two projected nuclear powered carriers on the navy roster. The CBO claimed that potential savings to the government added up to $37 billion. CNO Hayward opposed the swap, and he ended with battleships plus both carriers.

Congress voted money to start work on the *New Jersey* in the spring of 1981. The ship left Bremerton under tow for Long Beach on 27 July. She was completed under budget as Lehman had promised. Attending her recommissioning ceremony—her *fourth* commissioning—on 28 December 1982 was President Reagan himself.

The *Iowa* came on line next. Five yards competed intensely for the job. Lehman sent her first to Avondale at New Orleans for hull work and then to Ingalls at Pascagoula, Mississippi for the rest of her refit. That yard originally contracted to finish her by early 1985.

Typically, political considerations played a major role in the selection of yards and home ports. When the *Iowa* went south for reworking, the chairman of the House Defense Appropriations Subcommittee, Joseph Addabbo, vowed to slash the two new nuclear carriers from the Navy's budget. Lehman quickly made matters right by voicing his intention to base the *Iowa* permanently at Staten Island. Until the facilities there were readied, the ship would list Norfolk as her temporary home port.

Lehman made a virtue of necessity by arguing that this dispersal of major units to a larger number of port cities would render the Navy less likely to be closed up in a few harbors by a

One of the *New Jersey*'s outboard propellers, 18 feet 3 inches in diameter. The five-bladed inboard propellers are slightly smaller at 17 feet. The different types represent a reasonably successful attempt to damp down vibration. [USN]

when necessary. The eight large dehumidifiers had kept the air at 35 per cent humidity. One of the first people to enter the *Iowa* in 1982 remarked that the ship looked as if the crew had all gone off for the weekend. Old memos and other papers had not even yellowed. The paint on the bulkheads and overheads fell to the decks like snow once the ship was opened up.

And really, in terms of service age, they were young ships. Designed for a lifetime of 35 years, the *New Jersey* had spent 13.7 years on active duty, the *Iowa* 12.6, the *Wisconsin* 11.3 and the *Missouri* 10.1. All but three of the Navy's 13 active carriers were 'older'.

Of greater concern was the availability of spare parts to support systems designed in the 1930s and 1940s. For instance, a survey of the main battery fire control system showed that certain components, such as director train receiver regulators and the Mk 41 stable verticals, could not be supported. The Mk 13 radars and Mk 48 computers depended on vacuum tubes, resistors and capacitors which were leaving the marketplace. These problems were overcome in part by designing modern replacements which were manufactured by the Navy's Louisville ordnance facility and in part by cannibalisation. To get the *Iowa* and *New Jersey* to sea in a hurry, all ordnance spares were removed from the *Missouri*, and the mothballed cruiser *Oklahoma City* donated her Mk 48 computer and Mk 13 radar. The *Newport News* lost two Mk 41 stable verticals. In the long run, these parts would be replaced by Louisville production, and the whole matter of spares proved less vexing than many had feared.[14]

Many analysts wondered if the 16-inch rounds and guns were supportable. One authority maintained, in fact, that the *New Jersey* had been retired from the Vietnam conflict because of a shortage of liners for the 16-inch barrels.[15] In fact, ample numbers of the rifles were—and are—on hand. Of the 36 aboard the battleships, a 1981 survey showed their wear to average 42 per cent. That year, 33 spare barrels—24 at Hawthorne, Nevada and 9 at Subic Bay—were ready for immediate issue. The Dahlgren range held an additional seven weapons—three in storage and four used in tests. The Yuma Proving Grounds in Arizona had another barrel. If need be, the Watervliet Arsenal could even manufacture more. Although a registered national landmark, the

large surprise Soviet mining operation. However dubious this argument, the political advantages were indisputable. The *Iowa*, and the six other ships of her surface action group would bring to the New York area 3,600 permanent jobs and perhaps $500 million for the local economy over the life of their deployment.

Similar considerations have applied to the last two ships. The *Missouri* was delayed for a year when Congress turned down $55 million for the long-lead items requested in the 1983 budget. The money was voted the next year, and work began in 1984 on the battleship which will ultimately be based at Treasure Island, San Francisco. In May 1985, Congress rejected an attempt to strike money for the *Wisconsin*. Six Southern ports in five states were in the running at that point for the ship. Lehman ultimately announced the decision to spread the *Wisconsin*'s group among all the cities with the battleship herself going to Corpus Christi, Texas.

Not surprisingly, the three later ships cost more to refurbish—about $450 million—than did the *New Jersey*, since all three had to be brought up to that ship's 1969 standards. Despite the quarter of a century that the *Iowa*, *Missouri* and *Wisconsin* had spent in mothballs, they were all in excellent, albeit not perfect, condition. Cathodic protection guarded their hulls, and officers found the *Iowa*, when drydocked, to be surprisingly clean of marine growth. Workers had demossed their wooden decks every spring and painted their exteriors

'Big Gun Shop' there still has all the requisite equipment and at least 13 liner forgings.[16]

In the summer of 1984, Long Beach Naval Shipyard got a chance to replace a 16-inch rifle, something that no yard had done for almost 30 years. While the *New Jersey* was being refitted, an inspection showed that the middle barrel of No. 2 turret was suffering from 'flame wash'. To loosen the 100-ton gun, specialised wrenches, some weighing 50 lbs, were used. The yoke locking ring presented the yard workers with their greatest challenge. It defied all their efforts to unscrew it for two weeks. They finally broke it loose by using 360° wrenches and two 100-ton jacks that exerted 64,000 lbs of torque on the ring. The recalcitrant barrel was sent to Watervliet where it can be reworked if it is ever needed.[17]

Making a good situation even better is the fact that bore erosion is no longer a significant problem, partially because most rounds fired today are the lighter HC bombardment projectiles. The availability of Swedish additive, or titanium dioxide and wax, has further cut down on barrel wear. First used in Vietnam by the *New Jersey*, this substance, held in a jacket, is wrapped around the silk propellant bags. When the gun is fired, the Swedish additive forms an inert layer over the bore of the piece, rather like coating it in Teflon. With an AP projectile, the mixture cuts the wear to .26 of what it was originally. With the HC shell, it drops to only .11 of the original AP wear. Even more promising has been the introduction of jackets containing polyurethane foam. The upshot of these developments is that the gun situation looks satisfactory indeed.[18]

Big guns fire big shells, and here the state of affairs is not quite so comfortable. True, substantial stockpiles of the 16-inch projectiles exist at Hawthorne, Nevada, McAlester, Oklahoma and Crane, Indiana. Altogether, these three facilities held in 1981 15,500 rounds of HC ammunition, 3,200 of AP, and 2,300 practice rounds. This supply should be adequate for the foreseeable lives of the battleships, but if another Korea occurred (5,714 16-inch shells were expended there in six months in 1953, for example), no facilities exist at present to mass-produce 16-inch shells.

As to powder, the fleet stocks a variety of types including some cool-burning powders such as SPCG, a triple base propellant made of nitrocellulose, nitroguanidine and nitroglycerine. A special 'Navy Cool' (ethyl centralite

stabilised) powder is in the testing stage. Interestingly, some of the most consistent shooting with the tightest patterns has been done with propellant made for 8"/55 cruiser guns on 16"/45 rifles on the 27-knot battleships. In both cases, the powder has been precisely repacked by hand-stacking the grains, and contrary to some reports, powder that has been carefully handled has an almost indefinite lifespan.[19]

For the future, the Navy has experimented with extending the range of the 16-inch gun. Before her Vietnam deployment, the *New Jersey* did test fire a rocket-assisted 11-inch projectile fitted with a sabot from a 16-inch barrel. The shell reportedly reached out to 50 miles. However, Marine Corps proposals in the early 1980s to incorporate RAP technology to produce infra-red (heat-seeking) 16-inch shells unfortunately received no funding in 1984 or 1985.[20]

The battleships perhaps carry some of the advanced RAP rounds for the 12 5-inch guns still on board. The *New Jersey* had used a few

The *Iowa* was the next to get the treatment. She went first to Avondale at Westwego, Louisiana, and then to Ingalls at Pascagoula, Mississippi. In this view, she has been stripped of all electronic gear, of rangefinders, and even of her 5-inch mounts. [USN]

The *Missouri* leaves Bremerton, Washington, on 14 May 1984. Local people were sorry to see her go. In 1981, she drew 202,833 tourists, and Paramount Pictures filmed part of *The Winds of War* aboard the ship. [USN]

Bremerton's loss was Long Beach's gain. As the tugs *Saco* (YTB-796) and *Sea Otter* nudge her into the shipyard on 25 May, another vessel on her far side welcomes the *Missouri* with fountains of water. She is due to enter service 1 July 1986 at an estimated cost of $422 million. Naval thinking at the beginning of 1986 anticipated the creation of four BBSAGs (Battleship Surface Action Groups), one to operate with the Sixth Fleet in the Mediterranean, one with the Second Fleet in the North Atlantic, and two with the Seventh Fleet in the Pacific. [USN]

to good effect in Vietnam. During the 1970s, dramatic improvements were made in the range of the 5-inch shell by providing rocket boost and in accuracy by adding such esoteric guidance systems as infra-red and laser homing. The rub is that the new ordnance was designed for the 5″/54 and whether it has been modified for the 5″/38 aboard the 'Iowas' is unclear. In any case, the Navy has an adequate stockpile of conventional 5″/38 rounds (over 720,000 projectiles in storage) for the few such weapons still in service.

The 'Iowas' each lost some 5-inch guns to provide space for the new missile systems which give the ships their long-range punch and much of the rationale for their reactivation. With their great size, the battleships are capable of accepting substantial missile loads without endangering stability or hopelessly crowding their superstructures. Here lay a major reason why the Reagan administration chose the 'Iowas' rather than the 'Des Moines' heavy cruisers for modernisation.

The battleships carry two types of modern missiles. The Tomahawk, a cruise missile, flies only meters above the surface at a speed of 550 mph. A versatile weapon, it can be equipped with a shaped charge, high explosive, or nuclear warhead. Depending on the type, the missile has a range from 300 miles for the ship-killing model to 1,500 miles for the nuclear land attack version. With its fire-and-forget tracking system, the Tomahawk has extraordinary accuracy—over one-half can be expected to land within 10 yards of their target. When the *New Jersey* fired her first test round on 10 May 1983, the Tomahawk flew 400 miles to the Tonopah Range in Nevada where it hit a target the size of a house.

As reconfigured, the 'Iowas' carry 32 of these powerful weapons in eight box launchers armored to withstand the blast of 16-inch guns as well as significant splinter damage. Because of the priority given to her modernisation, the *New Jersey* received eight launchers originally slated for two 'Spruance'-class destroyers. To make room and weight for the launchers, four 5-inch mounts were removed. Incidentally, the dredger hoist holes for those guns then provided the necessary routing for the new cables and pipes required by the missiles, thus obviating cuts in the armored decks. These speedy modifications paid off: the *New Jersey* was the first ship in the Navy to carry Tomahawks operationally, the destroyer *Merrill* the

second and the *Iowa* the third. It has been suggested that a battleship armed with Tomahawks and covered by a carrier outside of enemy missile range would present 'a virtually unsolvable tactical problem for any potential enemy surface admiral'.[21]

Against medium range targets, the 'Iowas' can fire the Harpoon. With a range of 60 miles,

One of the first test launches of a Tomahawk SLCM (Surface Launched Cruise Missile) from the *New Jersey*, 10 May 1983. The missile has extendable cruciform tail fins and two mid-body wings. The BGM109B anti-ship version has a modified Harpoon guidance system with a radar altimeter, inertial guidance and active homing. The two land attack types (one nuclear armed, one not) are equipped with TERCOM-aided inertial guidance and DSMAC scene matching terminal guidance. [USN]

One of the armored box launchers for the Tomahawks on the *Iowa*. Each container holds four missiles. [Author]

Right: The Phalanx CIWS (Close-In Weapons System). The electrically controlled, hydraulically-driven barrels fire 3000 rounds per minute at any low-level, pop-up anti-ship missiles that evade the other defenses of the task group. This particular weapon is aboard the cruiser *Jouett* (CG-29). [USN]

this sea-skimmer is designed to pop-up as it nears its target and make its final attack in a steep dive. Like the Tomahawk, the Harpoon is a fire-and-forget weapon, although it apparently does not possess a nuclear capability. Carrying the standard 570-lb warhead, the missile has a high subsonic speed. The battleships are equipped with 16 of these weapons sited next to the after funnel. Positioning them in the fantail 40-mm tubs was considered but ruled out as too dangerous because of the helicopter pad close by.

Anti-ship missiles such as the Harpoon and Tomahawk pose a grave threat to modern surface warships. Similar weapons have already shown their effectiveness in combat starting in 1967 when Styx missiles sank the Israeli destroyer *Eilat*. The Argentine Exocet which mortally wounded HMS *Sheffield* in the Falklands struggle led some sensationalist commentators to pronounce all surface warships obsolete. Unquestionably, such sea-skimming missiles are tough to counter: when a Mach .9 Exocet is one kilometer away, it will hit in less than four seconds.

Thus, the 'Iowas' must be prepared to battle a threat rather similar to the Kamikaze—a terminal homing high speed missile. Off Okinawa, the best solution to the problem seemed to lic in a high volume of anti-aircraft

An amidships view, 6 August 1985, of the *Iowa* showing most of the additions made to her armament. Above and slightly to the left of the 5-inch gunhouse are the empty racks for Harpoons. Forward, but on the same level are the large rectangular boxes for the Tomahawks. Standing out above them in the center is the rounded radome of a Phalanx gun. [Author]

fire, coupled with a heavy 3″/50 shell to stop maimed aircraft dead in their tracks. Too often, badly damaged planes continued on to crash their targets. Similarly, to counter the cruise missile, the navy has developed the Phalanx—or the CIWS (Close-In Weapons System).

A self-contained, bolt-on weapon, the Phalanx requires of its parent ship only electricity for power, seawater for cooling and the ship's course inputs. In one mount, the CIWS features both search and track radars, digital weapon controls, an on-mount magazine, a six-barrel 20-mm gun and a closed-loop spotting system. The last tracks not only the target but its own projectiles and thereupon corrects the gun's aim while it is firing. The CIWS projectile is a heavy metal, depleted uranium penetrator fitted with a plastic discarding sabot to give it great velocity. The combination of mass plus speed means that the shot strikes with terrific force. As with the 3″/50 against the Kamikaze, the CIWS is designed to shatter cruise missiles to prevent damaged missiles from 'going ballistic' and continuing on into the target ship. To maximise the chances of hitting in the short length of time that the missile will be within range, the Phalanx shoots its heavy projectiles at a rate of 3,000 rounds per minute—or 50 per second. Anyone who hears this weapon fired for the first time is surprised by its sound which is quite different from the noise made by a conventional machine gun, 'Like a giant sheet being torn', one observer remarked. Perhaps the only drawback to the CIWS is that it cannot track other targets while it is engaging a missile because its surveillance radar tilts as the gun bears on its target. Since the battleships, as modified, are equipped with four Phalanx weapons, two per side, an enemy could theoretically saturate an 'Iowa's' defenses, assuming he fired enough missiles simultaneously.

It is difficult to generalise about the effects of a cruise missile hit on a battleship. Much would depend, of course, on where the missile struck the ship. A hit topside might very well take out some electronic equipment. An Exocet-type missile, hitting the *New Jersey* where the *Sheffield* was struck, would probably punch through the outermost plating, but it would almost certainly fail to penetrate the armored belt. It is important to remember that the 'Iowa' was designed with enough armor to protect the vitals of the ship against one-ton Mach 2 16-inch AP shells. Interestingly, an Exocet-type missile would have about the same force on impact as a Kamikaze, the plane

being slower but substantially more massive than the missile. Only one fast battleship, the *Missouri*, was hit by a Kamikaze—admittedly at an oblique angle, and that plane did no significant damage at all.[22]

Assuming the Soviets possess hollow charge warheads of adequate size, those could penetrate the side armor. No ship is unsinkable, not even the 'Iowas', but they are easily the most damage-resistant ships in existence. Their very presence would complicate a Soviet commander's job enormously. As Norman Friedman has written:

Even the big Soviet armor-piercing missiles would generally hit well above the waterline, where they would generally be unlikely to strike the ship's magazines. Apart from the Soviet weapons, there are few armor-piercing weapons left in the world's inventories, simply because there are so very few armored warships left. In this sense, the gross obsolescence of the battleship is a major asset. This is not to say that a ship like the *New Jersey* cannot be sunk, only that sinking it is no easy matter.[23]

John Lehman has stated publicly that the Soviet cruise missiles are a lesser threat to the battleships than the Japanese 18.1-inch shells were.

Contributing to the cruise missile defenses are the updated electronic suites on the 'Iowas'. The new AN/SLQ 32 electronic warfare system, controlled by computers, can detect and track multiple threats. An ECM component can jam several enemy sensors simultaneously. At close range, the ships are able to further confuse the enemy weapons with decoys. Four Super Rapid-Bloom Off-board Chaff (SRBOC) launchers are designed to confuse cruise missiles in the terminal phase of their approach. Two new radar systems have upgraded the vessels' long range air and surface search capabilities. Most of this equipment is monitored in the Combat Engagement Center (CEC), set up where the World War Two flag quarters were once located. The CEC requires so much power that dockyard workers made their only cut through armor when the ships were refurbished. The hole was started by patient drilling; then the rest of the circle was burned out.

Planners were challenged at reconciling all of this modern, and often sensitive, equipment with the blast overpressures of 16-inch gunfire. Despite forecasts from pessimists that the job

In upgrading the aviation facilities, the crane was removed from the stern, where a landing pad, raised two feet above the rest of the deck, was built. A helicopter control station was added under the after 5-inch director and tankage provided for 9,040 gallons of aviation fuel. The helicopter seen here on the *Iowa* is a Marine Corps CH-53 practicing landings. Note the high-line transfer gear fixed atop No 3 turret. [Author]

was impossible, it was accomplished in some cases by hardening the equipment—as in placing the Tomahawks in armored box launchers. Training arc restrictions for the big gun proved far less drastic than first feared. The only major new system not compatible with 16-inch blast was the modern encapsulated liferafts whose original cases and hydrostatic releases could not accept the overpressures.

Much other new equipment was worked into the ships as they rejoined the fleet. A rather extensive helicopter servicing facility with fueling, maintenance and firefighting equipment was set up in the fantail. The ships can stow three helicopters and operate a fourth even at night or in bad weather.

Habitability has been upgraded to current standards. The living quarters of the ships are air conditioned by seven 125-ton units. The old open racks have been replaced by bunks with privacy curtains, rubber mattresses and reading lights. A vending machine area supplements modernised messing facilities. Garbage grinders and waste-holding tanks bring the ships into compliance with environmental legislation.

One of the most difficult alterations involved converting the steam plant's black oil to distillate fuel (DFM, or diesel fuel marine). Each of the 130 riveted fuel tanks had to be cleaned of the bunker fuel residue—often of the consistency of asphalt. The tanks were then sealed from the inside with epoxy. The fuel pumps, valves and sprayer plates had all to be modified to accept the new, lighter fuel.

The 600-lb steam engineering plant presented another challenge to the Navy: by the 1980s, it was obsolescent and thus might be difficult to man. Fortunately, two ships, the carriers *Midway* and *Coral Sea*, used very similar installations. Better yet, the machinery in the combat support ships *Sacramento* and *Camden* was identical to that in the battleships—hardly surprising since the machinery for the auxiliaries had been removed from the *Kentucky* when that ship was scrapped. In consequence, there were enough navymen with the necessary experience to train new engineering personnel.

Planners were justifiably more worried about manning big gun turrets and gave some thought to reconfiguring the weapon system. A quick appraisal showed that only a major turret redesign would lead to any significant reduction in personnel. Such a large project was clearly out of the question.

The only feasible approach lay in re-establishing the 36–42 week training courses in main battery gunnery. Naval Sea System Command hired civilian companies such as RCA to write course syllabuses. These companies, in turn, hired former battleship gunners to teach the courses. Prime source materials for the courses proved to be plans, blueprints and the old turret manuals, particularly OP 769—upgraded for the *New Jersey* in 1968. But nothing could replace the actual experience of working with the weapons. As one gunner later wrote, for '... competent turret crews and main battery fire control personnel, continuous on-board training with hands on the equipment is the order of the day'.[24]

When Congress debated the reactivation of the ships in 1981, crew size figured once again

The new refueling boom on the *Iowa*: to make easier what the fast battleships have done so well for so long. [Author]

as a key point of controversy. Critics charged that the vessels were voracious of manpower and would soak up many scarce ratings. Proponents countered that the 'battleship mystique' would lure some sailors out of retirement and would virtually man the ships. Actually only five per cent of the *New Jersey*'s crew was made up of recall volunteers, in large part because of some restrictive Navy re-enlistment policies. However, the chance to be 'a battleship sailor' looked attractive enough to active duty personnel that three men volunteered for each billet. As to total crew size, the battleships went back to sea with 62 officers, 1,500 enlisted men, plus a marine detachment of 2 officers and 42 enlisted men. Assuming a shore support force of approximately 30 per cent of the ship's company, each 'Iowa' requires about 2,000 people to keep her on line. When all four ships are back in service, they will absorb about 1.5 per cent of the navy's total manpower—not an insignificant figure, but hardly an overwhelming drain. The 'Iowas', after all, are not insignificant ships.

Integral to early arguments in favor of their reactivation was the idea that they would ultimately be reconfigured to a much more advanced standard: the so-called Phase II modernisation. Charles Myers' 'Basis for Advocacy' that went the rounds of Congress visualised the removal of the aft 16-inch turret and its replacement with a vertical launch system for missiles plus a flight deck for marine helicopters. This proposal sparked a host of imitators, including one in the *Naval Institute Proceedings* for a canted flight deck with steam catapult and arresting gear so that the ships could operate the Navy's latest fighters, presumably the F/A-18 Hornet. The firm of Martin Marietta advanced a double flight deck plan with an 11° ski ramp on each side of the ships to enable them to fly the marine AV8 Harrier V/STOL aircraft.[25]

In late 1981, the Navy's Systems Analysis Division produced a study with six separate options ranging from the modest to the extreme. The least expensive would have retained all three turrets; four of the six plans would have removed turret No. 3 in exchange for vertical missile launchers and helicopters in varying numbers. The last option called for the replacement of all three big gun turrets with 400 vertical missile launchers.[26]

All of these projects were eventually put on the shelf, in part because of cost, even more

because of marine opposition. With the puny gun armament on the newest warships (a 'Ticonderoga' cruiser costs over $1 billion and mounts two 5-inchers), the marines were loath to give up a single 16-inch gun barrel. If a dozen helicopters went aboard, so would their fuel, and the ships would be much more vulnerable to enemy fire from shore. One marine officer even wrote to protest the use of the 'Iowas' as flagships. He argued that an admiral might find it difficult to command his fleet from a heavily engaged battleship. Perhaps Jocko Clark's antics off Korea reinforce this point.[27]

Ultimately, the Navy dropped Phase II. It was '... expensive, time-consuming, and

The return of the *New Jersey* to service was important enough to warrant the president's attendance at the ceremony. Ronald Reagan has just stepped away from the speaker's stand; Secretary of the Navy John Lehman is close behind it. The date is 28 December 1982; the place, Long Beach Naval Shipyard. [USN]

At sea in the Pacific, the *New Jersey* operates with the oiler *Kansas City* (AOR-3) and the guided missile destroyer *Buchanan* (DDG-14). It cost less to reactivate an *Iowa* than to build another *Buchanan*, and the US Navy got a ship with 20 times the firepower. This photograph was taken on 12 August 1983. [USN]

The *New Jersey* back in action off Beirut. The guns in each turret fire at an interval of .06 seconds, with the left gun firing first, then the right, and finally the center. The delay is to ensure that the projectiles do not interfere aerodynamically with each other in flight. Note the eight Tomahawk canisters and the Harpoon launchers clustered around the after funnel. [USN]

reduced the conventional gunfire support capability unique to a battleship', said Vice Admiral Walters, the head of the Surface Warfare branch.[28] Instead, the Navy has continued work on upgrading the gunfire capability of the battleships, especially by improving accuracy and developing submunitions rounds. The HC shell is being reworked to hold 'hundreds' of M242 army grenades, and a totally redesigned projectile body to carry submunitions of any sort is in the offing. So is a projectile tracking radar that will be able to follow precisely the ship's own shells as well as enemy projectiles, making possible an awesome counter-battery capability.

A 1985 proposal envisions the replacement of four more 5-inch mounts by an assault ballistic rocket system (ABRS). An offshoot of an Army program, the system can dump in a matter of minutes several tons of ordnance on targets up to 32,000 yards away. The marines are naturally interested, but the battleships would lose all but two of their 5-inch mounts. Costs, estimated at from $40 million to $105 million per ship, are substantial.

At the time of writing, two of the battleships have not yet returned to active duty. The *Missouri*, despite the protests of the Kitsap County Historical Society, is currently in the yard. Congress provided funding for the *Wisconsin* in the 1986 budget, although this author saw her still at the Philadelphia reserve facility in December 1985. That they are coming out is an indicator that the lead pair have satisfactorily demonstrated their capabilities.

After her commissioning at the end of 1982, the *New Jersey* joined the Pacific Fleet. Her gunnery qualification scores at San Clemente with marines calling fire were well above the fleet average. She began her first operational deployment to East Asian waters in June 1983 when she called at Pearl Harbor, Manila and Subic Bay. She then worked with the Seventh Fleet in the Gulf of Siam, but these exercises were interrupted when she was diverted at the end of July to Central America because of the tense Nicaragua situation. Her planned three month shakedown cruise was turning into an odyssey. In September, her startled crew received orders to head for the eastern Mediterranean at 26 knots.

Once off Beirut, she kept to an 'operating box' 10 by 20 miles in size. From this position, her lookouts could see with telescopes snipers in wrecked buildings. Sailors called the const-

After a first cruise that saw her travel from the Caribbean to Thailand to Lebanon, the *New Jersey* returns home to Long Beach. She had been away for eleven months. [USN]

ant night fireworks above the city 'the Disneyland Light Parade'. The battleship constantly changed speed and course to foil Syrian guns reportedly aimed at her. Stringent precautions were taken against suicide attackers. Officers considered measures to counter boats, light planes, gliders and even the remote threat of a hijacked suicide airliner. Several times the crew went to battle stations following warnings of kamikaze attacks. At one point, an unidentified freighter headed directly for the *New Jersey* at night. Capt. Richard Milligan, the *New Jersey*'s skipper, backed his ship at full reverse and took aim with 5-inch guns whereupon the mysterious cargo ship abruptly veered away.

After 12 alerts, the ship finally opened fire on 14 December 1983 against Syrian anti-aircraft batteries which had downed two Navy A-6 Intruders 10 days earlier. In this action, just weeks short of the 40th anniversary of her first battle, she shot only 11 rounds of 16-inch ammunition. On 8 February however, she expended almost 300. Details of these bombardments are still sketchy, and evaluators have differed sharply on the effectiveness of the battleship's gunnery. Admiral Walters, the boss of surface warships, characterised the vessel's shooting as superb and pointed out that whenever the ship fired, the enemy bat-

The *Iowa* less than five months from recommissioning. Lying at Ingalls, she is covered with dockyard detritus, but the six of her secondary turrets that she will keep are back on board, as is her large new foremast. Her missile installations and the Phalanx guns are in advanced stages of completion. By this point (1 January 1984), work was proceeding around the clock in order to get her out to Lebanon. [USN]

Fittingly, Secretary John Lehman gave the keynote address at the recommissioning of the *Iowa* at Pascagoula on 28 April 1984. [Author]

Operating in the Caribbean, the *Iowa* leads the Columbian frigate *Caldas* during Operation UNITAS XXV, in July 1984. The large radar on the *Iowa*'s new foremast is the air search SPS-49; barely visible under it is the SPS-67, a solid-state surface search set. Note that the housing for the SLQ-32 ECM system is more streamlined than that on the *New Jersey*. The new refueling boom is quite evident from this angle. [USN]

In spite of all the new missiles and electronic gear, some ties remain to the 1930s. The decks are still teak, signals still come out of the flag bag, and the old reliable 5″/38s are still protected by 2.5 inches of armor. [Author]

teries fell silent. Other defense analysts have been less sanguine. Edward Luttwak, an *enfant terrible* of the defense establishment, charged that the ship's shells were '... largely wasted because its guns were fired on map coordinates without concurrent target finding or correction'.[29] But other assessors have maintained that new Marine Corps target acquisition radars did allow precise correction '... to within about 13 meters accuracy—well within the lethal radius of the battleship *New Jersey*'s 16-inch guns. Unfortunately, the battleship's 16-inch gunfire proved nowhere near as accurate.'[30] Such speculation is perhaps borne out by the care with which the Navy began rebagging charges using 16″/45 and 8″/55 powders.

In any event, the *New Jersey* showed, if nothing else, she possessed plenty of stamina. Most of her crew, prepared for a short break-in cruise, went 111 days without liberty, although in January 1984, 200 men did win shore leave in a lottery. The ship ran out of milk, fruit and ice cream. Echoing a popular TV advertising refrain, *New Jersey* sailors answered the question, 'How do you spell relief?' with 'I-O-W-A.' The crewmen did receive double sea credit to compensate for their lengthened deployment. Upon her return in the spring, the *New Jersey* underwent a lengthy refit and finally ran her final acceptance trials in January 1985, over two years after she had commissioned—surely a record of some sort.

To provide the necessary relief, the refitting of the *Iowa* was accelerated greatly. Originally scheduled to enter service in early 1985, Lehman ordered the date to be advanced to 30 June 1984 and then to 28 April. The ship's company and Ingalls workers met this deadline by round-the-clock work. The importance of her return to active duty was underlined by the presence at her commissioning ceremony of Vice-President George Bush and Secretary John Lehman. Also attending the festivities— and most vigorously applauded by the large audience—was John L. McCrea, who had first taken the *Iowa* to sea in 1943.

Ironically, this great effort to get the *Iowa* ready for the Middle East proved unnecessary because the Reagan administration drastically lowered the American presence in Lebanon. But the *Iowa* had plenty to do. She tested most satisfactorily some of the rebagged charges at Vieques Island, east of Puerto Rico, in the late spring. She then took part in exercises off Nicaragua in the summer, during which her crew performed civic action chores in friendly Central American countries. For instance, dentists from the battleship flew by helicopter to provide their services to impoverished peasants. The *Iowa* performed so well that she earned a Meritorious Unit Commendation for her first active deployment in 27 years.

After upkeep in the spring of 1985, the *Iowa*
achieved such operating standards that she
won the Battenburg Cup in July as the best
allround ship in the Atlantic Fleet—hardly a
year after her shake-down. Beginning in September, she confirmed this judgment during
the month-long NATO exercise called Ocean
Safari. Teamed with the new anti-submarine
frigate *Halyburton* and the modern Aegis
cruiser the *Ticonderoga*, the *New Jersey* was
ordered to protect the northern flank of a
hypothetical convoy during its Atlantic transit.
The three ships crossed the Arctic Circle
between Greenland and Iceland while observing complete electronic silence. The battleship
demonstrated her prowess with her big guns
off Greenland. Using optical fire control
because of the ban on radar transmissions,
Iowa gunners hit an iceberg at 12,000 yards
with 6 out of 11 16-inch shells. Following the
NATO exercise, the *Iowa* stopped at Oslo,
where she welcomed King Olav V and then
entered the Baltic for further drills, especially

for work with the brand-new anti-submarine
Seahawk helicopter. As the first battleship to
sail the Baltic since World War Two, the *Iowa*
was greeted by large crowds at Copenhagen
and Kiel as well as by the East German flagship
Berlin, which steamed close across her bow.
On her return to the United States in December, the *Iowa* was awarded the coveted Battle
'E' Efficiency honor.

She had worn that 'E' earlier in her career,
but her achievement in 1985 showed how
sound her basic design had been. Conceived
for battle against ships which had been sunk
more than 40 years earlier, the *Iowa* and her
sisters combine protection, speed, range and
firepower into a package that had always been
unusual, and by the 1980s was obviously
unique. For little more than the cost of four
new destroyers—a type with perhaps 5 per
cent of a battleship's offensive power, the
Reagan administration had gained four im-
mensely impressive weapons systems.

APPENDICES

APPENDIX A

ORIGINAL SPECIFICATIONS FOR THE
'IOWA' CLASS, 9 JUNE 1938

The General Board recommends the following characteristics for the proposed 45,000-ton Battleships:

Hull

1 *Displacement :* Not exceeding 45,000 standard tons.
2 *Beam :* Not to exceed 108 ft 3 inches.
3 *Draft :* Not over 36 ft at extreme full load.
4 *Length :* Approximately 860 ft on waterline.
5 *Subdivision :* Designed with special view to as complete protection as practicable by subdivisions with intact bulkheads, with best protection against underwater damage.
6 *Damage control :* Fitted with latest approved devices for control of damage.
7 *Gas protection :* Most efficient means to protect against chemicals.
8 *Fueling arrangements :* Fitted to fuel destroyers.
9 *Towing :* Fitted for emergency towing.
10 *Quarters :* One to be fitted as Force Flagship, others of the type as Division Flagships.

Armament

1 *Main battery :* Nine (9) 16″/50 caliber Mark II guns mounted in triple turrets on centerline, two forward and one aft.
2 *Secondary battery :* (a) Twenty (20) 5″/38 caliber double purpose guns mounted in twin turrets.
(b) Three (3) quadruple 1.1″ machine guns, and twelve (12) .50 caliber machine guns.
3 *Ammunition allowance :* (a) Main battery— 675 rounds 16-inch, with space for mobilization supply.
Mobilization supply 495 rounds.
(b) Secondary battery—5″/38 caliber; 6,000 AA and common, 800 illuminating.

Magazine space for additional 2,800 rounds. Mobilization supply 2,800 rounds.
(c) Machine guns: Standard.
4 *Searchlights :* Six (6) high power, fitted for high angle searching.
5 *Aircraft :* Fitted to carry three (3) seaplanes; two (2) catapults.

Protection

1 *Vertical armor :*
(a) *Belt armor :* To be internal armor of sufficient thickness, tapered and sloped at the most suitable angle, to give protection at 18,000 yards against 16-inch 45 caliber 2,240 lb armor piercing projectiles at 90° target angle; and so designed to give reasonable protection against underwater trajectories. This belt armor to extend from forward of No. 1 turret to abaft No. 3 turret with upper edge at the second deck level, and from No. 3 turret to abaft the steering engine room, with upper edge at the third deck level.
(b) *Transverse armor :* Transverse armor to be of such thickness as will give protection at 18,000 yards against 16-inch 45 caliber, 2,240 lb armor piercing projectiles at 50° target angle.
(c) *Barbette, conning tower sides and conning tower tube :* To be of such thickness as will give protection at 18,000 yards against the above mentioned projectile at 90° target angle, except the centerline portion of barbettes for which a 50° target angle is sufficient. The 90° angle will result in a thickness of about 17.3 inches.
2 *Horizontal armor :*
(a) Main deck (bomb deck) from forward of No. 1 turret to abaft No. 3 turret to be 1½″ S.T.S.
(b) Second deck (protective deck)—As necessary with main deck to give proection at an outer limit of 30,000

yards against the 16-inch projectile mentioned above.

  (c) Third deck, from transverse armor abaft No. 3 turret to after end of steering gear compartment—of sufficient thickness to give protection at 30,000 yards outer limit against the above mentioned projectile.

  (d) Splinter deck (under second deck)—From transverse armor forward of No. 1 turret to transverse armor abaft No. 3 turret to be 25 lb S.T.S.

3 *Turret armor and top of conning tower :* To be of thickness that will give protection somewhat in excess of 30,000 yards outer limit. Actual thicknesses required are as follows: turret face plates—18 inches; turret sides—10 inches; turret tops—7.25 inches; conning tower top—7.25 inches.

4 *Secondary protection :* Major caliber fragment protection: $2\frac{1}{2}''$ S.T.S. to be provided for flag plot, flag radio, 5" gun houses and handling rooms, and Battle signal station.

  Splinter protection ($1\frac{1}{2}''$ S.T.S.) to be provided for all directors and director tubes, except that $2\frac{1}{2}''$ S.T.S. to be fitted on director tubes below navigating bridge level.

  Outer hull in vicinity of waterline, between No. 1 and No. 3 turrets, to have splinter protection of about $1\frac{1}{2}''$ S.T.S.

Propulsion

1 *Speed :* Full speed of 33 knots with smooth sea and clean bottom, which includes oil for full radius, full allowance (as specified in these characteristics) of stores and ammunition, and full supply of fresh and reserve feed water.

2 *Fuel :* Oil.

3 *Endurance :* 15,000 miles at 15 knots on fuel supply in regular fuel tanks.

4 *Lubricating oil :* Equal to or exceeding maximum fuel endurance at all speeds.

Communications

1 *Radio equipment :* Equipped to meet Fleet Communication Requirements.

2 *Visual equipment :* Standard day and night equipment.

3 *Sound equipment :* Echo-sounding only.

Provisions and Stores

		Battle endurance	Min. total capacity
1	G.S.K. stores:	6 weeks	16 weeks
2	Dry provisions:	6 weeks	16 weeks
3	Clothing and small stores:	6 weeks	12 weeks
4	Cold storage:	3 weeks	6 weeks

(SGD) THOS. C. HART

Source: General Board, File 420.6, NHC.

APPENDIX B

ALTERNATIVE GUNS FOR THE 'IOWAS': THE 16"/56 AND THE 18"/48

The following estimate of the capabilities of these two artillery pieces was submitted by the General Board on 21 April 1938 to the Secretary of the Navy:

If we look only at the power of the individual gun, the 18-inch is the best gun available. Against a target with 16" side armor and $6\frac{1}{4}''$ deck it allows an immunity zone of only 1,500 yards (27,500–29,000 yards) for the 3,200-lb projectile and if we increase the projectile weight to 3,850 lbs the immunity zone disappears and we penetrate both deck and side between 25,000 yards and 30,500 yards. The principal disadvantage of the 18-inch gun is the weight of the installation and the consequently greatly increased tonnage required to carry it. For an installation of nine 18-inch guns in three triple turrets with acceptable protection and speed, we can expect to exceed a displacement of 48,000 tons. It would be possible to mount a battery of six 18-inch guns in twin turrets on a displacement under 45,000 tons, but a main battery of only six guns is believed to be unacceptable for a tonnage of this magnitude. If we consider eight 18-inch guns in twin turrets, the required tonnage will be almost as much as for nine guns in triple turrets. Incidentally, there may well be considerable hesitancy in going directly to a triple 18-inch turret without first obtaining experience with the twin turret. A really vital point in deciding against the 18-inch gun for the present is that if we go to the 18-inch other countries will of necessity follow and we will be forcing the pace in bigger and bigger capital ships. This may soon result in reaching a size which cannot transit the Panama Canal. If we are willing to reduce speed to 21 knots or 23 knots, the 18-inch gun can be carried on a reasonable tonnage, but at present there appears to be no tendency among nations to reduce battleship speed. As regards the probability of other nations going to the 18-inch gun, we know that Great Britain is in favor of smaller battleships and smaller caliber of guns. Japan's position is uncertain. It is probable that she would like to bring out the first 18-inch capital ship as a matter of pride, as well as for the advantage which would accrue to her. However, in spite of Japan's present success in safeguarding her naval secrets, we should be able to obtain early information of the production of 18-inch guns in any quantity. Our present superiority in the battle line is such that we can afford to leave to Japan the decision to take the first step, if by so doing we can avoid having the 18-inch gun injected into the rearmament race and the attendant terrific expense.

The 16″/56 gun installation is almost as heavy as the 18-inch, but not so powerful as regards deck armor, muzzle energy and weight of projectile, with consequent smashing effect. It would not be the answer to an 18-inch installation by another nation. Neither would it give us the maximum offensive power possible on the tonnage involved.

Source: File 420–6, NHC.

APPENDIX C
ORDNANCE DATA: 16″/50 TURRET

A turret on an 'Iowa' class battleship is a most complex piece of equipment. It is designed, of course, to protect, feed and house the 16-inch guns, each of which weighs close to 150 tons. These massive weapons must be aimed precisely, and they must be supplied with their projectiles and propellant. The enormous recoil forces generated by the guns must be somehow managed. The whole turret needs a great deal of electrical power for the operation of its many motors. The men who work the guns must be able to communicate with one another and with men elsewhere in the ship. The turret crew requires adequate ventilation and protection against noxious gasses generated by the guns. The resulting piece of equipment is so complicated that the ordnance manual governing its operation (OP 769) covers almost 500 pages of small print. These diagrams and photographs can only cover a small part of the layout and working of the turret.

Internal ballistics

Length of gun, inches: 816.0

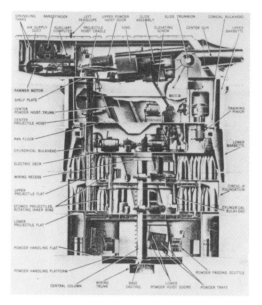

Turret arrangement—longitudinal section. The turret is rotated by its training pinions on the electric deck level just above the upper projectile flat. Most of the turret structure rotates. The components that do *not* are (from bottom to top): the powder handling flat, the outer projectile rings and the circular foundation, the lower barbette, and the upper barbette. [OP 769]

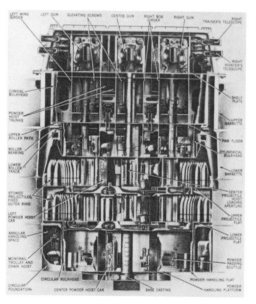

Turret arrangement—transverse section. In this view, the reader is looking at the gun breeches. Note the elevating screws for the big rifles and the space (called the gun pit) provided under each weapon for its elevation. [OP 769]

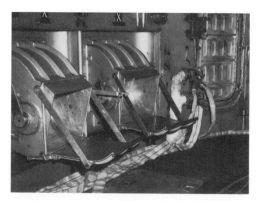

Powder scuttles in the powder handling room—*Iowa*, May 1943. The 60-lb powder bags are passed through these scuttles which are so designed that when one side is open, the other is closed making a fire resistant barrier. Note the hoses. Large water-filled tanks (out of the picture) provide a safe dumping ground for any spilled powder or split bags.

The powder handling flat lies at the very base of the turret structure. A sailor here is approximately 20 feet below the waterline. [NARS]

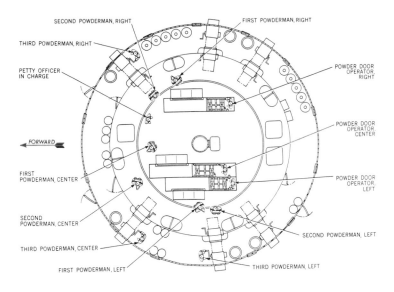

SECOND POWDERMAN, RIGHT
FIRST POWDERMAN, RIGHT
THIRD POWDERMAN, RIGHT
PETTY OFFICER IN CHARGE
POWDER DOOR OPERATOR, RIGHT
FORWARD
FIRST POWDERMAN, CENTER
POWDER DOOR OPERATOR, CENTER
SECOND POWDERMAN, CENTER
POWDER DOOR OPERATOR, LEFT
SECOND POWDERMAN, LEFT
THIRD POWDERMAN, CENTER
FIRST POWDERMAN, LEFT
THIRD POWDERMAN, LEFT

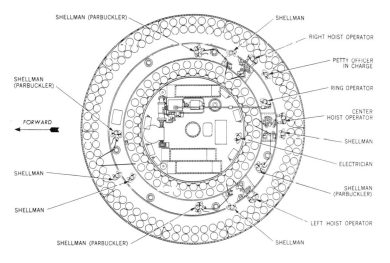

SHELLMAN (PARBUCKLER)
SHELLMAN
RIGHT HOIST OPERATOR
PETTY OFFICER IN CHARGE
SHELLMAN (PARBUCKLER)
RING OPERATOR
CENTER HOIST OPERATOR
FORWARD
SHELLMAN
ELECTRICIAN
SHELLMAN
SHELLMAN (PARBUCKLER)
SHELLMAN
LEFT HOIST OPERATOR
SHELLMAN (PARBUCKLER)
SHELLMAN

Powder handling room—overhead view. Note the double circle denoting the division between the stationary (or outer) powder handling flat and the rotating, inner powder handling platform. [OP 769]

Projectile flat—overhead view. This view illustrates how the shells are moved to the hoists by the parbuckling gear. To allow the projectiles to slide more easily, the rotating rings which make up the deck are coated in a light machine oil. The gunner's mates are supposed to put down a thin film; they are often too generous with it. The rings are usually slippery with oil. [OP 769]

Bore diameter, inches: 16.0
Bore length, inches: 800.0
Projectile travel, inches: 689.67
Powder chamber length, inches: 105.82
Powder chamber volume, cubic inches: 27,000.0
Powder chamber pressure (service charge), pounds per square inch: 35,000.0
Number of grooves: 96
Length of grooves, inches: 682.46
Depth of grooves, inches: 0.15
Twist: Uniform, right hand, one turn in 25 cals.

External ballistics

Muzzle velocity, AP Projectile (service charge), feet per sec.: 2425
Muzzle velocity, HC Projectile (service charge), feet per sec.: 2690
Range, AP Projectile (service charge), yards: 40,185
Range, HC Projectile (service charge), yards: 41,622

Range tables

Armor-piercing 16-inch projectile: OP 1457
High-capacity 16-inch projectile: OP 1100

Weight pounds, each turret

Turret roller path load: 4,030,000
Total ordnance installation: 1,540,000
Gun assemblies, right, center, left, each:
  Gun, with screw box liner: 239,156
  Gun, with recoiling parts: 292,000
  Yoke: 38,500
Elevating gear, right, center, left, each:
  Electric motor (inc. speed reducer): 1880
  Electric motor controller: 165
  Receiver-regulator: 240
Training gear:
  Electric motor: 4500
  Electric motor controller: 1800
  Reduction gear: 3100
  Receiver-regulator: 320
Projectile ring, upper or lower:
  Electric motor: 1200
  Electric motor controller
    First design: 130; Second design: 150
Parbuckling gear, upper or lower:
  Electric motor: 650
  Electric motor controller: 110
Projectile hoist, each:
  Electric motor: 1900
  Electric motor controller: 235
  Speed reducer: 375
  Cradle: 755
  Spanning tray: 184
Rammer, each:
  Electric motor (inc. speed reducer): 1750
  Electric motor controller: 165
Powder hoist, each:
  Electric motor: 2550
  Electric motor controller: 235
  Powder car (empty): 2050
Train limits, all turrets:
  Right train, degrees: 150

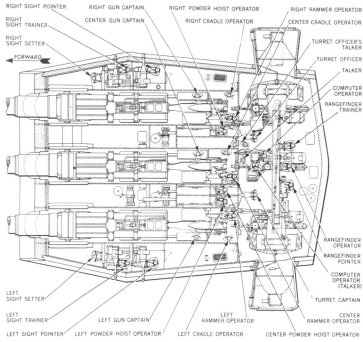

RIGHT SIGHT POINTER · RIGHT GUN CAPTAIN · RIGHT POWDER HOIST OPERATOR · RIGHT RAMMER OPERATOR

RIGHT SIGHT TRAINER · CENTER GUN CAPTAIN · RIGHT CRADLE OPERATOR · CENTER CRADLE OPERATOR

RIGHT SIGHT SETTER · TURRET OFFICER'S TALKER · TURRET OFFICER · TALKER · COMPUTER OPERATOR · RANGEFINDER TRAINER

← FORWARD →

RANGEFINDER OPERATOR · RANGEFINDER POINTER · COMPUTER OPERATOR (TALKER) · TURRET CAPTAIN

LEFT SIGHT SETTER · LEFT SIGHT TRAINER · LEFT GUN CAPTAIN · LEFT RAMMER OPERATOR · CENTER RAMMER OPERATOR

LEFT SIGHT POINTER · LEFT POWDER HOIST OPERATOR · LEFT CRADLE OPERATOR · CENTER POWDER HOIST OPERATOR

Projectile hoist control station—USS *Iowa*, July 1944. The hoist operator (at the right) is facing the upper hoist control and interlocks. Level with his waist is the control for the solenoid operated interlock. His right hand (out of the camera's view) is on the control handle; directly in back of his left hand is the hoist control indicator with six lights (three obscured by the control shaft) which visually signal safe hoist conditions or flash a warning. On the back side of the support bracket (away from the camera) is a hoist-ready gong. The circular object several inches to the lower left of the hoist control indicator is a contact maker for the emergency alarm. Note the solenoids (two visible) attached to the underside of the control handle bracket. These lock the control levers at hoist or lower so that they cannot be moved until the loading cycle is completed. Otherwise, an accidental reversal of the projectile hoist would seat one

projectile in the hoist on the nose of another lower down, possibly jamming the hoist and damaging the shells.

The shellman is kneeling before a capstan or gypsy head. Part of the parbuckling gear, the six gypsy heads in each projectile flat are driven by electric motors and rotate at 90 rpm. Each can slide a 2700-lb armor-piercing projectile against a 15° roll of the ship. The 'bullets' to the right are standing on the inner, rotating ring which can store 72 shells on each of the two projectile flats in all three turrets (thus 432 in all). The number of shells stowed on the outer, stationary ring depends on the level and the turret (see text). At present, the number of projectiles stowed exceeds the number of powder charges because several magazines were preempted for other uses (such as the CIC). The shells here are Mk 8 AP projectiles probably fitted with Mk 21 base detonating fuzes. [NARS]

Left train, degrees: 150
Elevating limits, each gun:
  Elevation, degrees: 45
  Depression, degrees: − 2
  Depression, (turret II), degrees: 0

Ammunition data

Armor-piercing projectile, 16-inch:
  Designation: Mk 8 Mod 0
  Weight, pounds: 2700
  Length, inches: 72
  Radius of ogive, inches: 144
High-capacity projectile, 16-inch:
  Designation: Mk 13 Mod 0
  Weight, pounds: 1900
  Length, inches: 64
  Radius of ogive, inches: 144
Powder charge, 16-inch:
  Number of bags (service charge): 6
  Total weight (service charge), pounds: 650

Projectile stowage

Service projectiles:
  Turret I:
    Upper projectile flat, outer ring: 120
    Lower projectile flat, outer ring: 126
    Each inner ring: 72
    Total stowage: 390
  Turret II:

Gunhouse arrangement—overhead view. Twenty-seven men work in this space. Of that number, only nine directly handle the projectiles and charges. [OP 769]

Upper projectile flat, outer ring: 70
Lower projectile flat, outer ring: 125
Each inner ring: 72
Fixed stowage, third level: 121
Total stowage: 460
Turret III:
Upper projectile flat, outer ring: 100
Lower projectile flat, outer ring: 126
Each inner ring: 72
Total stowage: 370
Drill projectiles:
Turret I: 9; Turret II: 9; Turret III: 9

Gun data

Center of gravity, from breech, inches: 280.6
Distance of recoil, design length, inches: 47
Distance of recoil, max., inches: 48
Gun oscillating weight, pounds: 387,900
Gun laying speeds:
Max. training gear rate, deg. per sec.: 4
Max. elevating gear rate, deg. per sec.: 12
Gun firing order: L, R, C
Firing delay period, sec.: 0.06

Firing load, trunnion pressure, gun at 45°
elevation, pounds, each gun: 1,677,648
Gun brake load, pounds: 1,380,782
Recoil system pressure, 42° elevation (service charge), psi: 2900
Counterrecoil buffing pressure, 0° elevation psi: 7200
Counterrecoil system air pressure, psi: 1550
Counterrecoil pressure, full recoil, psi: 2153
Counterrecoil force, full recoil, pounds: 372,857
Recoil period, 15° elevation, sec.: 0.43
Counterrecoil period, 15° elevation, sec.: 0.90
Gun spacing, center centerline gun to centerline right and left guns, inches: 122
Lines-of-sight data:
Depression of line-of-sight (includes 20° of roll) degrees: 50
Elevation of line-of-sight (for 20° of roll) degrees: 20
Deflection movement (left), mils: 100
Deflection movement (right), mils: 175

Source: NAVORD OP 769, NHC.

APPENDIX D
16″/50 TURRET

1. **Spanning tray—** *Missouri*, fall 1950. A gun captain (C. G. Reeves, Jefferson, Ga.) in turret No 1 signals to ram the 16-inch projectile. The tongue of the folding spanning tray fits neatly into the breech. Right above the gun captain's head is the gas ejector valve from which a blast of compressed air automatically scours the bore clean of powder gases and burning fragments of powder bag after every round. At 175 psi, the air blast creates a 60-knot wind in the bore, and there is an auxiliary gas ejection system for use in the event of an emergency. The gun captain is charged with inspecting the bore after each air blast to guard against a blowback (see text). He then depresses the bore clear switch. Immediately above Reeves' left index finger is one of the gas ejection nozzles located in the breech plug threads. [NARS]

2. **The rammer—** *Iowa*, July 1944. A complex piece of equipment, the rammer requires 25 pages of coverage in the turret manual. The head link (at bottom center) is made of cast bronze and drives the shell and powder charges home by means of a 297-inch chain, four links of which are visible. A 60 horsepower electric motor provides the power to drive the projectile into the gun at a maximum velocity of 13.9 feet per second (fps). An automatic decelerating device eliminated much trouble suffered by earlier rammers with their drives and chains.

The rammer operator is seated with his left hand on the lever that controls the ram. He also opens and closes the powder door (open directly to his front). The gun captain stands at bottom; to his left is the cradle operator. This ram serves either a center or right gun; on a left gun, the positions of the men are reversed.

This picture was taken from atop the gun yoke, that is, the large steel counterbalance at the breech end of the gun. Note the sprinkler to flush the chamber in an emergency. The plate above the rammer allows access to the tail link of the rammer chain in the chain housing. [NARS]

3. The rammer—ramming a 16-inch shell on the *Wisconsin* off Korea, fall, 1952. The rammer takes only 1.7 seconds to seat the projectile, and the clang that it makes is audible all the way on the bridge. The rotating band, visible at the rear of the shell, is 97.5% copper and 2.5% nickel. When the projectile is rammed fully home or in 'shot start condition,' the band seats on the band slope where the rifling begins inside the bore. Because some of the driving band is scraped off by the rifling lands, a packet holding 200 grams of lead foil for de-coppering purposes is stuck between the powder bags on each shot.

When the *Wisconsin* was shelling Okinawa,

24 March 1945, the rammer head of the left gun in turret No 2 slipped off the base of the projectile and struck the face of the breech. The projectile was moving fast enough to seat in the gun, and the crew loaded the powder bags by hand and fired the gun which then stayed out of commission for the remainder of the action.

The problem was caused by an overeager rammerman who rammed the shell before the cradle was horizontal, causing the head of the rammer to seat against the top of the base of the projectile. The rammer head and the first five links were bent and twisted. They took five hours to replace. [NARS]

4. Priming the firing lock—*Iowa*, July 1944. After firing a round, the breech plug is swung down and the spent primer case is automatically ejected. The primerman, standing on a platform below the shelf plate, inspects the mushroom stem hole and inserts a loaded primer. Due to safety interlocks, the primer cannot be fired until the breech is closed completely. In the event of a misfire, the gun can be reprimed without opening the breech.

The photographer is looking up from the bottom of the gun pit. Note the crewman in the gun house and the primerman's cartridge belt filled with primers. The sailor-spectator looking into the gun pit is not at action stations, and this is thus a staged photograph. [NARS]

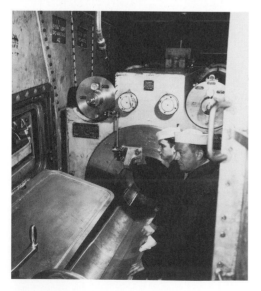

5. Spanning tray—*Iowa*, May 1943. The gun captain (nearest the breech) and his cradle operator await the powder bags, three of which will roll down the open door serving as a shelf between the powder hoist trunk and the spanning tray. The men will spread the bags apart (two forward, one aft) to make a space for the next batch of three. The powder bags are dumped on the order of the gun captain by the hoist operator stationed six decks below.

Note the 19-ton yoke which counterbalances the long gun. Set into the upper corners of the yoke are two large counterrecoil cylinders. These help stop the gun after it has recoiled 48 inches (in one-third of a

second). Note the depression buffer (the large pin) bolted to what appears to be the top of the yoke. The buffer limits the guns in turrets Nos 1 and 3 to a 2° angle of depression (zero in No 2). Attached to the bottom of the buffer is the yoke locking device (the notch of which is visible). A safety link, locked as it is here (and thus not visible) holds the gun in battery, at any angle of elevation, even with the counterrecoil cylinders drained of their hydraulic fluid. If the gun were fired with the link connected, the link would, by design, fail without other harm to the weapon. Nonetheless, the link would have to be replaced, and a

prominent plate on the yoke warns, 'DISCONNECT YOKE LOCKING DEVICE BEFORE FIRING GUN.' The fact that the safety link is fastened shows that the photograph was taken during a dry run.

The two smaller cylinders in the yoke are yoke rods which help connect the yoke to the larger counterrecoil cylinders. Out of sight under the surface of the yoke lies a maze of cylinders, plungers, and other components of the recoil system. The 16-inch gun, relatively simple at first glance, is actually a most complex piece of ordnance.

When the weapon is fired, the door to the powder hoist will have been closed and the men will have stepped at least four feet away. [NARS]

7. Retracting the rammer—*Wisconsin*, fall 1952. The gun captain (T. H. Eaton) signals the rammer operator to retract the rammer. The cloth on the gun captain's left arm is used to wipe the mushroom on the front of the breech plug clean of any burning powder fragments. The hole for one of the gas ejector jets can barely be seen about halfway in the threads of the screw box liner. The quilted black powder end of the powder bag is plainly visible. The arrow on the gun and the flange of metal on the bulkhead at upper right probably indicate when the gun has returned to its exact 5° loading angle. [NARS]

6. Dumping powder bags—*Iowa*, July 1944. The faint markings on the rearmost (left) powder bag indicate that these are dummy, practice charges. Note the cradle at left and the spanning tray leading from it at bottom center. It is just possible to make out the name of a crewman ('Wally') scratched onto the side of the powder car. The handle at the left is used to retract the projectile latch to permit the cradle to lower the projectile. [NARS]

8. Retracting the spanning tray—*Wisconsin*, fall 1952. The tray is mechanically attached to the cradle fulcrum by means of the spanning tray control link. Raise the cradle, and the tray retracts and folds; lower the cradle, and the tray unfolds and extends.

Hand signals are used because of the noise, from the electro-hydraulic drives for instance, although the sound of the firing itself is quite subdued within the turret. The turret is, however, shaken very perceptibly by the firing.

Note that the internal surface of the screw box liner of the breech is cut into 15 symmetrical stepped sectors. Consequently, a 24° turn locks the breech plug (24° × 15 steps = 360 degrees).

The inscription on the breech of the gun (No 296) shows that it was made by the Naval Gun Factory at Washington Navy Yard in 1942. [NARS]

9. Closing breech—*Wisconsin*, fall 1952. The breech plug, released by foot treadle, swings up through spring load and air pressure. As the plug is rotated by a cam to lock the breech, the operating lever swings up almost to its latch. To complete the process, the gun captain must step forward and push the lever home, as he is doing here with his left hand. When the *Missouri* was shelling Muroran on 19 July 1945, the center gun of turret No 1 missed four salvos when the operating lever latch jammed in the down position.

Once latched, the breech plug cannot be accidentally opened until after the gun has been fired. The salvo latch, attached by a lever cam to the counterrecoil cylinder at upper left, ensures this important safety feature. The cylinders do not move with the gun as it recoils. Note the analog counter on the right recoil cylinder which records the total rounds fired by the gun. The air gauges on the cylinders show no pressure. This then is a practice run.

The powder door can be seen at far left retracted flush into the turret bulkhead. [NARS]

145

10. Ready light switch— *Wisconsin*, fall 1952. After sealing the breech, the gun captain steps back and throws his ready switch. With its unlocking solenoid, this switch can be moved from the safe position only when the breech is closed. On one circuit, the switch is connected with the firing keys. On another, the switch is arranged with the turret officer's indicator panel. After the gun has been fired, the gun captain turns the switch back to safe, and the weapon is lowered to its 5° loading angle. [NARS]

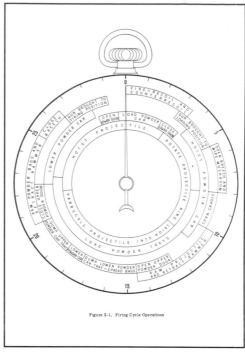

Figure 2-1. Firing Cycle Operations

11. All of these operations take only 30 seconds with an experienced turret crew. The variety of steps, keyed precisely into one another, is quite evident from this schematic view of the firing cycle. [OP 769]

APPENDIX E
ARMOR WEIGHTS

A Turrets:
188.93 long tons class 'A' armor on sides and rear

277.51 long tons class 'B' armor on front and roof

466.44 long tons total per turret

B Barbettes:
Turret No. 1 — 416.92 long tons class 'A' (7 segments)

Turret No. 2 — 770.9 long tons class 'A' (12 segments)

Turret No. 3 — 543.1 long tons class 'A' (11 segments)

C Belts:
Upper belt — 1085.79 long tons class 'A' per side

Lower belt — 1556.1 long tons class 'B' per side

Upper belt — 464 ft in length (Frames 50–166)

Lower belt — 556 ft in length (Frames 50–189)

Upper belt — actual plate depth — 11 ft 2.58 inches

Upper and lower belt depth combined — 38 ft 1.37 inches

D Decks:
2nd and 3rd decks — 4254.98 long tons class 'B' armor

E Armored end bulkheads:
Forward at Frame 50 — 405.38 long tons

Aft at Frame 166 — 151.31 long tons

Aft at Frame 203 — 44.41 long tons

F Steering gear armor box:
227.71 long tons Class 'A' and 'B'

G Conning tower:
Sides — 300 long tons approximately Class 'B' on the *Iowa*

202.61 long tons on the other three battleships

Bottom and top — 33.89 long tons

Doors — 9 long tons on the *Iowa*; 7.05 on the others

APPENDIX F
Construction Record   USS *Wisconsin* (BB 64)   Time—Labor—Material

Date	Months after keel laid	Months before launching	Months before commission	Structural tonnage erected on ship	Structural tonnage fabricated in shop	Man days expended shop and ship	Weld metal deposited (lb)	Rivets driven	Electric cable and wire installed (ft)	Percentage complete
	Keel Laid 25 January 1941			Launched 7 December 1943		Commissioned 16 April 1944			Completed 31 May 1944	
1 January 1941	—	35	39½	0	35	4,168	460	0	0	—
1 October 1941	8	26	30½	862	2,800	78,765	23,400	11,529	0	4.3
9 January 1942	11½	23	27	1,700	4,500	159,069	56,000	64,000	0	7.0
1 April 1942	15	20	24½	2,452	6,900	246,445	126,000	140,000	0	10.8
1 July 1942	18	17	21½	3,900	10,100	370,784	185,000	243,000	0	18.4
1 January 1943	23	11	15½	9,400	20,400	775,613	369,000	534,000	0	35.8
1 April 1943	26	8	12½	14,200	23,000	1,005,091	477,000	633,000	0	43.8
1 October 1943	32	2	6½	23,300	25,900	1,785,267	781,500	1,025,000	483,700	67.0
Completed May 1944	40	—	—	28,286	27,908	2,891,334	928,025	1,211,183	1,200,000	100.0

Source: 'History of the Philadelphia Navy Yard,' 568, NHC.

APPENDIX G
CAMOUFLAGE

During their careers, the 'Iowas' have worn a variety of standardised paint schemes, called measures.

  Ms 13—The normal peacetime system of haze gray.

  Ms 21—The 'navy blue system' with all vertical surfaces in navy blue and all decks in deck blue.

  Ms 22—The 'graded system'—the hull in navy blue to the lowest point of the deck sheer; above this, all vertical surfaces in haze gray and the decks in deck blue.

  Ms 32/22 D—A dramatic dazzle scheme with wave-like patterns in pale gray, haze gray and navy blue.

In addition the *Iowa* went out to the Pacific in 1944 wearing a most unusual paint scheme of dull black and haze gray, with the black feathered into the gray.

Over their years of service, the battleships were painted as follows:

  Iowa—Completion to January 1944: Ms 22

  January 1944 to November 1944 at minimum: the dull black and haze gray scheme

  By the summer of 1945: Ms 22

  Post-war: Ms 13

During the summer of 1952 and following her recommissioning in 1984, the *Iowa* wore a large American flag on the top of turret No. 2 and her hull number '*61*' on the top of turret No. 1.

New Jersey—Completion to the spring of 1945: Ms 21

  By May 1945: Ms 22

  Post war: Ms 13

Missouri—Completion through shakedown: Ms 32/22 D

  From the fall of 1944 to the end of the war: Ms 22

  Post war: Ms 13

Wisconsin—Completion to end of the war: Ms 22

  Post war: Ms 13

APPENDIX H
OPERATIONAL CASUALTIES SUFFERED BY THE *NEW JERSEY* DURING THE BOMBARDMENT OF MILI, 18 MARCH 1944

(1) On the 15th salvo by turret No. 2, the right projectile hoist failed, and the gun missed seven salvos. The casualty was due to worn shutter buffers on the upper shell flat which allowed an HC shell to cant inboard. Consequently, the rack pawls would not engage the

base of the shell which was thus only partially raised. It then dropped back on the nose of the next shell coming up the hoist from the lower shell flat. To keep the hoist operating, a man with a pinch bar kept succeeding shells from canting. After the action, the turret crew replaced the defective shutter buffers.

(2) After salvo 19, the powder car servicing the left gun in turret No. 1 failed to hoist, causing the gun to miss three salvos. The operator of the lower powder car had tried to close the powder car doors too early, and the doors had jammed slightly against a canted powder bag. Thus, the requisite switch (No. 4) did not make contact, and the open circuit rendered the hoist immobile. A petty officer, noticing the door slightly ajar, slammed it shut, whereupon service resumed.

(3) Several fire control radars became casualties during the action. The Mk 8 failed when electrodes in a vacuum tube were knocked together, shorting out the circuit and blowing a condenser. The Mk 4 in Sky 4 stopped working when blast knocked out a condenser. A condenser in the Mk 3 shut down because of excessive local heating. The search radars suffered momentary losses of power right after each 16-inch salvo.

Source: *New Jersey*, AR, 21 March 1944, NHC.

APPENDIX I
RADAR CASUALTIES SUFFERED BY THE *WISCONSIN* DURING THE BOMBARDMENT OF HITACHI MIRO 17–18 JULY 1945

The ship's action report illustrates how damaging blast pressure from the big guns could be to exposed electronic gear. All the equipment had been thoroughly checked after the Muroran shelling two days earlier and found to be operating 'at peak performance'.

After the fifth salvo, the Mk 27 radar was lost to the failure of a voltage regulator tube.

The forward Mk 8 stopped working early because tubes in the regulated rectifier and transmitter failed.

About the same time, the Mk 22 in Sky One failed when the main line fuse blew due to a short in the 'operate-standby' switch.

Later in the action, main battery shock knocked out a tube in the Mk 22 set in Sky Three. The set was out for the rest of the action.

Earlier, blast completely severed the co-axial line above the rotary joint serving the SK radar.

Finally, the bolts securing the reflector on the after SG antenna worked loose due to main battery shock, causing the reflector to tilt over.[1]

1. *Wisconsin*, AR, 25 July 1945. NHC.

APPENDIX J
FUEL CONSUMPTION

After some of the sweeps late in the war against Japan, the *Missouri* and *Wisconsin* submitted careful reports on their fueling needs. The following are truncated samples of such calculations:

The *Missouri* in the operations against Okinawa and Kyushu, 28 May to 10 June 1945, spent 336 hours underway, travelled 6,014 miles, and averaged 17.9 knots (highest speed reached = 27 knots). She fueled 3 times from tankers which gave her 33,301 barrels of oil, but she also dispensed 12,866 barrels to 17 destroyers. Overall, she consumed herself 25,024 barrels, for an average of 4.16 barrels per mile.

The *Wisconsin* steamed for 58 straight days from 17 March to 10 May 1945 (1,381 hours). During this period, she operated on 4 boilers for 553 hours; on 6, for 164 hours; on 7, for 64 hours; and on all 8 for 601 hours. She covered 25,706 miles at an average speed of 17.9 knots, took aboard 166,143 barrels from 13 oilers, and gave 48,267 to 41 destroyers. Her own consumption of 122,177 barrels yielded an average of 4.7 barrels (or 199.6 gallons) per mile.

From the cessation of hostilities to the surrender (16 August to 2 September), the *Wisconsin*'s figures reflect the more relaxed pace of operations: 420 hours underway; 5,541 miles travelled; 21,373 barrels burned for an average of 3.86 barrels (162 gallons) per mile.

Source: *Missouri* and *Wisconsin*, ARs, NHC.

APPENDIX K
DAMAGE SUFFERED BY THE *MISSOURI* ON THIMBLE SHOALS, 17 JANUARY 1950. (DATA TAKEN FROM THE SHIP'S REPORT, 14 FEBRUARY 1950)

A Grounding Damage
(1) Strake G starboard damaged by scoring,

indentation and rupture between frames 99 and 114, including three holes: two 8-inch and one 20-inch ruptures.

(2) A number of fuel oil tank heating coils required straightening or replacement.

(3) The starboard keel suffered a small 4-inch indentation at frame 104.

(4) NMC heads scratched slightly, but their operation was not impaired.

(5) The paint on the bottom was scoured.

(6) Two TBM motor generator armatures burned out due to lack of ventilation.

(7) Sand and debris plugged all injection and overboard discharges except for the after emergency diesel generator set.

(8) Casings, rings, and bearings were scored on four turbo-generator circulator pumps.

(9) Packing journals, casings, and rings were scored on one bilge pump, one main drain pump, four cooling water pumps and four fire and bilge pumps.

But the damage report noted that the equipment listed in points 8 and 9 was generally still operable.

B Salvage Damage

(1) Nos 2, 3, and 4 propeller edges suffered minor tearing, cracking, polishing, and furling caused by chain and cable passing.

(2) Salvage cables dished in, to a minor degree, the outboard side of the rope guards on No. 1 and No. 4 shafts.

(3) Explosive charges damaged 20 Tank-O-Meter gauges.

(4) The salvage cables caused minor hull damage to stanchions, scupper lips and the like.

To repeat, the ship's damage report concluded: 'All damage incurred in the grounding and salvage operations has been repaired by Norfolk Naval Shipyard and by the ship's force of the vessel. On 8 February 1950 [that is, after five days of yard work], a fully successful post repair trial was conducted at sea.'

One of her officers who served aboard the ship from December 1948 to early 1952 later wrote: 'As auxiliary, repair, and boiler division officer, as well as qualified engineering officer of the watch, I can testify that the BB-63 made 32 knots and better on every occasion required in support of carrier launch/recovery operations during the Korean Conflict.' (*US Naval Institute Proceedings*, June 1980, 85)

APPENDIX L
CLASS MILESTONES

Iowa (BB-61)

Authorised	17 May 1938
Laid down	27 June 1940
Launched	27 August 1942
(Sponsor: Mrs Henry A. Wallace)	
Commissioned	22 February 1943
Decommissioned	24 March 1949
Commissioned	25 August 1951
Decommissioned	24 February 1958
Commissioned	28 April 1984

New Jersey (BB-62)

Authorised	17 May 1938
Laid down	16 September 1940
Launched	7 December 1942
(Sponsor: Mrs Charles Edison)	
Commissioned	23 May 1943
Decommissioned	30 June 1948
Commissioned	21 November 1950
Decommissioned	21 August 1957
Commissioned	6 April 1968
Decommissioned	17 December 1969
Commissioned	28 December 1982

Missouri (BB-63)

Authorised	6 July 1939
Laid down	6 January 1941
Launched	29 January 1944
(Sponsor: Miss Margaret Truman)	
Commissioned	11 June 1944
Decommissioned	26 February 1955

Wisconsin (BB-64)

Authorised	6 July 1939
Laid down	25 January 1941
Launched	29 January 1944
(Sponsor: Mrs Walter S. Goodland)	
Commissioned	16 April 1944
Decommissioned	1 July 1948
Commissioned	3 March 1951
Decommissioned	8 March 1958

Illinois (BB-65)

Authorised	19 July 1940
Laid down	15 January 1945
Cancelled	11 August 1945

Kentucky (BB-66)

Authorised	19 July 1940
Laid down	6 December 1944
Launched	20 January 1950
Sold	31 October 1958

APPENDIX M

DAMAGE CLAIMED BY THE *NEW JERSEY*
DURING HER SECOND TOUR TO KOREA

Leaving Norfolk on 5 March 1953, BB-62 joined combat on 12 April 1953. By the end of the conflict on 27 July, the ship had steamed 37,519 miles and fired more than 4,000 16-inch shells in less than 5 months. She asserted that she inflicted the following casualties on the enemy during that time:

	Gun positions	Buildings	Tunnels	Highway bridges	Railroad bridges	Bunkers	Observation posts	Command posts
Damaged	124	37		3	7	182	4	2
Destroyed	144	75	18	3	3	255	8	1

Additionally, the *New Jersey* claimed to have put out of action 66 caves, four ammunition dumps, one radar station, one signal station and five oil storage tanks. She also claimed to have cut 130 yards of railroad track, 3,980 yards of trenchline and 24 roads, as well as causing 64 secondary explosions and 40 rockslides or landslides.[1]

1. *New Jersey*, cruise book, 1953, NHC.

APPENDIX N

EVALUATION OF THE EFFECTIVENESS
OF BATTLESHIP GUNFIRE SUPPORT IN
KOREA

The First Marine Division, facing an enemy deeply entrenched in heavy fortifications on steep reverse slopes, kept careful records of the effectiveness of naval artillery fired in its sector from January to March 1952.

Particularly interesting were the marine conclusions regarding long-range support.

Caliber	Number of missions	No. of rds fired	Average no. rds per mission	Average range
16″	43	977	23	32,500 yards
8″	103	1,661	16	22,000
6″	32	470	15	

Spotters reported the following results:

	Personnel casualties		Artillery pieces		Bunkers	
	KIA	WIA	Destroyed	Damaged	Destroyed	Damaged
16″	700	359	3	7	81	105
8″	239	47	2	3	116	127
6″	163	47	1	8	28	20

The report concludes that 16-inch projectiles were used in many cases against large enemy installations such as divisional and regimental CP's [command posts] where the expenditure of 50 to 60 rounds of fire for effect is not uncommon. The destructive and neutralization capabilities of the 16-inch projectiles have produced valuable results upon enemy installations and morale. It is felt that the expenditure of this ammunition is more than justified by the excellent results obtained on these targets, in view of the fact that in most cases the targets were located in positions that could only be attacked successfully by flanking and enfilade fire.[1]

1. Commanding General, First Marine Division to Commander, Seventh Fleet, 7 April 1952. Secret correspondence, p. 5–83 in CINCPAC, PACFLT OPS, interim evaluation, NHC.

APPENDIX O

A BATTLESHIP VS CARRIER COMPARISON, 1979

In November 1979, Charles E. Myers, Jr. published an influential article in the *US* *Naval Institute Proceedings* arguing for the reactivation of the 'Iowas'. The following tables gave battleship advocates some potent ammunition.

Table 1. Bombardment support alternatives

	Battleship	*Carrier*
Method of delivery	Gunfire	Strike aircraft
Personnel allowance	1,500–2,978	5,000
Tons per salvo or strike	12–15	70
Maximum tons per day	17,496*	210
Salvo rate	2 per minute	—
Strike rate	—	3 per day
Time to deliver 210 tons	9–80 minutes[1]	12 hours

* Theoretical maximum (exceeds magazine capacity).   [1] Depends on the number of gun tubes firing.

Table 2. Assault bombardment costs

	Battleship	*Carrier*
Crew pay per day $35 per man	$52,500	$175,000
Ship operations (less fuel)*	$250,000	$250,000
Combat losses:		
Ship	—	—
Aircraft (1%)	—	$2,028,000
Fuel costs	$15,000	$102,000
Cost per ton on target	$1,511	$12,156

* Although the same operations costs (less fuel) are assumed for both the battleship and the carrier, it is likely that carrier costs will be higher due to scale (size) as well as complexity of equipment.

Table 3. Typical bombardment rates

Ship	Displacement	Crew	Tons/hour	Tons/hour/personnel
Virginia	11,000	442	76.56	.1732
Spruance	7,800	296	76.56	.2586
Forrest Sherman	4,050	292	114.84	.3933
Coontz	5,800	377	38.28	.1015
Des Moines	21,500	1,803	948.6	.5261
Nimitz	91,400	6,600	17.5 (Alfa)	.00265
			26.67 (Cyclic)	.00404
New Jersey	59,000	1,700	1,458	.857

Source: C. E. Myers, Jr, 'A Sea-Based Interdiction System for Power Projection,' *USNIP* (November 1979), 105.

ENDNOTES

Chapter 1

1. William D. Hassett, *Off the Record with F.D.R. 1942–1945* (New Brunswick: Rutgers UP, 1958), 176.
2. 'Battleships 61 and 62,' File 420.6, NHC.
3. For the best discussion of these studies, see Norman Friedman, *U.S. Battleships: An Illustrated Design History* (Annapolis: U.S. Naval Institute, 1985), 307–311.
4. Cordell Hull, *The Memoirs of Cordell Hull*, Vol. 1 (New York: MacMillan, 1948), 568.
5. Sec/Nav to Chief, BuConRep, 18 April 1938, Confidential, RG19, NARS. Harold L. Ickes. *The Secret Diary of Harold L. Ickes*, Vol. 2 (New York: Simon & Schuster, 1954), 334.
6. FDR to Vinson, 25 April 1939, OF 18, FDRL.
7. General Board hearings, 9 July 1940, 249, NHC.
8. War Plans Division, 20 March 1939, NHC. General Board hearings, 28 July 1939, NHC.
9. Richard Hough, *Dreadnought* (New York: MacMillan, 1964), 219. Anthony Preston, *Fighting Ships* (London: Phoebus, 1980), 212.
10. General Board to Sec/Nav, 21 April 1938, File 420.6, NHC.
11. For a close look at these alternative weapons, see Emanuel Raymond Lewis, 'American Battleship Main Battery Armament: The Final Generation,' *Warship International* (No. 4, 1976), 276–303.
12. *Ibid.*, 299–300. BuOrd to General Board, 1 December 1938, File 420.6, NHC.
13. General Board hearings, 26 July 1939, File 420.6, NHC.
14. Hence, the contention of Anthony Preston in *Fighting Ships* (p. 212) that the 'Iowas' were battlecruisers rather than battleships is arguable indeed. BuEng to Commandant, New York Navy Yard, 27 November 1939, Confidential, RG19, NARS. CNO to BuEng, 30 November 1939, Confidential, RG 19, NARS.
15. General Board to CINCUS, 18 July 1939, File 803/4j, NHC.
16. FDR to Sec/Nav, 13 May 1940, OF 18, FDRL.
17. *Missouri* file, Ships Histories Branch, NHC.
18. War Plans Div., 20 March 1939, File 804/4 BB, NHC. General Board hearings, 28 July 1939, 125, NHC.
19. C. C. Bloch papers, LC. CNO to General Board, 13 December 1939, File 420.6, NHC.
20. General Board hearings, 1940, Vol. 1, 139.
21. BuShips to VCNO, 5 April 1943, CNO Central File, NHC. VCNO to CNO, 12 April 1943, CNO Central File, NHC. COMINCH to VCNO, 16 April 1943, CNO Central File, NHC.
22. King to Sec/Nav, 29 October 1943, King Papers, Series 1, NHC. Knox to Brainard, 2 November 1943, CNO Central File, NHC.
23. CNO to BuShips, 28 July 1944, CNO Central File, NHC.
24. USN, 'US Naval Administration in World War II: An Administrative History of the Bureau of Ships,' Vol. 3, 179, NHC.
25. General Board to Sec/Nav, 3 April 1941, File 420.6, NHC.
26. BuShips to NYNY, 11 July 1942, RG 19, NARS. VCNO to BuShips, 29 October and 9 December 1942, 14 July 1943, RG 19, NARS.
27. King Papers, Series 1, 7 July 1943, NHC.
28. NYNY to BuShips, 5 December 1941, RG 19, NARS.
29. 'History of the Philadelphia Navy Yard,' 571, NHC.
30. *Missouri* file, Ships Histories Branch, NHC.
31. 'History of the Philadelphia Navy Yard,' 572, NHC.
32. USN, 'US Naval Administration in World War II: Bureau of Ordnance,' part 2, Vol. 1, first draft narrative, 289, NHC.
33. 'History of the Philadelphia Navy Yard,' 576–578, NHC.

Chapter 2

1. *Wisconsin*, Action Report, 13 May 1945, NHC.

2. *Ibid.*

3. *Wisconsin*, Action Reports, 24 December 1944 and 3 March 1945, NHC.

4. *New Jersey*, Damage Report, 16 July 1951, NHC.

5. *Iowa*, ARs, 16 February, 12 and 28 November 1944, NHC.

6. Rear Admiral Frank Pinney to author, 13 January 1976.

7. Vice Admiral William R. Smedberg, III, interview transcript, USNI, *New Jersey*, 1968 narrative history, NHC. Capt. Gerald E. Gneckow, *Iowa*, to author, 6 August 1985.

8. *Missouri*, AR, 30 June 1945, NHC. *Wisconsin*, ARs, 24 December 1944 and 3 March 1945, NHC.

9. Smedberg, interview transcript, USNI.

10. Vice Admiral Charles L. Melson, interview transcript, USNI. Admiral Robert Lee Dennison, interview transcript, USNI. Gneckow to author, 6 August 1985.

11. Admiral Stuart S. Murray, interview transcript, USNI.

12. Smedberg, interview transcript, USNI.

13. *Ibid.*

14. *New Jersey*, 1968 narrative history, 7, NHC.

15. *New Jersey*, AR, 9 November 1944, NHC. Admiral U.S. Grant Sharp, interview transcript, USNI.

16. Rear Admiral Joshua W. Cooper, interview transcript, USNI.

17. Melson and Murray, interview transcripts, USNI. *Wisconsin*, Damage Report, 20 October 1944, NHC. *Wisconsin*, Cruise book, 1943–47.

18. *Missouri*, Storm Damage, 23 August 1950, NHC. Oscar Parkes, *British Battleships* (London: Seeley, 1956), 689.

19. Vice Admiral Olaf M. Hustvedt, interview transcript, USNI. Rear Admiral John L. McCrea to author, 7 April 1976.

20. *Iowa*, AR, 1 November 1944, NHC.

21. Cooper, interview transcript, USNI.

22. Dennison, Smedberg, Melson, and Cooper, interview transcripts, USNI.

23. Rear Admiral Raymond D. Tarbuck, interview transcript, USNI.

24. BuOrd, first draft narrative, vol. 2, 283–84, NHC.

25. OPORD, CTG 70.8, 320–69, NHC. *Surface Warfare Magazine* (October 1981), 11. 'Ammunition Handling,' NAVPERS 16194, pp. 9–28, NHC.

26. 'US Explosive Ordnance,' OP 1664, July 1947, NHC.

27. NAVPERS 16194, 4–25, NHC.

28. SW300–BB–GTP–010, 3–5, NHC. NSWC MP 83–23, 3–4, NHC.

29. *Wisconsin*, AR, 30 March 1945, NHC. *Missouri*, AR, 20, 22, 23 February 1951, NHC.

30. 'Naval Ordnance and Gunnery,' NAVPERS 16116–A, 481, NHC.

31. '16-Inch Three Gun Turrets: BB 61 Class,' NAVORD OP 769, 12–1, NHC.

32. *Wisconsin*, AR, 25 July 1945, NHC. NAVPERS 10798–A, 9–20, NHC.

33. *Iowa*, AR, 25 July 1945, NHC.

34. *Missouri*, AR, 14–19 March, 1951, NHC. *New Jersey*, 1968 narrative history, 12, NHC.

35. Joseph Bryan, III, *Aircraft Carrier* (New York: Ballantine 1954), 129.

36. Hustvedt, interview transcript, USNI. *New Jersey*, AR, 11 April 1945, NHC. *Wisconsin*, AR, 13 May 1945, NHC.

37. *Surface Warfare Magazine* (October 1981), 5.

38. W. H. Garzke, Jr. and R. O. Dulin, Jr., *Battleship's Axis and Neutral Battleships in World War II* (Annapolis: USNI, 1985), 283, 306, 497.

39. Thomas Hone and Norman Friedman, '*Iowa* vs. *Yamato*: The Ultimate Gunnery Duel,' *USNIP* (July 1983), 122–23.

Chapter 3

1. *Iowa*, Grounding Report 31 July 1943, NHC.

2. William M. Rigdon and James Derieux, *White House Sailor* (New York: Doubleday, 1962), 59.

3. *Iowa*, Report, 22 December 1943, NHC.

4. *Iowa*, Report, 22 December 1943, NHC.

5. Captain R. W. Faulk, interview transcript, USNI.

6. Letter to author from Admiral John L. McCrea, 7 April 1976.

7. *New Jersey*, AR, 16 February 1944, NHC.

8. Admiral O. M. Hustvedt, interview transcript, USNI.

9. W. Karig and E. Purdon, *Battle Report:*

Pacific War: Middle Phase (New York: Rinehart, 1947), 147.

10. Letter to author from Admiral F. L. Pinney, Jr. (fire control officer, *Iowa*, 1944), 13 January 1976.

11. *Iowa*, AR, 16 February 1944, NHC.

12. *Iowa*, AR, 28 March 1944, NHC.

13. Pinney to author, 13 January 1976.

14. *New Jersey*, AR, 21 March 1944, NHC.

15. *New Jersey*, ARs, 6 April and 1 May 1944, NHC.

16. *New Jersey*, AR, 12 July 1944, NHC.

17. *Iowa*, AR, 19 June 1944, NHC. Admiral O. M. Hustvedt, interview transcript, USNI.

18. *Iowa*, AR, 22 October and 1 November 1944, NHC.

19. *Iowa*, AR, 1 November 1944, NHC.

20. *Iowa*, AR, 28 November 1944, NHC.

21. *New Jersey*, ARs, 28 and 30 November 1944, NHC.

22. *Iowa*, ARs, 1 and 12 November 1944, NHC.

23. *Wisconsin*, Cruise Book, 1943–47, NHC.

24. *Wisconsin*, AR, 24 December 1944, NHC.

25. *Iowa*, AR, 31 December 1944, NHC.

26. Rear Admiral Ralph K. James, interview transcript, USNI.

Chapter 4

1. Captain R. W. Faulk, interview transcript, USNI.

2. *Missouri*, AR, 2 March 1945, NHC.

3. *Wisconsin*, ARs, 13 May and 26 August 1945, NHC.

4. *Wisconsin*, Cruise Book, 1943–7, NHC. *Missouri*, AR, 2 March 1945, NHC. *Wisconsin*, AR, 3 March 1945, NHC.

5. *Missouri*, AR, 2 March 1945, NHC. *Wisconsin*, AR, 26 August 1945, NHC.

6. *Wisconsin*, AR, 13 May 1945, NHC.

7. *Missouri*, AR, 2 March 1945, NHC. *Wisconsin*, AR, 13 May 1945, NHC.

8. *Wisconsin*, Cruise Book, 1943–7, NHC.

9. Captain R. W. Faulk, interview transcript, USNI.

10. *Wisconsin*, ARs, 3 March, 13 May and 26 August 1945, NHC.

11. *Missouri*, AR, 2 March 1945, NHC. *Wisconsin*, AR, 24 January 1945, NHC.

12. *New Jersey*, AR, 25 January and 16 April 1945, NHC. Joseph Bryan III, *Aircraft Carrier* (New York: Ballantine, 1954), 138.

13. *New Jersey*, AR, 16 April 1945, NHC. *Missouri*, AR, 2 March and 9 May, 1945, NHC.

14. *Missouri*, AR, 26 March 1945, NHC. *New Jersey*, AR, 31 March 1945, NHC. *Wisconsin*, AR, 30 March 1945, NHC.

15. Admiral S. S. Murray, interview transcript, USNI.

16. *New Jersey*, AR, 16 April 1945, NHC.

17. *Missouri*, AR, 9 May 1945, NHC. Captain R. W. Faulk, interview transcript, USNI.

18. *Wisconsin*, AR, 13 May 1945, NHC. *Wisconsin*, Cruise Book, 1943–47, NHC.

19. Admiral S. S. Murray, interview transcript, USNI. *Missouri*, AR, 9 May 1945, NHC.

20. *Wisconsin*, AR, 13 May 1945, NHC.

21. *New Jersey*, AR, 16 April 1945, NHC.

22. *Missouri*, AR, 30 June 1945, NHC.

23. W. F. Halsey and J. Bryan III, *Admiral Halsey's Story* (New York: McGraw-Hill, 1947), 260.

24. *Missouri*, AR, 19 July 1945, NHC.

25. Admiral S. S. Murray, interview transcript, USNI.

26. *Iowa*, AR, 25 July 1945, NHC.

27. *Missouri*, AR, 19 July 1945, NHC.

28. *Wisconsin*, AR, 25 July 1945, NHC.

29. *Wisconsin*, AR, 25 July 1945, NHC.

30. S. E. Morison, *History of United States Naval Operations in World War II*, Vol. 14: *Victory in the Pacific 1945* (Boston: Little Brown, 1960), 314.

31. *Wisconsin*, AR, 25 July 1945, NHC. *Iowa*, AR, 25 July 1945, NHC.

32. *Wisconsin*, AR, 25 July 1945, NHC. *Missouri*, AR, 20 July 1945, NHC.

33. Morison, 316. John Winton, *The Forgotten Fleet: The British Navy in the Pacific 1944–1945* (New York: Coward-McCann, 1970), 317, 329.

34. Naval Gunfire Training Section, Fleet Marine Force, Marine Corps Historical Center.

35. *New Jersey*, AR, 11 August 1945, NHC.

36. Admiral S. S. Murray, interview transcript, USNI.

37. *Missouri*, AR, 8 September 1945, NHC.

38. Admiral S. S. Murray, interview transcript, USNI.

39. *Ibid.*

40. *Ibid.*

41. *Ibid.* Rear Admiral Charles J. Wheeler, interview transcript, USNI. *Missouri*, AR, 8 September 1945, NHC.

Chapter 5

1. Admiral S. S. Murray, interview transcript, USNI.
2. Captain R. W. Faulk, interview transcript, USNI.
3. *Ibid. Missouri*, ship file, Marine Corps Historical Center.
4. Admiral C. K. Duncan, interview transcript, USNI.
5. Captain R. W. Faulk, interview transcript, USNI.
6. Admiral C. K. Duncan, interview transcript, USNI.
7. Vice Admiral J. B. Colwell, interview transcript, USNI.
8. Admiral R. L. Dennison, interview transcript, USNI. *Missouri* file, Ships Histories Branch, NHC.
9. Vice Admiral J. B. Colwell, interview transcript, USNI.
10. Vice Admiral J. V. Smith, Vice Admiral R. N. Smoot, and Vice Admiral W. R. Smedberg III, interview transcripts, USNI.
11. G. Newell and Vice Admiral Allan E. Smith, *Mighty Mo: The U.S.S. Missouri: A Biography of the Last Battleship* (Seattle: Superior, 1969), 74.
12. *Ibid*, 77.
13. Rear Admiral Edward A. Ruckner, interview transcript, USNI.
14. Vice Admiral Charles L. Melson, interview transcript, USNI. Vice Admiral John V. Smith, interview transcript, USNI.
15. Vice Admiral R. N. Smoot, interview transcript, USNI.
16. Newell and Smith, 85–92. Rear Admiral E. A. Ruckner, interview transcript, USNI.
17. Letters to the *U.S. Naval Institute Proceedings* by Dennis Moore, March 1982, p. 73 and by Terry W. Jackson, February 1980, p. 75.
18. R. O. Dulin, Jr. and W. H. Garzke, Jr., *Battleships: United States Battleships in World War II* (Annapolis: Naval Institute Press, 1976), 134.
19. Narrative '1968' History of the USS *New Jersey* BB-62, NHC.
20. Anthony Preston, *Fighting Ships of the World* (London: Phoebus, 1980), 213.
21. *Missouri*, Damage Report, 14 February 1950, NHC.

Chapter 6

1. *Missouri*, Storm Damage Report, 23 August 1950, NHC.
2. Walter Karig, *Battle Report: The War in Korea* (New York: Rinehart, 1952), 330.
3. Malcolm W. Cagle and Frank A. Manson, *The Sea War in Korea* (Annapolis: U.S. Naval Institute, 1957), 299. CINCPAC, PACFLT OPS, interim evaluation, NHC.
4. *Missouri*, AR, 15–17 September 1950, NHC.
5. Cagle and Manson, 298.
6. James A. Field, Jr., *History of United States Naval Operations: Korea* (Washington: USGPO, 1962), 218.
7. *Missouri*, AR, 12–13 October 1950, NHC. Karig, 336.
8. Karig, 424. *Missouri*, AR, 23–24 December 1950, NHC. Donald M. Weller, Jr. papers, MCHC.
9. *Missouri*, AR, 30 January–1 February 1951, NHC.
10. *Missouri*, ARs, 5–7, 9–14, 20, 22, and 23 February 1951, NHC.
11. *Missouri*, AR, 14–19 March 1951, NHC.
12. *Ibid*.
13. Newell and Smith, 117.
14. *New Jersey*, AR, 19–21 May 1951, NHC.
15. *New Jersey*, ARs, 3–6, 28 June 1951, NHC.
16. *New Jersey*, AR, 4–18 July 1951, NHC.
17. *New Jersey*, Damage Report, 16 July 1951, NHC.
18. *New Jersey*, AR, 17–31 August 1951, NHC.
19. *New Jersey*, AR, 1–17 October 1951, NHC.
20. *Ibid*.
21. *New Jersey*, ARs, 1–17 October, 2–6, and 14 November 1951, NHC.
22. *Wisconsin*, AR, 2–22 December 1951, NHC. *Wisconsin*, War Diary, 1951–52, NHC. *Wisconsin*, Cruise Book, March 1951–March 1952, NHC.
23. *Wisconsin*, AR, 11–16 January 1952 NHC.
24. Donald M. Weller, 'Naval Gunfire Support of Amphibious Operations: Past, Present and Future' (Dahlgren: Naval Surface Weapons Center, 1977), 150.
25. *Wisconsin*, AR, 23–30 January 1952, NHC.
26. *Wisconsin*, ARs, 4, 20–24 February and 15–19 March 1952, NHC.

27. *Wisconsin*, AR, 15–19 March 1952, NHC.
28. *Wisconsin*, Cruise Book, March 1951–March 1952, NHC.
29. Vice Admiral William R. Smedberg III, interview transcript, USNI.
30. *Ibid.*
31. *Iowa*, AR, 1 May 1952, NHC.
32. Smedberg, interview transcript, USNI.
33. *Ibid.*
34. *Iowa*, AR, 1 May 1952, NHC.
35. Smedberg, interview transcript, USNI.
36. *Iowa*, AR, 13 May 1952, NHC.
37. Cagle and Manson, 348. This work wrongly dates the bombardment as 25 April.
38. Smedberg, interview transcript, USNI.
39. *Iowa*, ARs, 19 June and 29 August 1952, NHC.
40. *Iowa*, AR, 19 June 1952, NHC.
41. *Ibid.* Smedberg, interview transcript, USNI. Cagle and Manson, 435.
42. *Iowa*, AR, 16 July 1952, NHC.
43. *Iowa*, AR, 29 July 1952, NHC.
44. *Iowa*, ARs, 29 August and 14 September 1952, NHC.
45. *Iowa*, AR, 29 July 1952, NHC.
46. Rear Admiral Joshua W. Cooper, interview transcript, USNI.
47. Smedberg, interview transcript, USNI.
48. *Iowa*, ARs, 9 and 24 October 1952, NHC.
49. *Iowa*, AR, 18 October 1952, NHC.

Chapter 7

1. *Missouri*, ARs, 24–27 October; 2–6, 15–17 November; 7–10, 17–22, 30–31 December 1952, NHC.
2. *Missouri*, ARs, 6, 25–28 January; 6–7, 24–26 February; 8–10 March 1953, NHC.
3. *Missouri*, AR, 3–6 March 1953, NHC.
4. *Missouri*, ARs, 16–22, 24–25 March 1953, NHC. Cooper, interview transcript, USNI.
5. Vice Admiral Charles L. Melson, interview transcript, USNI.
6. *New Jersey*, ARs, 12–13, 15–16 April 1953, NHC.
7. *New Jersey*, ARs, 17–20 April 1953, NHC.
8. *New Jersey*, ARs, 23–24 April; 1–7 May 1953, NHC. CINCPAC, PACFLT OPS, interim evaluation, p. 5–220, NHC.
9. *New Jersey*, ARs, 24–31 May 1953, NHC. Weller, 'Naval Gunfire Support . . . ,' 160.
10. *New Jersey*, ARs, 6–27 June 1953, NHC.
11. *New Jersey*, ARs, 4–28 July 1953, NHC.
12. *New Jersey*, AR, 22–26 July 1953, NHC.

Melson, interview transcript, NHC.
13. *New Jersey*, AR, 22–26 July 1953, NHC.
14. Karig, 338. CINCPAC, PACFLT OPS, interim evaluation, p. 1304, NHC.
15. CINCPAC, PACFLT OPS, interim evaluation, p. 1–50, NHC.
16. Cagle and Manson, 371.
17. CINCPAC, PACFLT OPS, interim evaluation, p. 5–204, NHC.
18. *Ibid*, p. 5–32, NHC.
19. *Ibid*, p. 5–23, NHC.
20. *Iowa*, AR, 1 May 1952, NHC.
21. Weller, 'Naval Gunfire Support . . . ,' 130.
22. *Wisconsin*, Operations Report, January 1954, NHC. BuShips to Ship Characteristics Board, 14 June 1955, NHC.
23. Norman Friedman, *U.S. Battleships: An Illustrated Design History* (Annapolis: U.S. Naval Institute, 1985), 392. A Katie nuclear round was on display for a time at Los Alamos, New Mexico.
24. Dean Allard to author, 31 July 1985. *New Jersey*, visit reports, 1955, 1956, NHC.
25. *Wisconsin*, operation report, 25 February 1954, NHC.
26. Dulin and Garzke claim incorrectly that the *Eaton* sank as a result of the collision.
27. FCCM Stephen Skelley, USS *Iowa*, to author, 10 November 1985.
28. C. S. Morse and C. C. Bream, 'The Activation of U.S.S. *New Jersey* (BB-62) at Philadelphia Naval Shipyard,' *Naval Engineers Journal* (December 1968), 859–864.
29. Duncan, interview transcript, USNI.
30. For details on all of these projects, see Friedman, *U.S. Battleships*, 389–402.

Chapter 8

1. Vice Admiral Edward B. Hooper, interview transcript, USNI. Admiral Roy L. Johnson, interview transcript, USNI.
2. USS *New Jersey*, Ships Histories Division, NHC.
3. Morse and Bream, 865.
4. *New Jersey*, Material SITREP, 1 August 1967, NHC. *Navy Times*, 17 April 1968.
5. *New Jersey*, ship alteration material summary, 1967–1968, NHC.
6. Paul Stillwell, 'The Last Battleship,' *USNIP* (December 1979), 46–50.
7. Howard W. Serig, Jr., 'The *Iowa* Class: Needed Once Again,' *USNIP* (May 1982), 144. C. E. Myers, Jr., 'Reactivation of *Iowa*

Class Battleships: A Basis for Advocacy.' (September 1980), 6, 25, Ships Histories Branch, NHC.

8. Narrative 1968 history of the USS *New Jersey* BB-62, 7, Ships Histories Branch, NHC.

9. Heinl, *USNIP* (March 1969), 60–62.

10. Narrative 1968 history, *New Jersey*, 43–44, NHC.

11. Stillwell, 49.

12. Narrative 1968 history, *New Jersey*, passim, NHC.

13. *Ibid.*, 45.

14. *Ibid.*, 48–50.

15. *Ibid.*, 52.

16. Major James Bell to author, 22 February 1986.

17. Narrative 1968 history, *New Jersey*, 52–53, NHC.

18. *Ibid.*, 53–54.

19. *Ibid.*, 55.

20. *Ibid.*, 56–59.

21. *Ibid.*, 61–65.

22. Narrative 1969 history, *New Jersey*, 2, NHC.

23. *Ibid.*, 5.

24. *Ibid.*, 6–7.

25. *Ibid.*, 7–10.

26. *Ibid.*, Appendices.

27. Weller, 'Naval Gunfire Support . . . ,' 40.

28. Bell to author, 22 February 1986. John H. Tennent, 'Bigger Punch for BB's,' *Surface Warfare* (October 1981), 5.

29. Bell to author, 22 February 1986. Stillwell, 49.

30. Narrative 1968 history, *New Jersey*, 57, NHC.

31. *Ibid.*, 51.

32. *Ibid.*

33. U.S. Congress, Senate, 97th Cong., 1st sess., 7 April 1981, S3449.

34. Narrative 1969 history, *New Jersey*, 10–12, NHC.

35. *Ibid.*, 15–22. Stillwell, 47.

36. Narrative 1969 history, *New Jersey*, 23, NHC.

37. Senate, 97th Congress, 1st sess., 7 April 1981, S3454.

38. *Ibid.*, 25–26. Robert C. Peniston, 'The Big Ship in My Life,' *USNIP*. (December 1979), 52–53.

39. Narrative 1969 history, *New Jersey*, appendix, NHC.

40. Peniston, 53.

41. Serig, 'The *Iowa* Class,' 138.

42. Vice Admiral W. P. Mack, interview transcript, USNI.

Chapter 9

1. Gibbs and Cox, BB 62 Class Feasibility Studies, April 1975, NHC.

2. Serig, 'The *Iowa* Class,' *USNIP* (May 1982), 138.

3. CINCPACFLT to CNO, 15 April 1978, NHC.

4. Charles E. Myers, Jr., 'A Sea-Based Interdiction System for Power Projection,' *USNIP* (November 1979), 103–106.

5. *New York Times*, 4 April 1982, 89.

6. Senate, 7 April 1981, S 3457.

7. *Ibid.*, S 3447, S 3456.

8. *Washington Star*, 26 July 1981.

9. *Chicago Sun-Times*, 7 June 1981.

10. *New York Times*, 4 April 1982, 28.

11. Kitsap County Historical Society to Casper Weinberger, April 1982, Ships Histories Branch, NHC.

12. *Washington Star*, 26 July 1981.

13. *Surface Warfare Magazine*, October 1981 and November 1982.

14. RCA Service Company, 'Supply Support Posture for BB-62,' 3 July 1983, NHC.

15. Preston, *Fighting Ships*, 212.

16. FCCM (SW) Stephen Skelley, USS *Iowa*, to author, 10 November 1985, *Surface Warfare Magazine*, October 1981.

17. *Surface Warfare Magazine*, November 1984, 23–24.

18. Skelley to author, 10 November 1985.

19. Skelley to author, 10 November 1985.

20. Stillwell, 'Riding Shotgun . . . ,' *Sea Power* (November 1984), 16.

21. J. F. Downs, *USNIP* (February 1980), 75.

22. Captain Gerald E. Gneckow, USS *Iowa*, to author, 6 August 1985.

23. Friedman, *U.S. Battleships*, 395.

24. Skelley to author, 10 November 1985.

25. Letter from Gene Anderson, *USNIP* (July 1981), 21–22. Ronald T. Pretty, 'US Battleship Reactivation Progress,' *Jane's Defence Review*, 1982, 405.

26. Serig, 'The *Iowa* Class,' *USNIP* (May 1982), 148.

27. Mark F. Cancium, 'Battleships: A Different View,' *Marine Corps Gazette* (February 1982), 62.

28. *Jane's Defence Weekly*, 14 April 1984.

29. *Armed Forces Journal*, April 1985, 100.

30. *Ibid.*, February 1985, 75.

ABBREVIATIONS

AA	Anti-aircraft
ABRS	Assault Ballistic Rocket System
AP	Armor Piercing
ARVN	Army of the Republic of Vietnam (the South Vietnamese Army)
BATDIV	Battleship Division
BDF	Base Detonating Fuse
CAP	Combat Air Patrol
CEC	Combat Engagement Center
CIC	Combat Information Center
CINCPAC	Commander-in-Chief, Pacific Fleet
CIWS	Close In Weapons System (the Phalanx gun)
CNO	Chief of Naval Operations
CO	Commanding Officer
COMCRUDIV	Commander, Cruiser Division
CRUDIV	Cruiser Division
DMZ	Demilitarised Zone (the zone separating North and South Vietnam)
ECM	Electronic Counter Measures
HC	High Capacity (the bombardment shell)
KMAG	Korean Military Advisory Group
LSD	Landing Ship Dock
MSR	Main Supply Route
PDF	Point Detonating Fuse
RAP	Rocket Assisted Projectile
ROK	Republic of Korea (South Korea)
SHP	Shaft Horsepower
TF	Task Force
TG	Task Group
USNI	US Naval Institute
USNIP	*US Naval Institute Proceedings*
V/STOL	Vertical/Short Take Off and Landing (Aircraft)
WP	White Phosphorus (a smoke round often called 'Willie Peter')
XO	Executive Officer

BIBLIOGRAPHY

This book was based primarily on the records held at the Naval Historical Center (NHC), the Marine Corps Historical Center (MCHC), the National Archives (NARS) and the Library of Congress (LC)—all in Washington, D.C. I have also gleaned useful materials from the Naval War College, Newport, Rhode Island (NWC), the Franklin D. Roosevelt Library, Hyde Park, New York (FDRL) and the US Naval Institute, Annapolis, Maryland (USNI). The Oral History Collection compiled by the Naval Institute is of special value.

Certain official publications intended for service use were of great assistance. Among them were *Naval Ordnance and Gunnery*, published by BuPers in 1958 (NAVPERS 10798-A) and its 1946 predecessor (NAVPERS 16116-A). Written by the same body was *Ammunition Handling* (NAVPERS 16194), 1945. *The 16-Inch Three Gun Turrets BB-61 Class* issued by NAVORD (OP 769) is a model of clear technical writing and is utterly invaluable to anyone wishing to understand the workings of the big guns.

Several secondary sources contain some important insights on the 'Iowas'. Among the most significant are: Cagle, Malcolm W. and Manson, Frank A. *The Sea War in Korea*. Annapolis: USNI, 1957. Dulin, Robert O., Jr and Garzke, William H. Jr, *Battleships: United States Battleships in World War II*. Annapolis: USNI, 1976. Field, James A., Jr *History of United States Naval Operations: Korea*. Washington: USGPO, 1962. Friedman, Norman. *U.S. Battleships: An Illustrated Design History*. Annapolis: USNI, 1985.

INDEX